Urban Spaces and Lifestyles in Central Asia and Beyond

This volume contributes new insights to the scientific debate on post-Socialist urbanities. Based on ethnographic research in cities of Central Asia, the Caucasus and Russia, its contributions scrutinise the social production of diverse public, parochial and private spaces in conjunction with patterns of everyday encounter, identification, consumption and narration. The analyses extend from the transnational entanglements between a Dushanbe bazaar and hyper-modern Dubai to the micro-level hierarchies in a flat-sharing community in Astana. They explore competing notions of urban belonging and aesthetics in Yerevan, local perception of Central Asian Muslims in Kazan and Saint Petersburg, and more, providing a rich tapestry of academic study. Taken together, the case studies address cities as gateways to 'new worlds' (both local and global), discuss ambitions of states at taming urban landscapes, and illustrate current trends of economic, religious and other lifestyles in urban Central Asia and beyond. This book was originally published as a special issue of *Central Asian Survey*.

Philipp Schröder is a lecturer and postdoctoral researcher at the Institute for Asian and African Studies, Humboldt-Universität zu Berlin, Germany. His teaching and research focuses on urban spaces and mobilities, identities and integration, youth cultures and political economies in Central Asia, Russia and China.

ThirdWorlds

Edited by Shahid Qadir, University of London, UK

ThirdWorlds will focus on the political economy, development and cultures of those parts of the world that have experienced the most political, social, and economic upheaval, and which have faced the greatest challenges of the postcolonial world under globalisation: poverty, displacement and diaspora, environmental degradation, human and civil rights abuses, war, hunger, and disease.

ThirdWorlds serves as a signifier of oppositional emerging economies and cultures ranging from Africa, Asia, Latin America, Middle East, and even those 'Souths' within a larger perceived North, such as the U.S. South and Mediterranean Europe. The study of these otherwise disparate and discontinuous areas, known collectively as the Global South, demonstrates that as globalisation pervades the planet, the south, as a synonym for subalterity, also transcends geographical and ideological frontier.

For a complete list of titles in this series, please visit https://www.routledge.com/series/TWQ

Recent titles in the series include:

Urban Spaces and Lifestyles in Central Asia and Beyond

Edited by
Philipp Schröder

Routledge
Taylor & Francis Group

LONDON AND NEW YORK

First published 2017 by Routledge

2 Park Square, Milton Park, Abingdon, Oxfordshire OX14 4RN
52 Vanderbilt Avenue, New York, NY 10017

Routledge is an imprint of the Taylor & Francis Group, an informa business

First issued in paperback 2018

British Library Cataloguing in Publication Data
A catalogue record for this book is available from the British Library

ISBN 13: 978-1-138-74319-9 (hbk)
ISBN 13: 978-0-367-21866-9 (pbk)

Typeset in Myriad Pro
by RefineCatch Limited, Bungay, Suffolk

Publisher's Note
The publisher accepts responsibility for any inconsistencies that may have
arisen during the conversion of this book from journal articles to book chapters,
namely the possible inclusion of journal terminology.

Disclaimer
Every effort has been made to contact copyright holders for their permission to
reprint material in this book. The publishers would be grateful to hear from any
copyright holder who is not here acknowledged and will undertake to rectify
any errors or omissions in future editions of this book.

Contents

Citation Information

The chapters in this book were originally published in *Central Asian Survey*, volume 35, issue 2 (June 2016). When citing this material, please use the original page numbering for each article, as follows:

For any permission-related enquiries please visit:
http://www.tandfonline.com/page/help/permissions

Notes on Contributors

Tsypylma Darieva is teaching at Humboldt-Universität zu Berlin, Central Asian Studies Program, and is an associate member of the Department for Slavic and Caucasus Studies at Friedrich Schiller University of Jena. He is also a research grantee at the Centre for East European and International Studies, Berlin (ZOIS).

Susanne Fehlings is a faculty member at the Institute of Social and Cultural Anthropology, Goethe University, Frankfurt am Main, Germany.

Philipp Frank Jäger is a PhD researcher at the Institute of History, Chair of History of Azerbaijan, Humboldt-Universität zu Berlin, Germany.

Abdullah Mirzoev is a PhD researcher in the junior research group 'The Demographic Turn in the Junction of Cultures' at the Cluster of Excellence 'Asia and Europe in a Global Context', University of Heidelberg, Germany.

Emil Nasritdinov is a faculty member in the Anthropology Department, American University of Central Asia, Bishkek, Kyrgyzstan.

Kishimjan Osmonova is a postdoctoral researcher who obtained her PhD from the Institute for Asian and African Studies, Humboldt-Universität zu Berlin, Germany.

Philipp Schröder is a lecturer and postdoctoral researcher at the Institute for Asian and African Studies, Humboldt-Universität zu Berlin, Germany.

Wladimir Sgibnev is a senior researcher at the Leibniz Institute for Regional Geography, Leipzig, Germany.

Manja Stephan-Emmrich is a junior professor at the Institute for Asian and African Studies, Humboldt-Universität zu Berlin, Germany.

Andrey Vozyanov is a PhD researcher at the Graduate School for East and Southeast European Studies, University of Regensburg, Germany.

Urban spaces and lifestyles in Central Asia and beyond: an introduction

Philipp Schröder

Institute for Asian and African Studies, Humboldt-Universität zu Berlin, Germany

Chunkurchak is a marvellous place. Just 40 kilometres south of Kyrgyzstan's capital, Bishkek, and into the forelands of the Tian Shan mountain range, its picturesque landscape offers everything that has come to be associated with a *jailoo,* a summer pasture: looking up, the snow-capped peaks appear closer than they are, a mountain river meanders through alpine meadows and passes forest belts – and in the further distance the Chuy Valley, with its bustling centre, Bishkek, seems far away in many ways.

But Chunkurchak is more than that. It is a winter ski resort and features diverse dining and accommodation opportunities. Unique among them is Supara, an 'ethno-style' restaurant and hotel complex. It serves Kyrgyz national dishes, and the interior is dominated by wooden furniture with traditional ornament. Yet the main feature of Supara is that the architecture of both the restaurant building and the cottages offered for overnight stays resemble a *boz ui* (or *yurt*), the round felt tent that is a key element in Kyrgyzstan's nomadic heritage.

Supara is interesting for this volume because it connects to the city and to contemporary urban lifestyles in Bishkek in multiple ways. Nowadays, a place like Supara not only attracts 'Western' tourists, but is also a getaway for Bishkek's affluent middle and upper classes. It caters to the recent trend of celebrating and commodifying Kyrgyz culture and ethnic identity, the conspicuous consumption of which has become an integral part of the urbanites' self-presentation (Comaroff and Comaroff 2009). However, the interiors of the *boz ui* cottages at Supara have not kept to the actual simplicity of previous days, but offer such 'modern' comforts as a shower cabin, air conditioning and a flat-screen TV, with Kyrgyz-, Russian- and English-language channels to choose from.

These different materialities of Supara and the experience it aspires to convey to its clients aim at blurring the boundaries of rural authenticity and urban progress. Away from Chunkurchak or Supara, that exact binary opposing civilized city life to 'backward' rural existence has since the Socialist era remained essential for social classifications and antagonistic discourses within many of the urban domains presented in this volume. Besides, this brief reflection on Supara already alludes to some further themes that will become relevant in the following pages, notably the emergence of urban middle-class subjectivities and their consumption of transnational lifestyle goods.

The intention of this volume is to complement previous efforts towards an anthropology of post-Socialist urban spaces. These have been rather recent, as during the first decade of research on the former Soviet Central Asia and the Caucasus, urban phenomena were not among the prominent topics on the social science agenda. Instead, insights on some of the most salient 1990s transformations in these regions – such as the (re)awakening of religious spirituality, the (d)evolution of civil society, and the repercussions on local livelihoods of state withdrawal and new market economy principles – have evolved either from fieldwork in rural areas, or at least without a specific attention to urban contexts.

Only after the turn of the millennium did publications such as Nazpary's (2002) ethnography on the experiences of post-Soviet moral decay and social chaos among city residents in Almaty emerge. Subsequent works provided new insights on topics such as the binding and alienating forces between newly independent states and their citizens in urban contexts of 'Post-Soviet Asia' (Alexander, Buchli, and Humphrey 2007), or public spaces and the ways these have been socially produced and (re)conceptualized in different urban settings of Eurasia 'after socialism' (Darieva, Kaschuba, and Krebs 2011).

While drawing on these earlier publications, the contributions to this volume try to add new angles – first, by focusing on cities like Aktobe, Dushanbe, Kazan, Khujand and Bishkek, which until now have been rather blank spots on the social science map. Moreover, the urban spaces examined here refer to all levels on the spatial 'hierarchies of privacy or intimacy' (Liu 2012, 132). This means that aside from the public arenas of parks, bazaars and mass transportation, the contributors approach parochial city spaces, such as the yards within neighbourhood communities, but also the very intimate domain of shared flats.

With ethnographic attention to the intricacies of urban lives, the case studies assembled in this volume investigate the social production of spaces in conjunction with patterns of everyday encounters, consumption, identifications and narrations. The analyses extend, for example, from the transnational entanglements between a Dushanbe bazaar and hyper-modern Dubai to the micro-level hierarchies within flat-sharing communities in Astana; and from competing notions of urban belonging and aesthetics in a city such as Yerevan to the insight that rural migrants in Bishkek over time may synchronize with the rhythms of this city as part of an urban socialization. In that way, each contribution develops its own unique insights on the collective topic of Urban Spaces and Lifestyles in Central Asia and Beyond. In the remainder of this introduction, I provide an overview of the main research themes that this volume addresses.

Urban gateways

The contributions to this volume show that urban spaces are gateways to new worlds. Within the former Soviet sphere, the opportunities to connect to and to experience previously unfamiliar flows of people, goods and ideas increased significantly after 1991, when cities such as Almaty, Dushanbe and Yerevan became capitals of newly independent states. During the preceding 70 years or more, Soviet regulatory regimes had encapsulated these urban domains in two directions.

Inwards, within the territory of a Soviet Socialist Republic, the *propiska* system of residency permits – which were literally 'written in' (*propisat*) the passport – aimed to manage internal migration and restrict free movement, in particular relocations to urban centres (Buckley 1995; Sahadeo 2012). Aside from administrative measures, the founding document of Socialist ideology already established a separation between the city and the countryside. As Fehlings reminds us in her contribution on urban Yerevan,

Marx and Engels remarked as early as the Communist Manifesto of 1848 that only the modern urban domain would free people from the 'idiocy of rural life'. Taken together, these influences shaped a strong binary, whereby urban residents could attach (themselves) to civilizational progresses of intellectualism and professionalism, enjoy material advantages and cultivate cosmopolitan attitudes (Alexander and Buchli 2007, 9), whereas the rural hinterlands and their inhabitants were looked down upon as comparatively backward and unsophisticated.

As regards the other, outwards direction, the Soviet Union maintained rigid border controls, preventing its citizens from emigration and travel, and 'protecting' them from foreign influences. As Chandler (1998, 3) remarks, 'border controls epitomized the power of the Communist party-state, its control of both the society and domestic economy'. In that way, the Soviet Union and its residents became detached from regions and networks they had historically been closely integrated with in terms of ethnic belonging, linguistic practice and shared religious beliefs. One such case concerned Tajikistan and Afghanistan, where the vibrant exchange between traders and the ties between kin communities across the Panj-Amu Darya River were interrupted when the Soviet power finally sealed off this border in the mid-1930s (Abdullaev and Akbarzadeh 2010, 48). For Tajiks and other Muslims of the Soviet Union, the regime's ambition for isolation meant that their opportunities to connect to the global *umma* were limited and often used as a tool of foreign policy.

Nowadays, the contribution by Stephan-Emmrich and Mirzoev reveals that 25 years into Tajikistan's independence Tajik Muslims have, through the bazaars of urban Dushanbe, become active agents in spreading and consuming a Dubai-branded Islamic lifestyle. They show that not only does selling goods such as the latest *hijab* fashion open up precious income opportunities within Tajikistan's otherwise fragile economy, but also trading links with an Arab nation enhances their personal sense of participation in a wider Muslim world.

Other contributions illustrate still other ways that cities have become gateways to global trends and commodity flows unknown during the Socialist era. Sgibnev and Vozyanov (this volume), who examine the *marshrutka* (routed shared taxi) mobility phenomenon in Khujand (Tajikistan), remark that during different periods of the post-Socialist era the vehicles used for this kind of privatized urban mass transportation were imported from countries as far away as Latvia, Germany, Russia and China. Furthermore, their contribution indicates that nowadays a significant part of the financing to purchase vehicles and local licences originates from the remittances of Tajik labour migrants in Russia.

Jaeger focuses on the MEGA shopping mall, built in 2009 in Aktobe (Kazakhstan), which marks a recent step in Central Asian urban economic development. Compared to the 'wild' and 'dirty' bazaar trade that picked up in the 1990s, the finely crafted merging of entertainment opportunities and presentation of 'Western' retail goods is perceived especially by youth as a symbol of (imported) modernity. Without the pickpockets and other bazaar annoyances, the mall is not only regarded as a safe place, in particular for young women, but also turns into a stage for experimenting with unconventional fashion styles and behaviours, such as public kissing, which cannot be observed in other spaces of the city.

Darieva's contribution illustrates the vital role the Islamic Republic of Iran has come to play in contemporary Armenia through the prism of Yerevan's Blue Mosque complex. She demonstrates that in the former imperial borderland of Russia and Persia transnational links extend beyond the trade, energy and tourism sectors. In fact, the Blue Mosque has become a hybrid focal point, both for the re-emergence of Shia Muslim lifestyles and for secular cultural exchange between Iranian migrants and the local Armenian population.

Certainly, these new worlds are plural and diverse, yet at the same time they are far from arbitrary. The contributions gathered in this volume demonstrate that in each city the pathways of contemporary incorporations of the global are significantly shaped by these urban locales' histories and imagined futures. Examining male youth in the southern Kyrgyz city of Osh, Kirmse (2011) has recently suggested the term 'nested globalization' to understand how, depending on the particular setting, cultural repertoires with very different origins and contents are made available, translated and then absorbed. Amongst others, in Kirmse's case this entailed the mobilizing rhetoric of transnational Islamic groups, Turkish pop music and the key role that the Russian language continues to play in the mass media and as a professional skill.

In terms of nested routes and patterns of global flows, the Russian Federation emerges as an important point of reference across this volume. For countries such as Armenia, Kyrgyzstan and Tajikistan this primarily relates to the significant role that remittances sent home by migrants working in Russian cities play in their national economies (Isabaeva 2011; Reeves 2012). In his contribution on the changing urban landscapes and rhythms in Bishkek, Schröder mentions that these money transfers from abroad were a vital factor in the city's recent construction boom in the residential housing sector (see also Nasritdinov undated). Also, the MEGA shopping mall in Aktobe, described by Jaeger in this volume, found its way into the Western Kazakh steppe from Moscow, where the first such 'trade and entertainment centre' was opened in 2002 by the Russian branch of IKEA.

Going beyond economic factors, Nasritdinov (this volume) investigates the everyday encounters and perceptions of Muslim Central Asian migrants and long-term residents in two Russian cities, Saint Petersburg and Kazan. He finds these relations and the 'readability' and 'legibility' of urban space to be better in Kazan for those relocating from Central Asia. He attributes this to the settlement's distinct spatial identity, which is crucially tied to the historical co-residence of Tatar Muslims and Russian (Orthodox) Christians since the mid-sixteenth century. Nowadays, this can be noticed in a city divided into an Islamic *rayon* and other neighbourhoods. This spatial manifestation of difference equips incoming Muslim migrants from Central Asia with an obvious point of reference, on the basis of which they develop ties of friendship and affection with ethnic Russian locals as well.

One further point of interest on urban spaces as gateways that arises from Nasritdinov's observations concerns the ambivalent perception of links to Russia. For the Central Asian respondents Nasritdinov encountered in Saint Petersburg, this westernmost Russian metropolis is associated with good earning opportunities in the familiar setting of a shared Soviet past and with Russian as the lingua franca. On the other hand, experiences of discrimination, potential deportation and other uncertainties may prompt Central Asian migrants to develop strategies of 'invisibility' and lead to sceptical assessments of life in these urban environments (for Moscow, see Reeves 2013).

In conjunction with Russia's necessarily reduced political and economic reach into the national affairs of other post-Soviet states, alternative orientations for desired lifestyles, cultural exchanges, new business partnerships and visions of urban modernity might gain in appeal in the capitals of the latter. Stephan-Emmrich and Mirzoev point to this tendency in their contribution, arguing that the embrace of Dubai Islamic attire, or the ways some of Dushanbe's new construction projects emulate the spectacular architecture and urban 'hyper-modernity' of Arab and Asian metropolises, could be understood as the adoption of a critical stance towards 'Russian', 'Soviet' and 'Western' influences.

Finally, aside from being the focus of transnational networks and global flows, the cities discussed in this volume have also become gateways for internal rural migrants. Although the Soviet-era *propiska* system is still formally in place in most successor states, its current interpretation by local authorities seems to be less rigid. Accordingly, the cities covered in this volume have experienced significant inflows of internal migrants seeking to escape the dire post-Socialist conditions in their neglected rural areas to find a better life in the urban domain. For each city, however, specific aspects of these movements towards urban centres can be identified. For Yerevan, people left homeless by the 1988 earth-quake, and refugees of the Nagorno-Karabakh War, can be mentioned (Fehlings, this volume); for Dushanbe as well, refugees of the civil war (1992–97) and people affected by the ensuing economic collapse make a sizeable group (Stephan-Emmrich and Mirzoev, this volume); for Bishkek, the time around the 'revolution' of 2005 was a period of especially strong in-migration (Schröder, this volume); and in Aktobe, an increase in relocations from the countryside can be tied to the 'oil boom' in western Kazakhstan since the early 2000s (Jaeger, this volume). Astana again presents a particular case, which as a planned city and Kazakhstan's new capital since 1998 has attracted all kinds of newcomers, including government officials and businessmen who relocated from the previous capital, Almaty (Osmonova, this volume).

Before such newcomers arrived, most cities had seen a wave of emigration in the early 1990s. In Central Asia and the Caucasus, among those leaving were many of so-called European ethnicity (Russians, Ukrainians, Germans, etc.), but also elites of the titular nations who moved on towards Russia, the US or Western Europe. Still, in most cases the overall population in the urban centres increased significantly. One example is Bishkek, which grew from around 600,000 in 1989 (the last Soviet census) to unofficially 1.3 million in 2015 (Schröder 2010; this volume). Alongside other challenges during the transformations in the 1990s, this meant that the social structures in many of these cities changed radically in terms of ethnic composition and the regional origins of new inhabitants (see below).

As gateways to new post-Socialist worlds, the urban spaces discussed in this volume are incorporated into transnational flows of goods and ideas, while simultaneously they have become an accessible national destination for citizens from rural areas. As a result, these cities have quite literally changed their faces as many newcomers have claimed urban belonging and as new post-Socialist materialities have emerged. This relates again to various forms of everyday lifestyles, urban mobilities and social classifications that are ana-lyzed in detail in the case studies to follow.

Urban lifestyles and materialities

The changing demography of many urban spaces has often received a critical reception. In fact, many established city-dwellers shared the binary template of an urban-elitist domain versus a backward countryside, and anxiously projected that strong in-migration would lead to a 'ruralization' and 'degradation' of urban life. From that viewpoint, citizens of rural origin and disposition embodied a relapse into 'premodern forms of living and sociality' (Alexander and Buchli 2007, 30).

In her contribution on urban Yerevan, Fehlings clarifies the context of this divide, linking it to the urban intelligentsia's post-Socialist experiences of collapse, which entailed deteriorating urban industry, architecture and nature, but also feelings of spiritual decay. She also points to an ambivalent perception of rurality among the urbanites, who refer to some of the natural landmarks in Armenia, most notably Mount Ararat, as both sacred and dangerous. Consequently, this qualifies the country's rural population as the true carriers of national identity; however, to refer to Fehling's intuitive title, for some this 'savage' transforms from 'noble' to 'ignoble' once he traverses the countryside and enters the urban domain.

Schröder's contribution illustrates that in Kyrgyzstan's capital stigmas of violation and violence similar to those of Yerevan are attached to rural migrants. In addition, he identifies so-called 'newcomers' to Bishkek as a group that escapes the common dual classification. After a period of post-rural socialization in the city, these former villagers may be seen to have adopted enough of an urban habitus, evidenced by adequate forms of dress, language and behaviour, to inconspicuously engage in everyday encounters and thus pacify the anxieties of 'true urbanites' about their city's ruralization.

Osmonova, in her contribution on Astana, also finds such people – 'liminal personae' in Turner's (1995 [1969]) classic terminology – at the threshold between rural origins and current attempts to settle in the city. She juxtaposes short-term co-residence in shared flats with the middle-class dream of home ownership in Kazakhstan's new capital, the material manifestation of successful integration. Furthermore, she follows how these particular living arrangements produce new forms of sociability and social hierarchy among temporary flat-mates, or between main tenant and subtenant, which are not captured by common notions of kinship or friendship.

These observations from Astana connect, in turn, to the ones made by Stephan-Emmrich and Mirzoev on the burgeoning trade of Islamic lifestyle goods in Dushanbe's bazaars. For both sellers and clients, many of whom share a rural origin, the Emirati attire on offer symbolizes urban belonging and material success. Beyond a middle-class fashion statement, Dubai-style veiling (hijob) aims to express female piety and thus legitimizes the presence of women in public domains, notably in the male-dominated, dangerous and 'immoral' setting of an urban bazaar.

Jaeger's contribution describes the socio-material details of quite a different commercial space, the MEGA shopping mall in Aktobe. He describes how by way of 'adjacent attraction', i.e. the presentation of consumables next to amusement opportunities such as restaurants or cinemas, a multi-functional environment through which diverse user groups may develop their associations of excitement, freedom and modern urbanity is created. In the absence of other, similar spaces in Aktobe, the MEGA in fact appears to be 'where the whole city meets' in order to see and be seen – from rural families taking their children to the skating rink, to young online acquaintances who have agreed to have their first non-virtual date there.

Urban imaginaries of upward mobility, as Osmonova remarks for her case of young Kazakhs pursuing the Astana dream, are driven nowadays by neoliberal subjectivities that emphasize 'individual risk-taking' and 'self-reliance'. In post-Socialist contexts, this stands in stark contrast to the recent past of a paternalistic state that made strong efforts to define its citizens' virtues and to provide for their well-being. The contributions to this volume thus offer additional insights into the different ways in which newly independent states in Central Asia and the Caucasus have redefined their role in terms of remaining involved in or withdrawing from certain domains of daily urban life.

In some cities the agendas of current regimes have unambiguously become inscribed in the urban landscape. In the most spectacular fashion, this is the case in Astana's Left Bank area, which for newcomers to the city, as Osmonova shows, did not fail to serve as a visible indication of their nation's and consequently their own future individual prosperity. Grandiose construction efforts can be noticed in Dushanbe ('the world's largest teahouse') and Yerevan as well. However, as Fehlings shows, established urbanites of Yerevan may in fact instantly declare a recent project such as that of the Northern Avenue unaesthetic and 'rural'. This judgement apparently refers as much to the cityscape's transforming facade as to the immorality of the corrupt 'new elites' behind these endeavours – a reality that may be even more upsetting when juxtaposed with the decay of a former workers' neighbourhood such as Errord Mass.

Other contributions to this volume provide additional illustrations of how social contracts have been reconfigured in the post-Socialist era, a dynamic that primarily depends on a particular nation-state's current financial capabilities as defined by GDP and the praxis of redistributing state revenues. A rare example of proactive government intervention is mentioned by Osmonova, who frames the Kazakh authorities' measures against a looming credit crisis in Astana's housing sector as a way of protecting the property-owning middle class in order to keep alive their belief in the state's ambitious pledge for a bright future.

While this could be expected of Kazakhstan, the most vigorous post-Soviet economy aside from Russia, in most other cities addressed in this volume the withdrawal of the formerly paternalistic state is undeniable. As regards urban landscapes this is very evident in the case of Bishkek's 'new settlements' (novostroiki). These have emerged alongside different waves of rural-to-urban migration since the late Soviet era and today host a sizeable share of the city's population (some estimates reach 30%). Schröder (this volume) points to some of the everyday challenges in place-making within such novostroiki, which aside from facing cultural stigmatizations as 'wild' rurals is also a struggle for basic civic rights and for connection to urban infrastructure such as energy or transport systems. This situation becomes even more complicated if a new settlement is considered 'illegal', which for residents may prevent access to social services, health care and education due to their lack of an official residence permit (propiska; see also Hatcher 2015).

For its residents, but also for those calling themselves long-term urbanites, the new settlements in Kyrgyzstan's capital are a source of persistent frustration. Disappointment is directed first of all at the weak performance of official institutions, which are seen as failing to provide appropriate urban conditions or to maintain 'order' (poryadok). Beyond Bishkek, other contributions to this volume make a similar observation, namely that a constant effort at taming urban environments may be an ambition of post-Socialist ruling elites, yet one that either remains unfulfilled or is contested among certain groups of residents (see also Laszczkowski 2014).

As regards the material environment, Fehlings reports that in Yerevan, whose master plan of 1924 rested on the British 'garden city' concept, many public parks and other green zones are abandoned and overgrown today, a situation that many urbanites take as a sign of the administration's loss of control and the city's further degradation into a 'village'. The same urbanites, whether in Yerevan, Bishkek or other cities, share the expectation that the state should contribute in other ways as well, for example through education or the rule of law, to domesticate rural migrants into proper city-dwellers in order to avoid socio-cultural 'ruralization'.

In contrast, the contribution of Stephan-Emmrich and Mirzoev shows that a regime's taming efforts may also be intended to restrict certain urban lifestyles. They suggest that the official plan for Dushanbe to replace the many 'chaotic' bazaars with 'civilized' shopping malls is not merely for the sake of appearances. In fact, it might be intended to advance the government agenda of gaining more control over externally inspired Islamic lifestyles that deviate from the 'national norm', and whose various goods and worldviews have spread more easily into Dushanbe's urban spaces through the city's less formalized trading venues.

Urban rhythms

State efforts at taming the urban environment, and residents' potential resistance to these, punctuate the city's rhythm. As discussed in the previous sections, further such impulses for urban rhythms emerge from a city's particular materialities and lifestyles and its (gateway) positioning within global networks.

The contribution of Sgibnev and Vozyanov on *marshrutka* mobility in Khujand (Tajikistan) speaks to all these dynamics. They remark that the first *marshrutka* route was opened in Khujand as early as the 1980s as an alternative to the overcrowded trolleybus lines. In particular since the independent Tajik state cut its funding of public mass transportation, the *marshrutka* services have filled the gap of inner-city mobility and have turned into a highly profitable sector in the urban economy (with supposedly 1 out of 10 local families gaining an income from it). Examining assemblages of different materialities (vehicles, infrastructure), persons (drivers, passengers) and sets of cultural practices, the authors cover various angles. They show that the '*marshrutka* mobility phenomenon' has reconfigured post-Socialist urban space and is understood as a token of modernity, promising accessibility, comfort and speed; that *marshrutka* mobility connects to transnational flows, both of vehicles, which are imported from European countries or China, and of remittances, which are sent home by Tajik labour migrants from Russia in order to purchase these vehicles; and that the *marshrutka* assemblages entail administrative regimes of regulation in the form of licensing, route specifications and requirements on operating hours.

Nasritdinov (this volume) employs cognitive mapping and other research techniques to visualize the everyday routes and rhythms of Central Asian migrants in Russian cities. With respect to urban transportation, he identifies the metro stations of Saint Petersburg, rather than ethnic neighbourhoods, as providing crucial points of orientation for migrant newcomers in a city environment otherwise perceived as dispersed and incomprehensible. The metro system constitutes an ambiguous, 'parallel' space underground: for Central Asian traders, it promises many passing customers to sell their small-time goods to, while at other times, as passengers, riding the metro means travelling in an enclosed space that it is difficult to escape from in case of racist attacks or police harassment.

Other contributions to this volume approach urban rhythms through processes of adaptation to city life. For some newcomers to the city, this might primarily be about its taking some time to acquire the basic sensory identifiers of proper city jargon and dress code and thus escape the cultural stigmatization attached to 'village backwardness' (Schröder, this volume). Yet for others, as Osmonova's contribution reveals, establishing oneself in a city like Astana may be about more than self-presentation and cultivating an urban habitus. In an environment of fleeting social ties, such as that of a flat-sharing community, access to the most essential information, for example on how to get a decent apartment, is frequently acquired by newcomers only through an arduous trial-and-error period (see also Schröder 2013).

Darieva's contribution looks beyond such micro-level processes of stop-and-go integration into urban life. The perspective she develops on the Blue Mosque complex in Yerevan traces the varied historical meanings and functions of this eighteenth-century building, from being a Friday mosque for the local Azeri-speaking Muslim population until the mid-1920s to serving as a secular exhibition centre for artists and intellectuals of Armenia's Socialist era after its closure during the anti-religious campaigns. Nowadays, the Blue Mosque complex has been rediscovered as a religious site for Yerevan's Shia believers. Yet it is also promoted by its Iranian administration as a cultural and educational institution for 'outsiders', such as urban (Armenian) Christians, who can attend free Persian-language classes or join public events. Most obviously during such common celebrations as for the Norooz holiday, the Blue Mosque complex defies any singular religious definition and is a shared space that references a type of regional integration dating back to pre-Soviet and pre-Islamic eras. Darieva vividly illustrates how Yerevan's urban rhythm has been influenced by the flux of contracting and expanding relations, which recontextualized the usages of that particular site within the cityscape during different periods and altered its perception by different groups of urban dwellers.

The pulses of urban middle-class subjectivities

Reeves (2011, 324) has recently argued for a 'dynamic approach to place' in Central Asia that investigates how certain spaces are socially co-produced, and how their materiality thus 'mediates experiences of belonging and exclusion'. As part of this, she also reflects on how ordinary residents engage in multiple ways of 'doing place', which may contest, ignore or appropriate statist efforts at 'taming space'. This volume follows on from this debate, taking it from (imperial and post-Socialist) borderlands, hydroelectric dams and rural areas into various cityscapes. At the same time, the present volume adds to the insight that Central Asia is nowadays integrated into diverse transnational networks in important ways, including even those of global financial institutions and the 'offshore world' (Heathershaw and Cooley 2015). Although the revenue streams from these high-profile operations are undeniably inscribed in the cityscapes as well, the focus of this volume is on non-elite urban dwellers and how they deal with everyday economic flows and other transactions within their urban surroundings.

In this respect, the ethnographic accounts assembled here document new nuances in the evolution of the post-Socialist urban fabric: from bazaar trade to shopping malls; from a singular reliance on remittances from Russia to trade in Islamic goods from Dubai; from an imagined cultural split between urbanites and rurals to the in-between classification of a non-stigmatized city 'newcomer'. Alongside this, previously unnoticed urban practitioners and their spatial niches have come into view: a young flatmate in Astana, a mobility entrepreneur in Khujand, or a female customer in a retail store in Aktobe. Often, their ways of 'doing place' define parochial urban spaces which become 'intimately public' when new sociabilities, hierarchies and mechanisms of control coalesce during the process of their appropriation. Such spaces remain contingent as mobile actors use, avoid or recontextualize them from different positions of power at different times. A Shia mosque, a new type of settlement or a *marshrutka* are thus both subject to and sources of the '(poly)rhythmicities' (Smith and Hetherington 2013, 4) that also underscore cities such as Yerevan, Kazan and Khujand. Future investigations into the dynamics of urban place-making in Central Asia and beyond would benefit from expanding their scope beyond the socio-spatial dimension to include the more complex temporalities of accelerating and dissipating daily micro-routines and routes through the city.

What the urban dwellers portrayed in this volume also widely share is less grief or anger about the social and economic entitlements of which they were 'dispossessed' after the Soviet collapse (Nazpary 2002). More than two decades into the 'unmaking of Soviet life' (Humphrey 2002), there is more to notice now than the sharp distinction between the (few) 'new rich' and the (many) 'new poor'. In fact, many respondents in the case studies of this volume express their (aspirations of) belonging to an emerging urban middle class (although this phenomenon has advanced at different speeds and to different extents in the nation-states covered here). Such identification habitually entails distinctive lifestyle aspirations of consumption and display, of sophistication and communication, of mobility and the attachment to multiple modernities (be these 'Western', 'Asian' or 'Muslim'). The more detailed examination of the formation of such 'middle-class subjectivities' (Heiman, Freeman, and Liechty 2012) promises to offer an interesting lens for an ethnographic approach to neoliberal global realities in post-Socialist contexts.

Finally, a great deal of the material in this volume links in to my introductory description of Chunkurchak's beautiful landscape. There, the Supara 'ethno-style' complex is a microcosm of Kyrgyz middle-class subjectivity that connects to Bishkek's urban rhythms. The person who first drew my attention to this place was a young ethnic Kyrgyz entrepreneur who had imported the shower cabins for the cottages from China. For him, Supara was a transnational business project that fed his young family – a place that was 'not too far from the city', where in the 'good company' of relatives or friends he felt momentarily reconnected to his ancestors' nomadic heritage while enjoying some glasses of *kumys* (the traditional drink of fermented mare's milk) – yet he could also rest 'comfortably' in a fully equipped cottage, and the wireless Internet connection enabled him to instantly share all his impressions via Instagram and WeChat with peers of equal standing, in Kyrgyz, Russian or Chinese, depending on his virtual audience.

Acknowledgments

Most of the contributions to this volume were first presented at the workshop 'Tracing Migration and Global Connectedness: Urban Contexts in Central Asia and Beyond' (Berlin, May 2013). We are grateful to Professor Manja Stephan-Emmrich (Humboldt-Universität zu Berlin), who generously funded this event. We also thank *Central Asian Survey* and its editor, Deniz Kandiyoti, for the opportunity to realize this collective project. Finally, the insightful comments and suggestions of all anonymous reviewers were highly appreciated.

Disclosure statement

No potential conflict of interest was reported by the author.

References

Abdullaev, A., and S. Akbarzadeh. 2010. *Historical Dictionary of Tajikistan*. Lanham: Scarecrow Press.
Alexander, C., and V. Buchli. 2007. "Introduction." In *Urban Life in Post-Soviet Asia*, edited by C. Alexander, V. Buchli, and C. Humphrey, 1–39. London: UCL.
Alexander, C., V. Buchli, and C. Humphrey, eds. 2007. *Urban Life in Post-Soviet Asia*. London: UCL.
Buckley, C. 1995. "The Myth of Managed Migration: Migration Control and Market in the Soviet Period." *Slavic Review* 54 (4): 896–916. doi:10.2307/2501398.
Chandler, A. 1998. *Institutions of Isolation: Border Controls in the Soviet Union and Its Successor States, 1917–1993*. Montreal: McGill-Queen's University Press.
Comaroff, J. L., and J. Comaroff, eds. 2009. *Ethnicity Inc*. Chicago: Chicago University Press.
Darieva, T., W. Kaschuba, and M. Krebs, eds. 2011. *Urban Spaces after Socialism: Ethnographies of Public Spaces in Eurasian Cities*. Frankfurt: Campus Verlag.
Hatcher, C. 2015. "Illegal Geographies of the State: The Legalisation of a 'Squatter' Settlement in Bishkek, Kyrgyzstan." *International Journal of aw in the Build Environment* 7 (1): 39–54. doi:10.1108/IJLBE-01-2014-0004.
Heathershaw, J., and A. Cooley 2015. "Offshore Central Asia: An Introduction." *Central Asian Survey* 34 (1): 1–10. doi:10.1080/02634937.2015.1008816.
Heiman, R., C. Freeman and M. Liechty, eds. 2012. *The Global Middle Classes. Theorizing Through Ethnography*. Santa Fe: School for Advanced Research Press.
Humphrey, C. 2002. *The Unmaking of Soviet Life. Everyday Economies after Socialism*. Ithaca: Cornell University Press.
Isabaeva, E. 2011. "Leaving to Enable Others to Remain: Remittances and New Moral Economies of Migration in Southern Kyrgyzstan." *Central Asian Survey* 30 (3–4): 541–554. doi:10.1080/02634937.2011.607917
Kirmse, S. B. 2011. "'Nested Globalization' in Osh, Kyrgyzstan: Urban Youth Culture in a 'Southern' City." In *Urban Spaces After Socialism: Ethnographies of Public Spaces in Eurasian Cities*, edited by T. Darieva, W. Kaschuba, and M. Krebs, 283–305. Frankfurt: Campus Verlag.
Laszczkowski, M. 2014. "State Building(s). Built Forms, Materiality, and the State Astana." In *Ethnographies of the State in Central Asia: Performing Politics*, edited by J. Beyer, J. Rasanayagam, and M. Reeves, 149–172. Bloomington: Indiana University Press.
Liu, M. 2012. *Under Solomon's Throne: Uzbek Visions of Renewal in Osh*. Pittsburgh, PA: University of Pittsburgh Press.
Nasritdinov, E. undated. "Building the Future. Materialisation of Kyrgyz and Tajik Migrants Remittances in the Construction Sectors of Their Home Countries." Unpublished Paper, American University of Central Asia.
Nazpary, J. 2002. *Post-Soviet Chaos. Violence and Dispossession in Kazakhstan*. London: Pluto Press.
Reeves, M. 2011. "Introduction: Contested Trajectories and a Dynamic Approach to Place." *Central Asian Survey* 30 (3–4): 307–330. doi:10.1080/02634937.2011.614096.

Reeves, M. 2012. "Black Work, Green Money: Remittances, Ritual, and Domestic Economies in Southern Kyrgyzstan." *Slavic Review* 71 (1): 108–134. doi:10.5612/slavicreview.71.1.0108.

Reeves, M. 2013. "Clean Fake: Authenticating Documents and Persons in Migrant Moscow." *American Ethnologist* 40 (3): 508–524. doi:10.1111/amet.12036.

Sahadeo, J. 2012. "Soviet 'Blacks' and Place Making in Leningrad and Moscow." *Slavic Review* 71 (2): 331–358. doi:10.5612/slavicreview.71.2.0331.

Schröder, P. 2010. "'Urbanizing' Bishkek: Interrelations of Boundaries, Migration, Group Size and Opportunity Structure." *Central Asian Survey,* 29 (4): 453–467. doi:10.1080/02634937.2010.537143.

Schröder, P. 2013. "Ainuras Amerikanische Karriere. Räumliche und Soziale Mobilität einer jungen Kirgisin." *Zeitschrift für Ethnologie* 138: 235–258.

Smith, R. J., and K. Hetherington, eds. 2013. "Urban Rhythms: Mobilities, Space and Interaction in the Contemporary City." *The Sociological Review* 61 (S1): 4–16. doi:10.1111/1467-954X.12050.

Turner, V. W. 1995 [1969]. *The Ritual Process: Structure and Anti-Structure.* New Jersey: Transaction Publishers.

The manufacturing of Islamic lifestyles in Tajikistan through the prism of Dushanbe's bazaars

Manja Stephan-Emmrich and Abdullah Mirzoev

Institute for Asian and African Studies, Humboldt-Universität zu Berlin, Germany

ABSTRACT
This article traces the multiple ways of 'manufacturing' Islamic lifestyles in the urban environment of Tajikistan's capital city, Dushanbe. The city's bazaars serve as a lens through which to observe the conjunction of its booming trade business with Dubai alongside its growing Islamic commodity culture and a religious reformism that is inspired by the materiality and non-materiality of a progressive and hybrid Dubai Islam. Bringing together long-distance trade, urban consumption practices and new forms of public piety in the mobile livelihood of three bazaar traders and sellers, the article provides insights into how the commodification of Islam informs notions of urbanity and modernity in Tajikistan. These notions correspond to the launching of urban renewal and the meta-narrative of Dushanbe's future as a modern city on the rise. Furthermore, the article illustrates the ways in which Dushanbe's Muslims turn bazaars into an urban laboratory for religious agency and cultural identities.

Introduction

A walk along Rudaki, Dushanbe's main avenue, provides frequent encounters with a great variety of urban fashions and lifestyles.[1] The manifold and creative ways schoolgirls combine their black-and-white school uniforms with traditional Tajik materials and European-style trousers or miniskirts are as striking as the colourful tunics and dresses, and the vivid and stylishly tied and draped *hijob*s (veils) of the many female students and teachers who are heading to their lectures at the Abu Hanifa Islamic Institute. This latter phenomenon – the *hijob* tied and worn in combination with trendy styles and materials – bears witness to a 'fashionalization' of Islamic clothing that connects Dushanbe's Muslims to the growing global market of Islamic lifestyles, commodities and identities. Moreover, these bodily practices demonstrate that in today's urban Tajikistan the 'modern' has become highly nuanced through cultural impulses that are inspired by trends not only from Eurasia but also from the Gulf region and the Middle East (Osella and Osella 2008, 325). One urban locale where these fashionable commodities and Islamic lifestyles are manufactured, negotiated and conflated with a new notion of Muslim modernity is in the bazaars of Dushanbe.

Catching one of the numerous private taxis that link the city centre with Dushanbe's more outward-situated main clothing bazaars, such as Kurvon and Sakhovat, is the quickest way to plunge into the varied world of what is on offer with regard to Islamic lifestyles. Trendy materials, such as glittery Islamic dresses and stylish headscarves in the 'Arabic' (*arabskiy*), 'Turkish' (*turetskiy*) or 'Iranian' (*eronskiy*) style, are available from lower-end vendors and luxury shops alike, while small media shops exhibit DVDs with Iranian, Turkish or Arabic movies, soap operas and video clips that act as visual guides into the manifold ways to wear or combine such fabrics and clothes in a fashionable way. Just around the corner, sellers display 'Islamic' wellness products, perfume or natural medicine from Arab countries. Others specialize in ritual paraphernalia or the basic necessities for Hajj pilgrims. Some sellers advertise their Islamic commodities from behind pious attire: female traders wearing fashionable *hijob* or Islamic clothes; male traders sporting long beards, Muslim headdress and 'Salafi-style' clothing.[2] When talking to their clients, some sellers use pious Arabic phrases such as *alhamdullilah* and *yo Allah*, even when selling kitchen appliances or the newer tech products. Strikingly, many sellers praise their products as *dubaiskiy* ('made in Dubai' or 'brought from Dubai') or they assure the prospective buyer that their products are imported from Arab countries (*az arabiston*) (Figure 1).

These varied sights and sounds of the bazaar are signs of a Muslim revivalism in Tajikistan's capital city, which cannot be separated from the material and non-material flows fuelled by a global Islamic economy. Moreover, the new Islamic consumerism involves a religious reformism in Dushanbe that promotes the engagement in projects of Muslim self-making. Furthermore, it combines the individual's aim for moral perfection – the desire to cleanse oneself of 'un-Islamic' local or Soviet traditions and Western values – with economic needs and educational aspirations (Schröder and Stephan-Emmrich 2014, 8ff.; Osella and Osella 2009; Frisk 2009). As such, Dushanbe's religious reformism is simultaneously local and transnational: it emerged from the specific social, political and historical context of the Soviet and post-Soviet eras (Babadjanov and Kamilov 2001; Dudoignon 2011; Epkenhans 2011) but has adopted global Islamic impulses towards

Figure 1. Assemblage of Iranian and Arabic movies, soap operas and music offered in Kurvon bazaar, Dushanbe (photograph by A. Mirzoev, 2014).

purification, progress and modernity (Osella and Osella 2008). These impulses, as we argue, can be traced in large part to Dubai's cosmopolitan history, transregional trading centres and global and historic Muslim networks, which challenge one-dimensional depictions of the Gulf states as exclusively Middle Eastern (Vora 2013, 3). Due to the many successful careers of Tajiks working and studying in Dubai, the religious reformism is associated with upward mobility, spiritual well-being and a cultural sophistication resulting from travel and work experiences in the urban hubs of the Gulf and the wider Arab world. This sense of a 'progressive' and 'modern' Islam finds its expression in new forms of public piety, such as the fashionable 'Dubai-style' veiling, or the conversion of traditional names into Koranic or Arabic ones. Furthermore, in an evolving moral urban soundscape, one can hear Arabic formulas in daily speech, mobile ringtones playing the prayer call (*a'zam*) or recitations of Koranic verses, and the growing presence of Islamic/Arabic pop music (*nasjid*).

Relying on Dushanbe's bazaars as a revelatory lens, this article aims to trace the multiple ways in which Islamic lifestyles are 'manufactured' in the urban environment of Tajikistan's capital city. Following anthropological studies on cultural consumption (Navaro-Yashin 2002; Fischer 2008), we use the term 'manufacturing' to link processes of producing, advertising and selling with the abstract local imagination to show how Islam has been turned into a brand to affix an imprint of piety onto the offered goods, which are also touted as prestigious and modern. The bazaar, in that context, becomes a place where modern urban identities are expressed through the medium of traded goods and through how these goods are advertised, sold and consumed according to the rules of the market economy. As we will show, the manufacturing of urban lifestyles is embedded in and fed by various intra- and inter-urban mobilities covering recent processes of urbanization, which include: rural-to-urban migration; the conjunction of long-distance trading and translocal business networks; and the intersection of business trips with religious mobilities, such as the Hajj pilgrimage or going abroad to study Islam. Ultimately, Muslim life and identity in Tajikistan have become increasingly inspired by the materiality and non-materiality of a Muslim modernity produced in the economic and urban hubs of the Gulf metropolis.

By linking the material semantics of the trading objects with the translocal trajectories of the traders' livelihoods and the ways their experiences of mobility are revealed by what they wear and how they wear it, the article offers a promising approach for understanding the materialization of Dushanbe's Muslim revivalism or 'how religion happens materially' (Meyer et al. 2010, 209). Moreover, exploring this configuration helps in understanding how the commodification of Islam informs urban notions of modernity in Tajikistan.

Tracing the work trajectories of each of three highly mobile urban actors who have successfully combined the careers of religious actor and economic entrepreneur, we illustrate how bazaar workers adapt to urban lifestyles and, at the same time, through their mobile livelihoods and by dwelling in translocal environments, gain agency and assume a major role in reshaping and creating urban lifestyles from a multitude of social, spiritual and economic opportunities.

Starting with the cultural strategies that the two saleswomen, Munira and Nasiba, developed in order to become fully accepted or economically independent 'urbanites' (*shahry*), we will argue that for single women fashionable veiling is a reputable way to respond to urban debates that decry the decline of female modesty. Moreover, fashionable veiling empowers women to gain a foothold in a traditionally male-dominated economy sector.

They thereby make use of the semiotics of 'Dubai-style' clothes that link modesty, urban cos-mopolitanism and modernity with 'proper trading'. By following the two women's transna-tional trading activities in and beyond the Gulf, as well as Abdurahmon's successful career as a cross-border trader vending 'Mecca perfume' and Hajj paraphernalia later in the article, we illustrate how the Dubai boom in the early 2000s facilitated successful urban careers as 'busi-nesswomen' or 'pious entrepreneurs' and accelerated the change of Dushanbe's public face through products and images of a progressive and cosmopolitan Islam. The three actors who are the focus of this article combine economic success with spiritual awakening and religiously defined sales strategies, and in this way they transform 'Islam' into a highly coveted brand that conflates existing romanticized and exoticized media images of the (Arab) 'Muslim other' (McBrien 2012) with urban notions of modernity, prosperity and pro-gress. The prestige goods and stylish clothing brought from Dubai create fictions of a modern Muslim identity and fuel a symbolic consumerism that is closely related to the spec-tacular architecture and urban 'hyper-modernity' of that very global city.

Blurring the boundaries of piety, consumption and urbanity, mobile Tajik Muslims turn Dushanbe's bazaars into an urban laboratory for cultural politics. The new commodity culture presents a stylish, modernized and urban 'Islam' (*Islom*) that is distinctly separate from traditional Muslim ways of life in villages and remote areas, which are labelled as 'reli-gion' (*din*), associated with 'culture' or 'tradition' (*urfu odat, an'ana*) and perceived as 'back-ward' (*qafomonda*). At the same time, Islamic lifestyle consumption expresses a critical attitude towards 'Western', 'Soviet' or 'Russian' values, as seen by contrast to dress styles and public habits commonly labelled as 'modern' (Russian: *sovremennyj*). Arguably, Tajikistan's Muslims resort to abstract images and concrete objects of a modern Islam to reject both the old Soviet legacy and the new Russian cultural hegemony. In that sense, the production of urban Islamic lifestyles in Dushanbe's bazaars contributes to the repo-sitioning of Tajikistan's Muslims by evoking a modernity that is imagined and shaped as 'Muslim' rather than as 'Western' or 'European'.

Urban renewal and the 'Dubai boom'

The expanding informal economy in the early post-Soviet era led to a 'bazaar boom' that constitutes an important pillar of Dushanbe's urban economy to the present day. Cur-rently, Dushanbe hosts 33 public and private bazaars. Numerous reopenings, overnight closings and mysterious fires in recent years confirm Dushanbe's markets as a highly con-tested urban space that creates uncertain livelihoods (Humphrey 1997, 2002). At the same time, private ownership and enterprises have facilitated the accumulation of new wealth in the city and turned the bazaar economy into a lucrative business.

The attitude of the city administration towards Dushanbe's markets, however, is rather ambivalent. As in the Central Asian neighbour states, recent urban planning in Dushanbe suggests economic modernization and development that clearly mirror the Soviet dis-course concerning modernity and progress (Alff 2013, 23). Perceived as a legacy of the Soviet 'economy of shortage' (Verdery 1991) and later of 'post-Soviet chaos' (Nazpary 2002), markets serve as an allegory of an 'uncivilized', 'disordered' and runaway economy that should be replaced, step by step, with 'civilized' and 'modern' supermarkets and shopping malls characterized by fixed prices, tax regulations and high-quality pro-ducts (Figure 2).

Figure 2. Young women strolling through the Kurvon bazaar, Dushanbe (photograph by A. Mirzoev, 2013).

The replacement of bazaars in the inner city by modern malls, trading centres or residential areas,[3] or the bazaars' relocation to the city's outskirts, is in line with a general construction boom that reflects the government's intention to 'tame' urban public space and shape Dushanbe into a civilized and up-and-coming modern city. The decreed urban renewal finds its expression in architectural superlatives such as 'the world's biggest teahouse' or 'Central Asia's biggest mosque'. Obviously, these projects can help Dushanbe in its attempt to overcome its marginalized position among Central Asian capitals, but they also can have a more global appeal. 'Jubilee projects' such as the National Library or the Presidential Palace have been recently constructed on the occasion of the twentieth anniversary (in 2011) of the republic's independence, but are perceived by city dwellers as 'dictator chic' rather than national symbols (Parshin 2012, 1). Additionally, city bazaars such as Putovsky have vanished in favour of high-rise elite apartments financed by Turkish agencies or the state of Qatar.

The most prestigious construction project currently underway is Diyar Dushanbe, along the waterfront of the Hisor Canal, an integrated community development project financed by the government of Qatar through Diyari Qatar. With its planned residential towers, office buildings, central plaza, shopping malls and leisure facilities, the residential area promises integrative lifestyles and consumption events for the new urban middle and upper classes. This reshaping of Dushanbe's urban materiality can be compared to the hyper-modernity and global futures produced in the urban narrative of cities such as Dubai (Vora 2013, 6ff.). Local fantasies of a new urbanity are awakened that correspond to global Muslim or 'Asian' rather than European, Western or Soviet values.

Urban notions of modernity and progress were also accelerated when the 'Dubai boom' reached Dushanbe's bazaars. In the mid-1990s Tajikistan's political elite of that time discovered Dubai not only as an exclusive tourist destination but also as a place for the lucrative automobile parts trade. Later, and based on the healthy cultural connections with Dubai's Afghan and Iranian diaspora,[4] trade flourished that involved luxury cars, smartphones, flat-panel televisions and modern kitchen appliances, replacing cut-rate imports from China and paving the way for a newly prosperous economic and pious elite, the 'new Tajiks' (*tajiki nav*). Their wealth, spiritual success and established cross-border networks induced many Tajiks to follow suit, fuelling a 'Dubai boom' that reached its apex around 2010 but now has begun to subside considerably.

The import of modern and high-quality products from Dubai was accompanied by the introduction of fashionable female fabrics labelled as 'Arabic' or 'Dubai veil' (*arabskiy* or *dubaiskiy satr*). Produced in Pakistan, China or India and ornamented in Dubai, these fabrics copy the national female Emirati dress and thereby merge different cultural styles, materials and applications into a hybrid 'Dubai style'. However, the fabrics still convey the semantics of the newly arisen elitist Arab (Emirati) nationalism, which distinguishes an 'authentic' Arab identity from Dubai's cosmopolitan history (Vora 2013). Symbolizing Arab cultural superiority, wealth and exclusiveness, fashionable Emirati dresses were brought home by Tajik traders for their wives, worn by tradeswomen or exhibited in the luxury *abaya*[5] shops that opened up in the city centre. In so doing, the Dubai trade business accelerated the fashionalization of women's Islamic clothing. Furthermore, the prestigious goods became markers of the lifestyles and aspirations of Dushanbe's 'new Tajiks'; i.e. members of a new urban, economically strong, upper and middle class, because they are marketed in the recently built city malls and supermarkets and worn by female family members.

Moreover, the imported Emirati female attire serves as an indicator of the spiritual awakening that many Tajiks experience in Dubai. During deep-into-the-night discussions about Islam and proper Muslimness that take place in the accommodations Tajik traders share with Afghan, Arab and Sunni Iranian migrants in the Dubai Creek area, through attending Koran courses in one of Dubai's Islamic education centres or performing the Hajj pilgrimage to Mecca, Tajik traders adopt globally circulating Islamic impulses and develop new Muslim identities. Therefore, the fashionable Emirati attire materializes the conflation of economic success, inner reform and moral self-perfection with a cultural sophistication that is embodied in cosmopolitan urban habits, knowledge and travel experiences. As such, the fashionable Emirati attire also feeds urban fantasies about a good life, which is modern, luxurious, 'purified' and pious and thus signifies the urban discourse of cultural differentiation from the 'backward' rural other.

When Dubai became accessible to non-elite Tajiks, the trade of 'Dubai goods' began to flourish and take over the city's bazaars. Since that time, hybrid Dubai lifestyles have increasingly shaped the consumption habits of the city's disadvantaged or 'dispossessed' (Nazpary 2002), such as newcomers from rural regions and single or divorced women. The semantics of prestigious Islamic goods brought from Dubai have fuelled their desires and aspirations to become 'urbanites' (*shahry*).

Rurals in the city

Dushanbe's cultural and social ties with the surrounding rural regions were strong in the Soviet era. However, after Tajikistan's independence the city experienced a rapid urbanization by way of several waves of rural-to-urban migration. Initially, the civil war in 1992 caused refugee flows from rural areas and remote regions into the city. After the civil war, a collapsing economy and rising poverty forced many more rurals to move to the city. The term 'Kulobization' refers not only to the transition of political power in 1994 to the reigning Rahmon clan, which originates from the Kulob region, but also to the many poor people from the republic's southern region who poured into the city and became involved in the bazaar trade. The consequent growth of the bazaar economy is best illustrated by the decreasing role of the Sakhovat bazaar and the rise of the Kurvon bazaar with respect to Dushanbe's central market of textile fabrics.

Sakhovat, which was built in the 1970s as an agricultural-products market, grew to be one of the biggest post-Soviet public wholesale markets until 2002. When the area became too crowded to accommodate all of the vendors with their shops and trailers, the city administration opened Kurvon at the southern edge of town, where a main road connects Dushanbe to Tajikistan's southern centres, such as Kurghonteppa and Kulob. Sakhovat remained a hub for trade in food and pharmaceuticals. But the territoriality of Kurvon strikingly revitalized the city. The once-deserted Soviet *mikrorayon* blocs around the market now serve as temporary residence for rural bazaar workers from the southern Khatlon region, and a bustling taxi service connects bazaar workers and consumers with both the inner city and the rural surroundings. Like Sakhovat before it, Kurvon has become a node in regional networks spanning rural–urban boundaries and thus ensures the continuity of cultural and social urban–rural relations (Nasritdinov and O'Connor 2010, 143).

With their local dialects and rural dress codes and ways of life, but also with their Muslim beliefs and practices, the newcomers have changed the city's image, which, as a consequence, has generated specific urban anxieties about a ruralization of the city. These anxieties surface in ironic comments and jokes, such as those intimating that the political elite has successfully transformed Dushanbe from a city (*shahr*) into a village (*qishloq*). They are also expressed in an urban discourse that posits the cultural superiority of the 'civilized' and 'modern' city and its inhabitants (*shahry*) over the 'uncivilized', 'backward' and 'traditional' rurals or rural migrants (*qishloqi*).

Market moralities and the 'feminization' of trade

Kaneff (2002, 41ff.) has illustrated in her ethnography of post-Soviet economies how markets shape and reshape identities and subjectivities through moral debates wherein the bazaar trade as a form of work is ambivalently characterized in terms of shame and pride. In Dushanbe, although the bazaar trade is often an essential livelihood strategy, it is sometimes viewed as 'bad work' (*kori bad*) or 'impure work' (*kori nopok*), a notion that derives from the association of the bazaar locale with strangers, disorderliness and a proclivity towards cheating and disreputable speculation (Kaneff 2002), as well as a dumping ground for inexpensive, low-quality goods from China. Here, old Soviet reservations join post-Soviet bazaar realities and find their expression in the Tajik proverb, *Bozor – maqomi shayton ast!*[6]

The urban debates about market moralities intensified when the bazaar trade in Dushanbe underwent an obvious 'feminization'. The post-Soviet economic transition, with its plunging incomes and declining employment opportunities, affected mainly women. Having previously worked as teachers or nurses or in the public sector, they were pushed back into domestic (re)production or driven into informal economies overnight. Post-Soviet private and cross-border trade is therefore predominantly female (Alff 2013, 21; Werner 2004).

In Tajikistan, however, the feminization of the bazaar trade is not merely an outcome of the rapid transformation from planned economy to private capitalism and its subsequent 'de-modernization' (Ishkanian 2003, 483). It is also a direct result of the lack or absence of men as family breadwinners. The widespread losses and mass displacement during the civil war between 1992 and 1997, as well as the male-dominated work migration to Russia,[7] left a significant number of single, widowed or divorced women who were pushed into the bazaar trade and undertook the formerly male role of family breadwinner. According to our survey among bazaar workers at the Sakhovat and Kurvon markets, there are many single newcomers to the city among the tradeswomen with children who, as the case of Munira will show, were driven to Dushanbe by poverty, an uncertain future and economic needs.[8] Once they arrived, they struggled to gain a foothold, and some managed to achieve a level of economic independence that allowed them to maintain their single status and to live alone in the city.

The appropriation of urban public space by women involved in private entrepreneurship and trade resonates with the reigning urban debates about the immorality and disorderliness of the market. Men complain that through their involvement in the bazaar trade, 'women have started to behave like men' – they 'speak in a loud voice', 'talk to strangers' or 'move like men'. As a consequence, it is feared that women will 'lose their female modesty' (*sharmu hayo*), which is marked by virtues such as shyness, obedience and grace. The new visibility of women in markets amplifies gendered anxieties in the urban public sphere about the bazaar as an obvious local 'anti-structure' (Turner 1969), in opposition to the traditional social order strongly built on patriarchal principles and gender segregation. Even when urban debates in Dushanbe on tradition and modernity were conducted with women as the focal point and at the same time excluded from participation (Kuehnast and Nechemias 2004, 3), tradeswomen responded to their heightened vulnerability in public through veiling (*satr pushidan*) (Tohidi 1998, 144). For many women involved in cross-border trade or in selling at the bazaar, the decision to veil themselves not only reveals their religious awakening but also serves as an appropriate cultural tool to protect their modesty while pursuing economic strategies in the male-dominated public sphere. In doing so, tradeswomen re-encoded the semantics of veiling from a solely public expression of a new and merely elitist Muslim consciousness (Stephan 2006) to what also becomes a marker or proof of female morality, modesty and piety. Such re-readings of the veil affirm the women's active and creative contribution to a growing Muslim reformism in Dushanbe and resonate with the urban narrative that places the origin of Dushanbe's post-Soviet Muslim revival in the city's bazaars.

As the following two case studies illustrate, Dushanbe's markets provide an important urban space where women encounter the moral semantics of the *hijob* and experience veiling as a reputable cultural strategy to successfully adapt to urban life and lifestyles. Moreover, through the bazaar trade women can earn their livelihoods in the city. They pursue both economic needs and religious aspirations and foster experiences of well-being through empowerment, economic independence, self-cultivation and social and moral betterment.

Selling trust: Nasiba and Munira

Nasiba's and Munira's careers as tradeswomen started at the Sakhovat bazaar. While Munira has always worked as a saleswoman in a shop for modern kitchen appliances, Nasiba sold tablecloths and kitchen napkins with her stepmother before she opened up her own bijouterie shop in the Chinese bazaar. As shopsellers both women gradually became involved in cross-border trade, travelling regularly to either Bishkek or Dubai to bring back new, high-quality and prestigious goods.

Although they share successful careers as tradeswomen, Nasiba and Munira come from very different backgrounds. Nasiba, forty years old, was born and raised by her Samarkandian stepmother in Dushanbe. After graduating from technical college she worked in a small microcredit bank that later collapsed. Afterwards, her husband decided to work in Russia, but instead of returning to Dushanbe he divorced her by phone. Left alone with a child, Nasiba decided to go to Russia on her own to find work but returned after six months. With the help of her stepmother she found employment as a court secretary in Dushanbe, but quit when her second husband ordered her to stay at home. After her second divorce, and now left with two children, she began to work as a seller at Sakhovat with her stepmother. In 2008 she opened up her own bijouterie.

Munira, thirty-six years old, first came to Dushanbe as a civil war refugee along with her family from the southern city of Kurghonteppa but later returned to her home village. There she was married to a man who spent most of the year working in Russia and divorced her after two years. She returned to her birth home, but moved to Dushanbe two years later to look for a job to support herself and her child. In Dushanbe she stayed with her aunt, who helped her find a family in the neighbourhood that needed a babysitter. Later on, that same family recommended Munira to a friend, who employed her as a seller in his shop. Since 2006 she has sold kitchen utensils at Sakhovat.

Nasiba's and Munira's careers as tradeswomen cannot be separated from their decision to veil. As the following statements demonstrate, the women justify their willingness to comply with pious urban dress codes and styles by referring to their daily cultural encounters and exchanges at the workplace:

> I started to wear the *hijob* in 2006, when I was working in the Sakhovat bazaar. I observed that many saleswomen and also many of my friends there started to wear the *hijob*. That's why my interest increased and I also began to wear the *hijob*. In the beginning, I was very unconfident but later I felt more comfortable because I realized that my body was protected from men's and strangers' glances. (Nasiba)

For Munira, besides protection the prospect of retaining a good reputation and high moral standing strongly influenced her decision to veil. After her arrival in Dushanbe she observed that women wearing the *hijob* were more respected in the community:

> People here [in my neighbourhood] respect women wearing the *hijob*. Through the *hijob* a women can show that she is modest and pious … that she protects herself from the inappropriate words [*gapi ganda*] of men. For me as a single woman the *hijob* is like a shield [*sipar*]. Walking on the street no man comes too close to me.

These statements are consistent with those of other tradeswomen we met in Dushanbe, who by veiling experienced self-confidence, freedom and empowerment in a work environment that is dominated by strangers and men. Zefi (in her forties), who considers herself one of the first tradeswomen at Kurvon, states:

> With the *hijob* my work became so much better. Now I feel comfortable and free to move. Since my body is fully covered I could give up putting emphasis on open parts of my neck or décolleté. Men no longer stare at me. They respect me as a pious woman [*zanaki dindor*]. I feel strong now and freely negotiate with them [*laughs*].

Studies on material religion have pointed out the affective power of things, and in particular how items of pious dress contribute to the formation of both Muslim subjectivity and public discourse. As Moors (2012, 286) contends in her work on face veiling in the Netherlands, Islamic dress affects both those who are involved in the practice themselves as well as the social environment around the practitioners, creating ambivalent feelings of disapproval and fascination. In Dushanbe, public disapproval is often sparked at the juncture of faith and commerce and involves a wide spectrum of Muslims' voices outside the realm of city markets that contest the 'authenticity' of veiling. From a more secularist viewpoint, many tradeswomen 'misuse' the *hijob* by utilizing it as an economic strategy, while others suspect them of misusing it to disguise a moral shortcoming (Stephan 2010, 478). Some Muslim women trained in Arab countries, in turn, allege that these women lack faith (*beiymon*) and knowledge (*'ilm*) and are driven solely by consumerist desires. At the same time, veiling is seen as a self-cultivating practice that exerts a disciplinary effect on women's behaviour, leading to a heightening of morality and pious habitus (McBrien 2010; Sabirova 2011, 334ff.). For many Muslims involved in the bazaar trade, therefore, veiling is an expression of 'authentic' or 'real' piety and compels respect from the social environment.

In the language of the market economy, the moral imagery of veiling can generate an important cultural resource for pursuing a successful business project, namely trust. According to Munira, her work career has been advanced by the religious metamorphosis she underwent in Dushanbe. Soon after she decided to veil, she also started to pray and live in accordance with Islamic principles. Through her religious labour and her Islamic lifestyle she accumulated symbolic capital that helped to establish her as a trustworthy businesswoman, and later to upgrade her work position and start saving money to buy a small apartment in the city:

> I found a job in the city because I wear the *hijob*. Look, I am illiterate.[9] But my appearance helped me find a job as a baby nurse. That family trusted me. … [Also] my boss [the shop owner] trusts me, due to my religiosity. [He knows that I started praying and that] I work honestly. We collaborate very well. Due to my honesty, he regularly sends me to Bishkek to buy new kitchen appliances for the shop.

The moral imagery ascribed to veiled saleswomen is also profitable for the employer and his economic enterprise. In the setting of urban markets, which is strongly associated with cheating, false claims and greed, the pious and trustful habitus of saleswomen like Munira serves as an appropriate advertisement strategy, promising honesty, propriety and sincerity. As such, Munira's pious habits correspond with the high moral standards of Dushanbe's new religious reformism, which enable Muslims to do proper business in a controversial economic setting (Ewing 1993, 70). Some male customers from Munira's shop with whom the authors talked stressed that they like to buy products from her because she has 'good manners' (*odob dorad*), she 'speaks respectfully' (*gapi shirin dorad*) and 'she is covered' (*satr pushidagy*), which implies that 'she is modest' and ensures that 'she would never cheat'.

Obviously, religion provides an important moral resource for single women to pursue economic strategies and gain a foothold in the city. Moreover, through their religious awakening and pious habitus Munira and Nasiba cultivate the appearance of appealing and trustworthy behaviour in the eyes of their clients, which forms a clear antidote to the climate of 'amorality' of the bazaar economy. In doing so, female traders contribute to the moralization of the bazaar trade and thereby to the conversion of an urban public space which is commonly perceived as 'uncivilized' and 'disorderly'.

Running a 'pious business': Abdurahmon

As the cases of Nasiba and Munira have shown, the new piety-minded Islam in Tajikistan cannot be dissociated from the economic everyday life of urban markets. However, not only individual reform projects pave the way for a successful economic integration into the city. Due to the strict secularization that Dushanbe's public has undergone since the 'law on religion' underwent several modifications between 2007 and 2010,[10] many pious Muslims have been driven by their religious convictions into careers as bazaar sellers and traders. As Abdurahmon's story will illustrate, markets can serve as a niche within a highly secularized urban public that provides a freer space for the harmonizing of religious ideals and economic necessities. By linking piety and bazaar work Abdurahmon, like Nasiba and Munira, has adapted to and at the same time created an urban lifestyle. Furthermore, through his efforts to run a 'pious business' by selling only 'proper' goods he enriches the growing market of Islamic commodities and contributes to the moralization of Dushanbe's markets as well.

We met Abdurahmon in an Afghan teahouse in Dubai in 2013. Sitting with fellow Tajiks, he talked about a planned trip to Mecca that would enable him to combine his pious intention to perform the Hajj pilgrimage with his idea of establishing a business selling perfume brought from Mecca. Abdurahmon was born in Tajikistan's southern Khatlon region. After graduating from secondary school in his village district in 1999 he moved to Dushanbe, where he lived with his older brother's family. In addition to his studies at the Institute of Physical Culture he helped his brother operate a small perfume shop, first at Sakhovat and since 2004 at Kurvon.

After graduating from university, he continued working in his brother's shop, 'because I wished to continue my religious studies', he explained. From early childhood he has shown a strong interest in studying the Koran and learning Arabic. In Dushanbe, he regularly attended private Koranic lessons in a religious scholar's house. His choice not to seek work in the public sector correlates with his evident religious appearance. Long-bearded and dressed in the traditional Afghani *shalvar khamez* – men's clothing perceived as solely 'Islamic' in Dushanbe – he is aware of the difficulties he would face if he wanted to work as, for example, a physical education teacher *and* cultivate an Islamic lifestyle. In Tajikistan, a rigid state secularism prohibits expressions of piety in public places such as schools, universities and state agencies. This covers both face veiling (Arabic, *niqob*; Tajik, *ninja*) and the wearing of long or uncut beards, as well as performing ritual duties publicly. For example, the law on religion bans praying in public places such as restaurants, teahouses, universities and government agencies. It therefore is hardly surprising that

Muslims such as Abdurahmon who wish to live in accordance with Islamic principles search for appropriate conditions and end up working in the bazaar.

Although an urban market is a 'public place' (*joy-i jamoat*), in Dushanbe religious practice at urban markets is only rarely targeted by the state's secular agenda. Before the government's recent anti-*hijob* campaign,[11] which also targeted bazaar sellers, the only noticeable restrictions concerned the distribution of DVDs, audiotapes, books and leaflets with Islamic contents. An official ban covers visual and audio material from foreign preachers and local scholars who are suspected of spreading 'uncontrolled' or 'dangerous' religious ideas and jeopardizing the state's interpretation of Hanafi Islam (*mazhabi hanafi*) as the moral and spiritual base of the Tajik nation and the foundation of a 'peaceful' (*orom*) and 'tolerant' (*tahammulpazir*) Tajik Islam (Rahmon 2009, 4–40). The associated bazaar controls, which accomplished little more than to encourage an under-the-counter trade in the above-mentioned products, expose how the Tajik state is willing and able to regulate Islam and Muslim life in Dushanbe's urban public. In neighbouring Uzbekistan the government has responded to the upsurge in public piety in the capital city of Tashkent by banning the sale of Islamic clothing (the *hijob*) that does not match the officially accepted 'national' Muslim dress codes.[12] In contrast, bazaars in urban Tajikistan are a lively testing ground, where the adaptation to, and the creation of, Islamic lifestyles and identities is actively contested. However, the strikingly disparate situations in Dushanbe and Tashkent indicate different scales of power and capacity in the two secular states with regard to the penetration of urban markets and the regulation of the Muslim revival in Central Asian capital cities.

The sellers and traders with whom the authors talked in Kurvon and Sakhovat praised the convenient conditions for combining bazaar work with the performance of religious duties. Using storerooms, trailers or panels of fabrics, bazaar workers temporarily convert public into private religious space in order to perform prayers (*namoz*) or ritual ablutions (*tahorat, ghuzl*). One tradeswoman who sells fabrics at Sakhovat and shares such a small prayer room with other saleswomen explained:

> When I used to work in a small kiosk near the city centre, I had to make up for my prayers in the evening or at night. But often I was too tired to be strict and therefore felt I was a bad Muslim. But here, I pray five times a day. [Here] I have perfect conditions. Nobody watches me. ... [The prayer room] is close to my shop, and if I need to speak an additional prayer I just ask my neighbour to keep an eye on my products.

Dushanbe's bazaars also provide a free space for an evolving Islamic commodity culture that stimulates the individual's striving for self-perfection through both pious business activities and 'proper' Islamic consumption. The 'Dubai boom' opened up new opportunities for traders to establish long-distance Muslim networks and pursue highly mobile livelihoods between Tajikistan, the Gulf and the wider Middle East. Dwelling in translocal urban environments, traders link the city and its residents (particularly those who are not mobile) both with the flow of Islamic goods, images, values and lifestyles and with the related urban hubs. Furthermore, the Dubai trade opens up new horizons to improve one's own piety and simultaneously pursue economic strategies.

When Abdurahmon's older brother established a perfume business in 2011, he sent Abdurahmon to Dubai and instructed him to select the products and to bring them to Dushanbe. The business idea succeeded, and the brothers' shop became known for its

'Mecca perfume' or 'Arab perfume' (*dukhy az Makka, dukhy az Arabiston*) that Abdurahmon brought from Dubai. Later, Abdurahmon utilized his frequent Dubai trips to become financially independent from his older brother. In 2012 he established his own business with Hajj dress and paraphernalia (including pilgrimage clothing, rosaries, carpets, and Koran books). Channelling his own religious demands into an innovative 'Hajj business' he fills a market niche and serves the needs of his pious fellow Tajiks. Abdurahmon explains how his new business concept is perfectly tailored to the needs of Tajik pilgrims:

> Every year almost six thousand Tajiks go on Hajj. For their trip they need many things: *ihram*,[13] light or white clothing because of the hot weather. … Also, when they return from Mecca, they should bring presents for their families, kin and all neighbours who visit them. They are expected to bring perfume, Koran books, *hijobs*, rosaries, *zam-zam* water or carpets. But on their flight they cannot carry more than 25 kilograms or else they must pay extra. Here [in my shop] they can buy presents before they leave [for Hajj]. Here, the products are 25% cheaper. … Originally, the products are from Pakistan, or Mecca, or *Arabiston*. But I bring them from Dubai.

With his 'Hajj business' and the 'Mecca perfume' he markets in his brother's shop, Abdurahmon emotionally links his customers with the sacred centres (Mecca) and economic hubs (Dubai) of the Arab region. Thus he feeds the customers' longing for, and their ability to imagine belonging to, a global Muslim community (*umma*). The religious values ascribed to the goods confirm the products' 'authenticity' and guarantee that Abdurahmon runs a pious business with 'Islamic objects' and does so without making false claims about his goods or trying to cheat his customers with regard to a fair price. But what makes a product Islamic?

Branding Islam, consuming modern urbanity

The question 'What makes a product Islamic?' leads us to the materiality of the product and the meaning that derives from its circulation, local adaptation and 'the affective and conceptual schemes whereby users apprehend' the product (Meyer et al. 2010, 209). In Dushanbe, a body oil or perfume is perceived as Islamic when the packing or the bottle is labelled with Arabic letters or decorated with an image of the Ka'aba or the Masjid al-Haram in Mecca. Thereby, a certain image of the product is created that appeals to a Muslim audience, promises authenticity and addresses the need of Dushanbe's Muslims to feel connected to the sacred centres of Islam. In addition, some headscarves or fabrics bear names such as Khurramsulton.[14] Such names evoke images of Islam or 'the Orient' and amplify the consumers' identification with the exotic Muslim 'other' that many Muslims in Tajikistan encounter when watching TV soap operas, viewing or reading media advertisements, or seeing the products first-hand in the newly opened luxury shops in the city centre.

Moreover, the religious value ascribed to an 'Islamic' product increases when the vendor advertises his or her products as imported directly from Mecca, Dubai or elsewhere in *Arabiston*. From that perspective, it becomes clear why Abdurahmon works hard at bringing his Hajj project to fruition in order to import the prophet's perfume directly from Mecca. The ability to import products directly from sacred places such as Mecca signifies a high point of individual spiritual endeavour. The marketed products thus become more 'authentic', and a pious business more credible.

Obviously, mobile urban actors such as Abdurahmon, Nasiba and Munira contribute to the manufacturing of Islamic commodities. Both their economic and spiritual trajectories serve to confirm that their traded products are 'Islamic'. In this way, the trader's body mediates his or her economic and spiritual success and links the traded objects with places people go 'to find themselves part of something larger' (Meyer et al. 2010, 209). Thus, with their marketed goods and pious habits, traders turn the bazaar into an urban locale that integrates the city and its residents into larger transregional or global Muslim spaces. These spaces facilitate the articulation of a religious 'homing desire' related to the sacred centres in the Hejaz as well as a cultural belonging to the ancient Persian tradition they share with the Afghan and Sunni Muslim Iranian community in and beyond Dubai. Through their circulation within these transregional Muslim spaces, the products brought from Dubai or *Arabiston* are therefore associated with 'authenticity' in the local imagination, even though they are often produced in China or another non-Muslim country.

*Hijob*s, perfume or Hajj paraphernalia brought from Arab countries, however, are not merely examples of piously coded objects marketed to Tajikistan's Muslims in an emerging 'semiotic landscape of faith and consumption' (Jones 2012, 617). They are also 'sign-commodities' and 'prestigious goods' (Nazpary 2002) symbolizing individual success, urban progress and elusive images of Muslim (Arab) progress and economic advancement. With their fashionable veils (black *hijob* with expensive rhinestones) and luxurious silk dresses (*abaya*) with white sleeves, saleswomen Nasiba and Munira became role models creating fictions of identity and feeding the consumers' identification with the exoticism, prosperity and attractiveness of Dubai's spectacular modernity (Elsheshtawy 2010), which is visualized through media images and reproduced in the luxury lifestyles and consumption practices of Dushanbe's 'new Tajiks'.

Ultimately, the significance of the *hijob* has extended beyond its moral implications and turned into a prestigious and desirable commodity that links Islam with notions of urban progress and modernity. The male clients we interviewed near Munira's shop explained their buying behaviour also in reference to her fashionable appearance. Comments such as Munira 'looks nice and is dressed up' confirm that through fashionable veiling saleswomen turn Islam into a brand that advertises the marketed products as 'modern' – i.e. that the products are Dubai imports and therefore of good quality. 'Modern' has to be understood not solely in terms of an alternative to cheap, low-quality imports from China; rather, the booming Dubai trade promotes the integration of Dushanbe's bazaars into a commodity culture that contributes to the rise of a new, global and cosmopolitan Muslim 'middle classness' (Fischer 2008; Jones 2012; Schielke 2012).

Thereby, the city's Muslim masses are able to consume a modernity that was previously accessible only in the luxury shops of the recently built city malls. Strikingly, the new public piety in urban Tajikistan contributes to the taming of the bazaar trade and turns the city's 'wild' and 'disordered' markets into a cultivated urban place where, as in the recently built city malls, urbanity can be consumed through images of the marketed products and the sellers' bodily practices. In that reading, Dushanbe's bazaars serve as an urban laboratory for new cultural distinction (Darieva and Kaschuba 2011, 8). The consumption of fashionable styles and products advertised as Islamic (*islomy*) distinguishes the modern and cosmopolitan urbanite (*shahry*) and sets him or her apart from the 'rural other', both from the latter's traditional way of life as well as from their 'traditional' and 'backward' Muslim

Figure 3. Fashionable Emirati women's clothing on display in Dushanbe's Saodat city mall (photograph by A. Mirzoev, 2013).

beliefs and practices, which are subsumed under the term 'religion' or 'religious' (*din* or *diny*) and depicted as traditional (*an'anavy*) and thus backward (*qafomonda*). Through fashionable veiling, saleswomen like Munira and Nasiba demonstrate their aspiration to shed their status as city newcomers or 'dispossessed' city dwellers and become modern urbanites. However, Munira's statement – 'I cannot work in the shop wearing village dress; I am in the city [*shahr*]!' – not only confirms the pervasive power of Dushanbe's urban culture, but also illustrates a new notion of urbanity, informed by Muslim or Arab role models rather than by old Soviet values. Moreover, the abstract image of Dubai as a clean, safe and Muslim-friendly place offers an antidote to the Russian nationalism that many Tajik migrants in Moscow and other Russian cities experience every day in the form of discrimination, racism, xenophobia and structural marginalization (Stephan-Emmrich forthcoming) (Figure 3).

Conclusion

In this article, Dushanbe's city bazaars have served as a lens through which to observe the conjunction of the booming Dubai trade business with a new religious reformism and the growing marketplace of urban lifestyles in Tajikistan's capital city. Taking the intra- and inter-urban mobilities of three traders and sellers as a starting point, the article has shown how Islamic lifestyles are created and re-created in the context of everyday trans-local bazaar economies. The authors proposed the term 'manufacturing' to illustrate how urban culture is produced and branded, as well as consumed materially (through trading goods) and non-materially (through the abstract images associated with the goods). Framing the social practices subsumed under the term 'manufacturing' in a particular public locale has helped reveal how urban culture is spatialized. Furthermore, the article's focus on bazaar trade and consumption has highlighted the micro-perspective of the traders' and sellers' mobile livelihoods and thereby provided insights into how urban space is produced, reproduced and imbued with a 'modern' and 'Islamic' meaning by human agency (Low 2009, 23).

Reflecting these case studies, Dushanbe's bazaars are highly dynamic public places that catalyse adaptation to Islamic lifestyles, promote encounters with the Muslim 'other' and produce cultural innovators and creative actors. These actors and innovators shape new urban lifestyles through how they express the experiences of their mobile livelihoods, multi-local embeddedness and new piety through their bodies. Thus, the body is not only the centre of agency but also the location where human experience and consciousness take material and spatial forms and where abstract translocal and transnational spaces materialize into a concrete form revealed by personal emotions, desires and social practices (Low 2009, 22, 26). Accordingly, the article linked the concrete locale of the bazaar with traders and their livelihoods and bodies and traced how bazaar traders transform that locale into a space of urban fantasy, desire and aspiration through the marketing and consumption of global Islamic goods.

Therefore, it is through the bazaar and bazaar trade that the city becomes integrated into translocal networks and the global circulation of commodities, values and images by which a progressive and hybrid 'Dubai Islam' is disseminated. Mobile urban actors such as Munira, Nasiba and Abdurahmon link Dushanbe and its Muslim residents with the sacred centres and economic hubs of the Arabian Peninsula and thereby provide a particular contribution to the city's image (Hahn 2012, 13). That image, however, mirrors a self-making, progressive and piety-minded Islam that absorbs significant impulses from urban bazaars.

Furthermore, the Dubai trade boom in the early 2000s clarifies that the reconfiguration of post-Soviet urban space takes place on very different scales. Tajikistan's 'post-colonial nationalism' broke fresh ground in the reconsolidation of the then-permeable national border. The resulting disconnectedness and immobility of Tajiks and other Central Asians in the region completes post hoc a core undertaking of Soviet modernity and consequently hampers cross-border trade with neighbouring countries (Kosmarski 2011). Simultaneously, long-distance trade flourishes and is decisively supported by Tajik migrants, pilgrims, business partners and students abroad. The new trading networks in the Gulf and the wider Middle East integrate Tajikistan's Muslims into new zones of global cultural influence that offer novel forms of Muslim belonging. The new Muslimness easily transgresses realigned state borders and follows supra-national configurations of cultural closeness that are grounded, as shown, in a shared Persian tradition. At the same time, Dushanbe's urban markets catalyse the 'Dubaisation' (Elsheshtawy 2010) of the local Muslim imagination that is predicated on the uncritical borrowing of abstract ideals and concrete examples simultaneously from Dubai's historical and new Islamic cosmopolitanism and from a new Arab (Emirati) elitism (Abaza 1996, 139; Vora 2013, 36ff.). Thus, the old Soviet cultural imperialism and Russia's new influence as a centre for oil production and labour migration (Lemon 2011, 310) are increasingly being replaced by an influential 'Dubai modernity' that both contradicts the secular state's attempts to protect Tajikistan's Muslims from 'foreign' influences and propagates a 'home-grown' Hanafi Islam that bolsters national identity and unity.

The repositioning of Tajikistan's Muslims in international and global contexts, however, was also brought about by the privatization of the city's bazaars. Hence, the state's power to 'tame' the capital city's public urban space turned out to be rather limited, which consequently prompted Dushanbe's Muslims to turn the bazaar into a laboratory for religious agency and Islamic lifestyles. Furthermore, pious Dubai traders such as Abdurahmon utilize the transnational spaces they create through their business practices as sites of resistance and to escape control by the state (Low 2009, 32).

At the same time, the three ethnographies illustrate that within the mobile livelihood of bazaar traders, geographic relocations not only combine social mobility (becoming a full 'urbanite') and religious mobility (becoming a pious Muslim); assessments of personal well-being and spiritual success also draw upon a person's particular position within social and cultural hierarchies such as gender or rural background (Schröder and Stephan-Emmrich 2014). Thus, Nasiba's and Munira's religious metamorphosis and Abdurahmon's pious business have a very local impact. They transform a 'wild', 'disordered' and 'morally reprehensible' urban locale into a moralized and cultivated space of trade and consumption comparable to the newly built city malls.

To sum up, the manufacturing of urban lifestyles in Dushanbe's bazaars prompted us to look at urban space outside, across and beyond the nation-state (Low 2009, 33) and to understand the (re)production of urban culture in Tajikistan as part of a larger, global figuration that links local Muslim reformism to the global Islamic economy. It is through individual Dubai trade enterprises that Dushanbe overcomes its former peripheral status as a Soviet capital city (Darieva and Kaschuba 2011, 10), and that its residents are presented with images of a global Muslim modernity. These global images are locally adapted, negotiated and inscribed with meaning. Thereby, the bazaar as a core site of these adaptations and negotiations turns out to be a highly contested public urban space where gender discourses criss-cross market moralities and interleave with new cultural politics. Moreover, the bazaar turns out to be an urban space where modern urban identities are expressed through the medium of consumer goods from the Gulf and produced in the context of an urban marketplace of identities (Navaro-Yashin 2002, 223; Kirmse 2013, 127). The resulting consumerism is marked by aspiration and imagination and offers the economic success and revitalized piety of Dushanbe's 'new Tajiks' as a local role model to imagine and imitate global 'middle classness' (Liechty 2012). At the same time, the cultural politics of bazaar trade are a very local expression of urban anxieties resulting from the rapid urbanization of the capital city, whereby rurals in the city are depicted as the 'cultural other'. Thus, Dushanbe's bazaars serve as a laboratory for social and cultural distinction (Darieva and Kaschuba 2011) that more or less undermines or contradicts secular state politics. At the same time, the manufacturing of modern urban identities is in line with the launched urban renewal that promotes the 'Dubaisation' or 'Gulfication' (Elsheshtawy 2010; Choplin and Franck 2014) of Central Asian's urban centres and repositions the meta-narrative of Dushanbe's future as a modern, rising and Muslim city. Meanwhile, the urban discourse on Muslim modernity and progress perfectly blends with circulating reformist thoughts that promote a progressive Islam combining moral perfection and striving for piety with economic success and upward mobility.

Notes

1. This article is based on the results of the authors' multi-sited ethnographies in Dushanbe and Dubai that encompass several fieldwork trips between 2012 and 2014.

2. Among male Muslims in Dushanbe, the 'Salafi style' is represented by uncut beards, tunics and single-colour wide, ankle-length trousers.
3. This transformation occurred, for instance, with the former Eighty-Two Bazaar (*Hashtodo du*) in 2004. Previously one of the most popular clothing markets, the bazaar was closed and replaced by a new residential area that includes the SAODAT trading centre.
4. Many Tajik families continue to maintain close relationships across the Tajikistan–Afghanistan border. Furthermore, because of the Persian language as well as the shared history of the Persian Islamic tradition, Tajiks feel a strong cultural bond with Sunni Muslim Iranians and the Dari-speaking Tajik population in Afghanistan.
5. Abaya is a traditional black Islamic garment worn by Emirati and other Arab Muslim women in Dubai's public places, usually combined with a face veil and often decorated with rhinestones or stylish braids.
6. The bazaar is the devil's home!
7. As of this writing, approximately one million Tajiks (10% of Tajikistan's population) work in Russia. Most of them are men ages 18–29 employed in the construction industry or in low-skilled jobs (Salimov 2014; Ganguli 2009).
8. The authors' survey in the Sakhovat and Kurvon bazaars comprised a total sample of 93 male and female sellers, traders and consumers. More than 40% of the sellers and traders originated from rural areas, mostly the Khatlon region. Ten of them were single women (divorced or widowed) who had moved to the city due to economic necessity.
9. Driven by uncertainty and anxiety during the civil war in Tajikistan, many parents kept their adolescent daughters at home, and thus the education of many young women of the civil war generation did not extend beyond elementary school.
10. Tajikistan's Law on Religion and its recent modifications comprise the Law on Traditions, Festivities and Ceremonies of 2007, the Law on Freedom of Conscience and Religious Associations of 2009/2010 and the Parental Responsibility Law signed in 2011, which deals with social responsibilities related to the raising of children.
11. In the celebration of Mother's Day in March 2015, Tajikistan's President Rahmon delivered a speech criticizing women who wore 'foreign' clothing, in particular the black veil associated with Arab Islam. Afterwards, officials began threatening shopkeepers who sold the *hijob*, and a few days after the speech, a state television campaign was launched that denounced *hijob*-wearing women as well as *hijob* sellers for promoting religious attitudes 'alien' to Tajikistan's national traditions (Eurasianet.org, "Islam-Fearing Tajikistan Says Hijab Is for Prostitutes", 1 April 2015, http://www.eurasianet.org/node/72816).
12. Refworld, "Islamic Clothing Vanishes from Markets in Uzbek Capital", 14 March 2012, http://www.refworld.org/docid/4f672f472.html.
13. The *ihram* is a special wardrobe to be worn when performing the Hajj pilgrimage. Wearing the *ihram* symbolizes the sacred state of the same name that the pilgrim enters when he or she performs the *hajj* (or *umrah*, the 'little Hajj').
14. The name Khurramsulton refers to the heroine in the historical Turkish soap opera *Muhteşem Yüzyıl* (*The Magnificent Century*). The television series is based on the life of Ottoman Sultan Suleiman the Magnificent and his wife Hürrem Sultan, also known as Roxelana.

Disclosure statement

No potential conflict of interest was reported by the author.

Funding

This work is part of the research project Translocal Goods: Education, Work, and Commodities between Tajikistan, Kyrgyzstan, Russia, China, and the Arab Emirates (https://www.iaaw.hu-berlin.de/de/querschnitt/islam/forschung/netz), which since May 2013 has been supported by VolkswagenStiftung (the Volkswagen Foundation) under grant number Az. 86870.

References

Abaza, M. 1996. "Islam in Southeast Asia: Varying Impact and Images of the Middle East." In *Islam, Muslims and the Modern State: Case Studies in Thirteen Countries*, edited by Hussin Mutalib and Taj ul-Islam Hashmi, 139–151. New York: Saint Martin's Press.

Alff, H. 2013. "Basarökonomie im Wandel: Postsowjetische Perspektiven des Handels in Zentralasien." *Geographische Rundschau* 65 (11): 20–25.

Babadjanov, B., and M. Kamilov. 2001. "Damulla Hindustani and the Beginning of the 'Great Schism' among the Muslims of Uzbekistan." In *Islam in Politics in Russia and Central Asia (Early Eighteenth–Late Twentieth Centuries)*, edited by Stéphane A. Dudoignon and Hisao Komatsu, 195–220. London: Kegan Paul.

Choplin, A., and A. Franck. 2014. "Seeing Dubai in Khartoum and Nouakchott: 'Gulfication' on the Margins of the Arab World." In *Under Construction: Logics of Urbanism in the Gulf Region*, edited by Steffen Wimpel, Katrin Bromber, Christian Steiner, and Birgit Krawietz, 271–284. Surrey, UK: Ashgate.

Darieva, T., and W. Kaschuba. 2011. "Sights and Signs of Postsocialist Urbanism in Eurasia: An Introduction." In *Urban Spaces after Socialism: Ethnographies of Public Places in Eurasian Cities*, edited by Tsypylma Darieva, Wolfgang Kaschuba, and Melanie Krebs, 9–32. Frankfurt/Main: campus.

Dudoignon, S. A. 2011. "From Revival to Mutation: The Religious Personnel of Islam in Tajikistan, from De-Stalinization to Independence (1955–91)." *Central Asian Survey* 30 (1): 53–80. doi:10.1080/02634937.2011.557857.

Elsheshtawy, Y. 2010. *Dubai: Behind an Urban Spectacle*. London: Routledge.

Epkenhans, T. 2011. "Defining Normative Islam: Some Remarks on Contemporary Islamic Thought in Tajikistan – Hoji Akbar Turajonzoda's Sharia and Society." *Central Asian Survey* 30 (1): 81–96. doi:10.1080/02634937.2011.554056.

Ewing, K. P. 1993. "The Modern Businessman and the Pakistani Saint: The Interpretation of Two Worlds." In *Manifestations of Sainthood in Islam*, edited by Grace M. Smith and Carl Ernst, 69–84. Istanbul: Edition Isis.

Fischer, J. 2008. *Proper Islamic Consumption: Shopping among the Malays in Modern Malaysia*. Copenhagen: NIAS Press.

Frisk, S. 2009. *Submitting to God: Women and Islam in Urban Malaysia*. Seattle: University of Washington Press.

Ganguli, I. 2009. *Tajik Labor Migration to Rusia: Is Tajikistan at a Crossroads?*. Scholar Research Brief. Washington: IREX (International Research and Exchanges Board). Accessed January 11, 2015. http://www.irex.org/sites/default/files/Ina_Gangulil.pdf.

Hahn, H. 2012. "Introduction. Urban Life-worlds in Motion." In *Urban Life-Worlds in Motion: African Perspectives*, edited by Hans Peter Hahn and Kristin Kastner, 9–28. Bielefeld: transcript.

Humphrey, C. 1997. "Traders, 'Disorder' and Citizenship Regimes in Provincial Russia." In *Uncertain Transition: Ethnographies of Change in the Postsocialist World*, edited by Michael Burawoy and Katherine Verdery, 19–52. Lanham, MD: Rowman and Littlefield.

Humphrey, C. 2002. *The Unmaking of Soviet Life: Everyday Economies after Socialism*. Ithaca, NY: Cornell University Press.

Ishkanian, A. 2003. "Gendered Transition: The Impact of the Post-Soviet Transition on Women in Central Asia and the Caucasus." *Perspectives on Global Development and Technology* 2 (3–4): 475–496. https://www.colby.edu/academics_cs/courses/HI398/upload/Gendered-Transitions.pdf. doi:10.1163/156915003322986361.

Jones, C. 2012. "Women in the Middle: Femininity, Virtue, and Excess in Indonesian Discourses of Middle Classness." In *The Global Middle Classes: Theorizing through Ethnography*, edited by Rachel Heiman, Carla Freeman, and Mark Liechty, 145–168. Santa Fe, NM: SAR Press.

Kaneff, D. 2002. "The Shame and Pride of Market Activity: Morality, Identity and Trading in Postsocialist Rural Bulgaria." In *Markets and Moralities: Ethnographies of Postsocialism*, edited by Ruth Mandel and Caroline Humphrey, 33–52. Oxford: Berg.

Kirmse, S. 2013. *Youth and Globalization in Central Asia: Everyday Life between Religion, Media, and International Donors*. Frankfurt: Campus.

Kosmarski, A. 2011. "Grandeur and Decay of the 'Soviet Byzantium': Spaces, Peoples and Memories of Tashkent, Uzbekistan." In *Urban Spaces after Socialism: Ethnographies of Public Places in Eurasian Cities*, edited by Tsypylma Darieva, Wolfgang Kaschuba, and Melanie Krebs, 33–56. Frankfurt/Main: campus.

Kuehnast, K., and C. Nechemias. 2004. "Introduction: Women Navigating Change in Post-Soviet Currents." In *Post-Soviet Women Encountering Transition: Nation Building, Economic Survival, and Civic Activism*, edited by Kathleen Kuehnast and Carol Nechemias, 1–22. Washington, DC: Woodrow Wilson Center Press.

Lemon, A. 2011. "Afterword for Urban (post)Socialisms." In *Urban Spaces after Socialism: Ethnographies of Public Places in Eurasian Cities*, edited by Tsypylma Darieva, Wolfgang Kaschuba, and Melanie Krebs, 307–314. Frankfurt/Main: campus.

Liechty, M. 2012. "Middle Class Déjà Vu: Conditions of Possibility, from Victorian England to Contemporary Kathmandu." In *The Global Middle Classes: Theorizing through Ethnography*, edited by Rachel Heiman, Carla Freeman, and Mark Liechty, 271–299. Santa Fe, NM: SAR Press.

Low, S. 2009. "Towards an Anthropological Theory of Space and Place." *Semiotica* 175: 21–37. doi:10.1515/semi.2009.041.

McBrien, J. 2010. "Muqaddas Struggle: Veils and Modernity in Kyrgyzstan." *Journal of the Royal Anthropological Institute* 15: S127–S144. doi:10.1111/j.1467-9655.2009.01546.x.

McBrien, J. 2012. "Watching Clone: Brazilian Soap Operas and Muslimness in Kyrgyzstan." *Material Religion: The Journal of Objects, Art and Belief* 8 (3): 374–396. doi:10.2752/175183412X13415044208952.

Meyer, B., D. Morgan, C. Pain, and B. Plate. 2010. "The Origin and Mission of Material Religion." *Religion* 40 (3): 207–211. doi:10.1016/j.religion.2010.01.010.

Moors, A. 2012. "The Affective Power of the Face Veil: Between Disgust and Fascination." In *Things: Religion and the Question of Materiality*, edited by Birgit Meyer and Dirk Houtman, 282–295. New York: Fordham University Press.

Nasritdinov, E., and K. O'Connor. 2010. *Regional Change in Kyrgyzstan: Bazaars, Cross-Border Trade and Social Networks*. Saarbrücken: Lambert Academic.

Navaro-Yashin, Y. 2002. "The Markets for Identities: Secularism, Islamism, Commodities." In *Fragments of Culture: The Everyday of Modern Turkey*, edited by Deniz Kandiyoti and Ayşe Saktanber, 221–253. New Brunswick, NJ: Rutgers University Press.

Nazpary, J. 2002. *Post-Soviet Chaos: Violence and Dispossesion in Kazakhstan*. London: Pluto Press.

Osella, F., and C. Osella. 2008. "Islamism and Social Reform in Kerala, South India." *Modern Asian Studies* 42 (2–3): 317–346. doi:10.1017/S0026749X07003198.

Osella, F., and C. Osella. 2009. "Muslim Entrepreneurs in Public Life between India and the Gulf: Making Good and Doing Good." *Journal of the Royal Anthropological Institute* 15 (1): S202–S221. doi:10.1111/j.1467-9655.2009.01550.x.

Parshin, K. 2012. "Tajikistan: Dushanbe Building Boom Blocks Out Economic Concerns." *EurasiaNet*. Accessed January 11, 2015. http://www.eurasianet.org/node/65340.

Rahmon, E. 2009. *Imomi A'zam va guftugūi tammadunho. Imomi A'zam va huvijati millī*. Dushanbe: Adib.

Sabirova, G. 2011. "Young Muslim-Tatar Girls of the Big City: Narrative Identities and Discourses on Islam in Postsoviet Russia." *Religion, State and Society* 39 (2–3): 327–345. doi:10.1080/09637494.2011.584710.

Salimov, O. 2014. "Tajikistan Ratifies Agreement with Russia on Tajik Labor Migrants." *Central Asia-Caucasus Analyst*. Accessed January 11, 2015. http://www.cacianalyst.org/publications/field-reports/item/12914-tajikistan-ratifies-agreement-with-russia-on-tajik-labor-migrants.html.

Schielke, S. 2012. "Living in the Future Sense: Aspiring for World and Class in Provincial Egypt." In *The Global Middle Classes: Theorizing through Ethnography*, edited by Rachel Heiman, Carla Freeman, and Mark Liechty, 31–56. Santa Fe, NM: SAR Press.

Schröder, P., and M. Stephan-Emmrich. 2014. "The Institutionalization of Mobility: Well-being and Social Hierarchies in Central Asian Translocal Livelihoods." *Mobilities* 1–24. doi:10.1080/17450101.2014.984939.

Stephan, M. 2006. "'You Come to Us Like a Black Cloud': Universal versus Local Islam in Tajikistan." In *The Postsocialist Religious Question: Faith and Power in Central Asia and East-Central Europe*, edited by Chris Hann and the 'Civil Religion' Group, 147–167. Münster: LIT.

Stephan, M. 2010. "Education, Youth and Islam: The Growing Popularity of Private Religious Lessons in Dushanbe, Tajikistan." *Central Asian Survey* 29 (4): 469–483. doi:10.1080/02634937.2010.538283.

Stephan-Emmrich, M. forthcoming. "Studying Islam Abroad: Pious Enterprises and Educational Aspirations of Young Tajik Muslims." In *Islam, Society, and Politics in Central Asia*, edited by Pauline Jones Luong.

Tohidi, N. 1998. "'Guardians of the Nation': Women, Islam and the Soviet Legacy of Modernization in Azerbaijzan." In *Women in Muslim Societies: Diversity Within Unity*, edited by Herbert L. Bodman and Nayareh Tohidi, 137–162. Boulder, CO: Lynne Rienner.

Turner, V. 1969. *The Ritual Process: Structure and Anti-Structure*. New York: DeGruyter.

Verdery, K. 1991. *National Ideology under Socialism: Identity and Cultural Politics in Ceausescu's Romania*. Berkeley: University of California Press.

Vora, N. 2013. *Impossible Citizens: Dubai's Indian Diaspora*. Durham, NC: Duke University Press.

Werner, C. 2004. "Feminizing the New Silk Road: Women Traders in Rural Kazakhstan." In *Post-Soviet Women Encountering Transition: Nation-Building, Economic Survival, and Civic Activism*, edited by Carol Nechemias and Kathleen Kuehnast, 105–126. Baltimore: Johns Hopkins University Press.

Where the whole city meets: youth, gender and consumerism in the social space of the MEGA shopping mall in Aktobe, western Kazakhstan

Philipp Frank Jäger

Department of History, Humboldt-Universität zu Berlin, Germany

ABSTRACT

The shopping mall entered Central Asia's commercial sector as a result of the economic transformation of post-Soviet space. Constructed near the centre of the city, the shopping mall overwrites the urban landscape, dominating it as a symbol of modernity. It functions as a gateway of global consumerist culture to the Eurasian steppe. Using the MEGA shopping mall in Aktobe, in western Kazakhstan, as an example, this article shows that the building acts as a stage for the construction of a new social and cultural space. This study focuses on the ways in which young women interact with the mall's spaces. The mall turns out to be a playground not only for children, but also for the whole younger generation, who come to this unique place to see and be seen. The mall became a hot spot of youth culture in the post-socialist worker's city by offering more than a mere shelter from dust and snow storms on the steppe. The available amenities made it a favourite place for meeting, consuming and dreaming. Young women especially are attracted to MEGA to experience the newest fashions and build social relationships.

Introduction

Marketplaces in Central Asia have substantially changed their faces since the post-Soviet economic transformation. Contemplating commercial sites in Central Asia, the first image that comes to mind for many is the bazaar. Ever since trade was first conducted along the Silk Road, commodities have been not only brought from China to the West and vice versa, but also sold at local markets along the way. Although the modalities of commodity exchange have shifted, market activities have been present throughout history, even during the Soviet period, when inter-regional trade was cut off and the bazaars functioned mainly as places to sell agricultural surplus from local collective farms (Carpenter 1978, 587).

After the breakdown of the Soviet Union, the bazaars enjoyed a revival. The increase in private consumption was assisted by markets supplied with commodities from the Far East. This led to enormous growth in Central Asia's main markets, such as the Barakholka in Almaty and the Dordoi in Bishkek. These bazaars can be seen as more than just trading hubs in the economic sense; they are also places for human contact. Merchants, buyers and other actors connected to the bazaar construct these places socially. The first studies on Central Asian bazaars have been published recently (e.g. Özcan 2011; Alff 2014). Another, more recent, kind of commercial site in Kazakhstan, however, has still not been widely researched: the shopping mall. This new trend in retail commerce began in North America about 90 years ago, then spread out all over the continent in the post-WWII period and has continued to conquer the world since the 1980s (Hahn 2007, 15). The mall reached Central Asia, beginning in Kazakhstan, only recently. Maybe it is too early to judge how the shopping mall will change the economic sphere, but it is nevertheless possible to say that shopping malls have had various social and cultural impacts on those Central Asian cities where they were built. Here, I analyse these impacts using ethnographic data collected during my fieldwork in 2012 in Aktobe, western Kazakhstan.

My research in western Kazakhstan was part of my PhD in social and cultural anthropology on migration, mobility and the labour market in the Caspian region on the examples of Aktobe (Kazakhstan) and Sumqayit (Azerbaijan). Using mainly the methods of participant observation and semi-structured interviews, I analysed mobility between the provincial capital Aktobe, the regional town Alga, and villages close to them. The main part of my research was centred in Aktobe, where I studied how Kazakh and Russian rural–urban migrants find a place to stay and a job as well as how they get familiar with their new home. A part of this was also questions about cultural interaction in the city they moved to.

In my anthropological research the MEGA shopping mall in Aktobe was a hot spot for participant observation. I met my informants here and conducted interviews. For many of my interlocutors, MEGA was a place to which they regularly returned for shopping and entertainment. I soon realized that the shopping mall was more than simply a place to meet and exchange thoughts and ideas. For many of my younger informants, MEGA was their favoured meeting point. The centrality of MEGA to so many of my informants' lives is what first sparked my curiosity about this place.

During my interviews with rural students, I noticed that when I asked them about cultural activities and urban culture in Aktobe, only one in five referred to cultural institutions established during the Soviet period, such as the theatre or cultural centres. Instead, the MEGA was for them the main symbol of urban culture and modernity. My research questions focus on the shopping mall as a social and cultural space. How are social spaces inside the MEGA constructed? Are there any kinds of cultural spaces unique to the mall in the steppe city?

In order to explore MEGA as a social space, I collected ethnographic material on young women (aged 17–40), who were mainly migrants to Aktobe. Why is the mall especially attractive to them? What role does the mall play for them in building social relationships? In this article I show how young women are influenced by commercial structures and how they deal with them. I found that these young women are the most frequent users of the mall. This trend does not seem to be unique to Kazakhstan. General observations of mall customers show that 'the stereotypical shopper is female' (Goss 1993, 21). Also, in the neighbouring region of Anatolia, Erkip (2005, 102) states that 'feminization of the *flâneur*' (literally, 'stroller') characterizes the Turkish mall.

The flat in which I lived for most of the time during my fieldwork was directly opposite the mall. This offered me an excellent view of the MEGA during holidays such as Nauryz[1] or Victory Day[2] as well as after business hours. During my year of fieldwork, I had the opportunity to talk to many people working at MEGA, the majority of whom were employees within the mall. Additionally, I used MEGA for shopping and recreation on a regular basis.

Discourses about shopping centres and modernity can be found in the whole Eastern Bloc. Bodnar (1998, 189–90) shows that in Budapest, the opening of shopping centres marked a transition towards consumerist culture in the 1990s. More recent studies indicate that the process of commercialization of urban landscapes continues in CIS[3] states. In her study of malls in Saint Petersburg, Zhelnina (2011, 48) discusses how ambiguously shopping malls are received by the inhabitants, which vary from a symbol of a 'Western', 'civilized' lifestyle to a symbol of new social inequality. In Saint Petersburg, malls play a role in the differentiation of taste for the middle class (61). Ryabchuk and Onyshchenko (2012) illustrate how an industrial plant was transformed into a shopping mall. Just as the physical space transformed, the once-united working-class collective in the plant morphed into a socially unequal urban society in which buying power enables individuals to differentiate themselves from each other by the choices of commodities they acquire as well as the distinction of taste. Supermarkets in Bishkek are seen more as shopping places for the rich (Botoeva 2006, 48–49) than places to buy basic commodities. As a symbol of 'civilization' and 'modernity', they 'boost the image of Bishkek, thus indicating urbanization and gradual modernization processes' (47).

Central Asia is one of the last regions on earth to be conquered by shopping malls. While the forerunner of today's shopping mall, the Parisian department store, opened around 1850 (Crawford 1992, 17), the first malls in Central Asia opened only in the early 2000s. The economic transformation paved the way for the mall in the CIS states, continuing the globalization of the shopping mall driven by Western investors after approaching the saturation point in North America in the 1980s (10–11).

The city of Aktobe and its commercial space

The city of Aktobe is located at the heart of the Eurasian steppes, midway along the railroad track between Moscow and Almaty. Aktobe functions as the administrative and educational centre of western Kazakhstan. The breakdown of the Soviet Union deepened the discrepancy in the development of infrastructure between Aktobe and the rest of the province. Grey is the dominant colour of the city's face. Along the streets the residential blocks continue, one after the next. Their uniform look is broken up only by the individualized balcony expansions, which are a common sight. These apartment blocks were planned and constructed in the latter decades of Soviet rule. In Aktobe, their basic layout remains. Large housing blocks were built next to the street, and in between the buildings there is space for kindergartens, schools and shops. The basic concept of the *mikrorayon* (microdistrict) can be traced back to the 'superblock' idea of the early Soviet Union, but it was only in the post-WWII period that the *mikrorayon* in its rationalized form was constructed in large quantities all over the Soviet Union (French 1995, 37–38; 77). As French (1995, 81) shows, the haste of construction often led to insufficient services and shops, so that the inhabitants of a *mikrorayon* nevertheless had to travel to other quarters to satisfy their needs.

In the Soviet era, *mikrorayons* were built as living complexes for 8000–12,000 people. Through the planned development of high-density residential settlements, equality in collective consumption was pursued (Molodikova and Makhrova 2007, 53). Usually the *mikrorayons* were built at the periphery of a city, but in Aktobe they occupy a central part. One reason for this is that Aktobe experienced rapid growth after WWII, from 48,600 inhabitants in 1939 to 143,700 in 1969 and 253,700 in 1989 (Department statistiki Aktyubinskoj oblasti 2008). Aktobe's new area reaches from the central bus station at the northern edge of the old town to the industrial area, which completes the city's northern border and consists exclusively of *mikrorayons*. From here the workers could easily reach the industrial complex by bus. At that time, heavy industry dominated Aktobe's economic life.

In the years following the independence of Kazakhstan, the housing situation became more problematic. The resource crisis which affected the Soviet Union during the *perestroika* period also hit Aktobe at the beginning of the 1990s. Not only did it become difficult to obtain food products, but shortages of power, water and fuel troubled city dwellers. At that time, a significant number of inhabitants left for the European part of Russia. They were partly replaced by people moving from the rest of Aktobe Province to the city, so that about a quarter of a million inhabitants lived in the steppe centre. Only after 2001 – at the same time as an economic boom hit all of Kazakhstan – did the number of inhabitants began to climb again. At first the growth was moderate, to 268,644 inhabitants in 2008, but then the number exploded to 371,357 in 2013 (Department statistiki Aktyubinskoj oblasti 2009, 15, 2012, 10). If we add the unregistered residents and the suburbs, the total number of urban dwellers reaches half a million (2012, 10).

Not all Aktobe urbanites live in *mikrorayons*. In Aktobe's historic centre, which dates from the original colonial outpost founded in 1869, one can find lower buildings. These are mainly *khrushchyovkas*, 3–4 floors high, which replaced the older buildings in the centre near the main train station after the 1950s. Of the former fortress (*krepost*), only the quarter names of Garnizonaya and Tatarska survive. Neither soldiers nor a significant Tatar minority can be found here any longer. The first Tatars had come as traders in the nineteenth century. They bought animals and products of the nomadic economy from Kazakhs, stopping by at the trading post, and then sold them to the European part of Russia (Tazhibayev et al. 2002, 195–98; Bisembayev et al. 2007, 215–19). The market in the historical centre is still here today. In Soviet times the Kolkhoznyj Rynok (Kolkhoz Market) was where people from the collective farms sold the surplus of their private plots. As an informant who worked at the market told me, the price was up to five times higher than in the shops; nevertheless, their overall availability in a shortage economy and their high quality made these goods desirable. Around the bazaar, commerce centres opened in the first decade of the new millennium. They specialize in clothes and wholesale trading for traders buying new commodities which they then resell in their own shops in regional towns.

In post-socialist Aktobe, the market witnessed a revival. At the bazaar, not only food but also household goods, clothes and tools can be traded. Nowadays the bazaar is a complex structure of open-air market lanes and two smaller buildings, one for meat, the other for fruit. The market's borders are blurred by smaller market stalls that spill into the streets. In the streets leading from the market to the centre of the old town, pensioners sell vegetables from their *dachas*,[4] teenagers try to give out advertisement flyers, and fortune tellers offer their services.

Pawnbrokers can also be found at the markets, along with dealers of stolen goods. Pick-pockets sell mobile phones stolen in the permanently overcrowded minibuses or in the market itself. Observing the bazaar, I was continuously warned by my informants to keep an eye on my belongings. Accompanying my informants on shopping trips at the market, I observed that they would quickly complete their purchases and then leave as soon as possible. The place was considered dirty and uncomfortable, the available food and drink possibly a health hazard.

The city's transformation after the breakdown of the Soviet Union took a similar shape as mentioned in other literature, which describes how living space was privatized and private business flourished (Kostinskiy 2001). The state loosened its control over the use of urban land. Urban development was given over to the city's administration, which had to raise its own revenues and set priorities in construction (Alexander 2007, 92). The ideological slogans and pictures painted along the main streets were exchanged for commercial advertisements. In Aktobe, not only did the number of single shops in the *mikrorayon*s expand, but also new shopping centres, mostly smaller, were opened. None of them offered any kind of entertainment section, and only two of them match the MEGA in size. The first of these is located at a market for construction materials near the central bus station, which has enjoyed a high level of customer demand since the start of the economic boom.[5] In contrast, the section where housewares are sold does not cause excitement. Many shops on the second and third floor are out of business. The second shopping centre also struggles with abandoned selling spots (*tochki*). Con-struction flaws such as uneven stairways, inaccessibility for disabled persons, and overly intense air conditioning quickly became obvious. Due to a lack of clients, many shops closed, leading to an eerie atmosphere in the half-empty upper floors, where through blue acrylic glass distorted sunlight shines on abandoned items and dust.

The processes of transformation in Aktobe were similar to those in Russia, where at the end of the 1990s retail and services transformed into semi-permanent structures as smaller shops emerged. Mostly, however, everyday trade continued to be concentrated at open bazaars. Over time, the shops grew larger, a process which in the 2000s led to the estab-lishment of the first shopping centres and malls (Stanilov 2007, 87–89). In Russian, the new buildings were called *torgovye centry* (trade centres) and *torgovo-razvlekatel'nye kompleksy* (trade and entertainment complexes), which brought together shops, cafes, entertainment facilities and sometimes banks and office companies under one roof (Zhelnina 2011, 52). The first generation of shopping centres in the European part of the Russian Federation had great success and marked the beginning of a significant retail investment in the 2000s (Stanilov 2007, 92).

The MEGA company was a pioneer in shopping malls. Part of the Russian branch of IKEA, the first MEGA opened near Moscow in 2002. Soon, more centres in larger cities such Kazan, Nizhny Novgorod, Yekaterinburg and the outlying areas of Saint Petersburg[6] were built, and the company is considering investing an additional €2 billion in new malls by 2020.[7] This may well be seen as proof of its continuing success, although competitors have begun to open their own malls. At the moment, there is no end to this Russian boom in sight.

The Kazakh businessman Nurlan Smagulov founded MEGA Kazakhstan and added it to his holdings in the Astana Group in 2003. The first MEGA opened in Almaty in 2006; three additional malls followed, in Astana and Shymkent in 2007 and in Aktobe in 2009. A second MEGA in Almaty was constructed in 2013. With a gross leasable area of 14,000–45,000 m^2, MEGAs look tiny in comparison to the world's largest shopping malls in East and South-East Asia, which exceed half a million square metres, but they appear enormously large in their local contexts.

MEGA Aktobe is in the geographical middle of the city, between the old and new sections. This area was long inaccessible due to underground springs, which created marshy land, impeding the construction of stable foundations. In the 1980s, technological advancements allowed the local authorities to construct the 11th *mikrorayon* close by, followed by the 12th in the 1990s. In between the 11th *mikrorayon* and the city's new part the Park Lenina was opened, but it became overgrown and neglected during the post-independence era. During the 2000s, the whole park was rebuilt into a memorial complex. Renamed the Park of the First President, it was extended further with a memorial complex consisting of a mosque and a Russian Orthodox Church connected by a square.

MEGA and its parking lot are located at the eastern end of the memorial complex, next to the church. Its front section faces onto a scenic fountain and a bridge leading to the bus stop facing the 11th *mikrorayon*. Although the MEGA is smaller than the 11-storey residential building next to it, it looks colossal in contrast to the much smaller church and mosque. The yard is used for stages and exhibitions during holidays. Here the security guards patrol and ask everyone to stick to the rules. Children are sent away from playing at the fountain, and brash taxi drivers offering their services loudly are driven out of the area.

In the post-war United States, malls were built in suburbia with the idea of making them accessible by car. In contrast, in Kazakhstan, the post-socialist transformation made plots in the inner parts of the cities, rather the outlying areas, available. The centrally located MEGAs are well connected to public transport. By choosing construction sites in open spaces at the edge of the centre, the company invests in the future of fast-growing Kazakhstani cities, while the area around is accessible to commercial business and residential construction. In the midst of Kazakhstan's immense urban growth, the commercial complexes with the shopping malls and surrounding shops soon began to function as a new urban forum.

MEGA's rectangular form, vertical expansion and central location demonstrate the influence of Turkish malls in Ankara (Ozdemir 2008, 238). However, similarities to the American mall concept also exist. Following the precepts of J.C. Nichols, who is regarded as the initiator of the shopping mall concept for his development of the Country Club Plaza in Kansas City (USA) in 1924, MEGAs put an emphasis on sufficient parking (Crawford 1992, 20), although car ownership in Central Asia is not as widespread as it is in North America or Europe.

The core concept, however, remains the same. The Kazakhstani shopping mall forgoes austerity by inviting customers into a comfortable environment, which in many post-socialist cities is in sharp contrast to the deprived centres of the early transition period. Informants living in Almaty or Aktobe felt that the first period of transition in the 1990s was a kind of breakdown of infrastructure. 'Vse bylo razvaleno' (Russian: everything was broken) was a phrase often used when talking about this time period. The municipal administration lacked the funds to maintain infrastructure and had to privatize public facilities in the centres. While Almaty recovered slightly at the beginning of the 2000s, the oil boom in the west manifested itself in Aktobe via a construction boom only some years later. In this regard, the 2009 opening of a MEGA is one of the main symbols of the current boom. Nowadays, while the streets are dirty and loud from the noise of the construction sites surrounding it, the MEGA in Aktobe itself offers a quiet place for recreation.

MEGA offers shops on four floors, a supermarket, a cinema, a food court, cafes and restaurants, a children's park and a small-scale ice skating rink. The French firm Design Architectural designed the building and applied a similar architectural style to different sites throughout Kazakhstan. The mall's homepage states that 'on weekdays the average attendance in MEGA is 30,000 people, on weekends it is over 60,000. The attendance record is 108,000 people'.[8] Conceptually, MEGA aims to offer well-known brands in clothing and offers shops from companies that can also be found in European cities.

When entering MEGA, one's view is drawn along the booths for mobile phone accessories to the atrium with the ice rink where trainers teach children how to skate. Around the square are prestigious brand shops such as Adidas, Promod, and Swatch. Opposite the entrance, a climbing wall lures the more active visitors. To the left and right, corridors lead shoppers in a semicircle. The same layout is copied on the second floor, except that a cafe and bar fill the area above the main and north entrances. The third floor consists of a spacious food court that seats approximately 400. Visitors can buy Central Asian, Russian, American, Mexican, Turkish, Italian or East Asian fast food. A franchise of the Kazakh Assorti restaurant chain, a cinema complex and a children's park are also located on the third floor.

The main attractions for customers include a technology store, the Happylon children's park and the seven-screen Kino Park movie theatre, which seats 959. An Internet hall populated mainly by boys playing video games connects to the theatre. Their cursing, shouting, and loud, colloquial speech scare away not only adult visitors but also teenage girls, who prefer to use social media services via their smartphones while sitting in the food court. The fourth floor used to feature a bowling alley, but it closed during the summer of 20102 for lack of patronage. A sporting goods store and the Fudze restaurant remain.

With this layout, the MEGA is following a general directive. In contrast to commercial centres and shops, the strategy of the shopping mall 'depends on "indirect commodification", a process by which non-saleable objects, activities, and images are purposely placed in the commodified world of the mall' (Crawford 1992, 14). The basic principle here is the 'adjacent attraction' in accordance with which cinemas, restaurants, video-game rooms and skating rinks were established in the mall. Consumption should be combined with the human need for recreation, public life and social interaction (14–15). North American malls have pioneered new trends such as the 'festival market', 'lifestyle centre' and 'hybrid centre' (Hahn 2007, 18). These first experiences can be transferred to other regions of the world.

In MEGA's hallways, benches and flower boxes were positioned, an architectural feature taken from Western malls, to prevent clients getting tired (Dörhöfer 2007, 63). The decoration begins immediately behind the entrance with a fountain. The benches around it are used as a meeting point for groups. Soft adaptations of pop songs are mixed with a kind of folk pop called *deko-musika*, pop versions of traditional Kazakh songs and instrumental performances of the string instruments called *dombyra* and *qobyz*. Pauses between the songs are used for commercials and notifications of upcoming MEGA events.

The shopping mall as a gendered social space

A mall has to attract as many groups as possible to be successful. As the first mall of its kind in Aktobe, MEGA has the potential to accomplish that task by creating an accessible space for visitors by playing with their expectations. On the one hand, visitors enter a new realm of fascinating things that should encourage them to buy commodities. On the other hand, they find known places they intended to reach like the cinema for a rendezvous, the food court to meet friends, and the skating rink for the children during a family trip. The shopping mall combines economic, social and cultural spaces.

For many migrants from other provinces who are not yet familiar with Aktobe, MEGA is the first place that springs to mind. Here they are able to blend in without being marked as an outsider. A young Kazakh woman, Manat[9] from Taraz, who had graduated from a medical university in Almaty and had come to Aktobe to work, called MEGA 'the only place in the city where I'm free'. Here Manat can move without hindrance, while she emphasized that other public and commercial sites are dirty and boring. Working as a medical resident completing her training, her monthly salary is less than USD 400, which forces her to live in a room at a *dacha* near the centre with an *azhe* (a Kazakh *babushka*), one of many elderly people renting their living space out to top up their pensions (which are on average about USD 100 per month). Once an area for recreation, *dachas* near the old town have become a residential area for regular use. Since *dachas* are not registered as living spaces, no one cares about correct documentation, contributing to the image of the neighbourhood as a hideout for bandits and *neudachniki* (the unfortunate). In an area with no streets or lights, Manat constantly feels threatened, which is intensified by her cultural shock as a southern woman newly arrived in the north-west. Manat differs from Aktobe Kazakhs in many ways, not just because of her geographical background. She descends from the southern Ulu Zhuz (Large Horde), a different clan federation from most residents of western Kazakhstan, who are mainly of the Kishi Zhuz (Small Horde).[10] Manat observed differences in customs and habits as well as mentality. She found it remarkable that her female colleagues at the hospital and the students at the medical university speak openly among themselves about relationships, love affairs and sex, which is unthinkable for her. She pointed out that in the south the sexual sphere is kept in absolute privacy and premarital sex is viewed as shameful.

Typically, students and trainees living in crowded dormitories or with relatives without their own room in Aktobe emphasize that they enjoy MEGA's atmosphere, which is dramatically different from the outside environment. Plants, waterways, coulisses and a heating system invoke a feeling of being outdoors, but an outdoors far removed from the harsh continental climate of the Eurasian steppes. Other negative aspects of the city, like traffic and poor people, can be kept out as well. In this way, 'shopping becomes a recreational activity and the mall an escapist cocoon' (Crawford 1992, 22). Nothing and no one hampers the visitors of the mall. At first glance, the mall's doors appear to be open to all, but its boundaries are clear-cut and guarded. Security is very visible at the entrance, and cameras survey every corner of the building (27). Entry is forbidden to unwanted people like beggars, but the barriers are tested in a similar way to what Anna Zhelnina (2011, 57) observes in her study on shopping malls in Saint Petersburg. Although adult panhandlers cannot pass the controls, homeless children manage to enter from time to time in order to ask for money. Similarly, beggars in Aktobe can be found around the bazaar, but not in front of MEGA. Even the beggars at the entrance of the Russian Orthodox Church, who meet there for regular prayer sessions, do not enter MEGA's territory right next to the church, a sharp but invisible borderline which reflects new social inequalities.

People living in the countryside often perceive MEGA as a place of entertainment, as the city's main attraction. On the weekends they are able to take a bus to Aktobe and walk the 500 metres from the central bus terminal to the shopping mall. The appearance of these visitors, for example regarding clothing, usually differs from that of city dwellers. The regulars in Aktobe are in permanent touch with the latest fashion trends, even if only through window shopping. In contrast, the clothes of provincial visitors often are considered to look 'Soviet or 'outdated Western'. In summer 2012 big sunglasses and hot pants were fashionable in Aktobe. Not attuned to current fashion styles, rural men prefer shopping for sports clothes, which resemble the everyday dress code in the villages. Depending on their financial capabilities, men buy at Adidas or Sportmaster, or they consider buying counterfeit brand-name clothes at one of the city's bazaars.

The cinema is the main attraction to MEGA for young adults. With entry fees of about USD 10–15 for an evening show, going to the cinema marks a special event for most people and is not an everyday experience. Groups of young adults going out in the evening connect cinema and having dinner at the food court with shopping. A meal at the food court costs about USD 5–12 per person. Many of the groups of friends who are only visiting Aktobe contain both boys and girls, but are monolingual.

A significant function of the mall in Aktobe is shelter. Like Canadian malls, MEGA offers a warm and cosy welcome when the outside world lies covered in snow. Together with sociologist John Manzo (2005, 84), I would argue that shopping malls have not received much attention in social research in countries such as Russia, Kazakhstan and 'Canada in which the climate has made enclosed malls preferred gathering spots in many communities'.

Some of my informants could not imagine an alternative to going to MEGA in winter. This is especially true of students who moved to Aktobe and who were less familiar with the city. Many of Aktobe's buildings do not seem inviting to newcomers. MEGA is an exception to that. Everyone who can buy commodities or participate in the entertainment section is welcome at the mall. It is easily accessible to both locals and newcomers. It is a space where people who do not feel native in Aktobe may feel accepted.

Offering clothes from global brands, the shops give the impression that a consumer is part of a world community. This refers to the 'imagined worlds' in the sense of Appadurai (1990, 296), who describes them as 'the multiple worlds which are constituted by the historically situated imaginations of persons and groups spread around the globe'. The decorated shop windows with pictures from New York, Paris or Tokyo as a background to the mannequins lead to a fluidity of space. Several cityscapes overlay Aktobe's steppe landscape, blurring the lines between reality and fiction. The pictures of MEGA's mediascape and ideoscape condense space and connect actors to imagined places (299). What Appadurai saw emerging in the nineties is intensified with the use of smartphones by actors actively adding and playing with media content while visiting nexus points like shopping malls. My informants used the free wi-fi in the restaurants and cafes to check prices and compared video clips of the clothes in the shop windows with the fashion of their favourite sports or music stars, cinema actors or models.

As Miller et al. (1998, 26) have shown, with reference to Mary Douglas and Pierre Bour-dieu, attention has to be paid to the 'process by which commodities communicate, and are communicated as, *social relationships*' (emphasis in the original). Through practices of shopping and identity, these relationships are refreshed (26–27). These processes can be observed in MEGA. Visitors to the mall not only buy fashionable items there; they also use it as a stage for the clothes they have previously bought. While men may show off their new sport outfits on the skating rink, the climbing wall or the sport yards at Hap-pylon, women may wear the clothes they purchased during their last visit and gain com-pliments for their urban style.

This cycle of buying and displaying the clothes works well in MEGA, while in other places like the bazaar or the workplace – and maybe a conservative family home – a Western (or Far Eastern, as Japanese and Chinese brands are now more and more accepted) dress code could be seen as negative or not be admired. From this image of seeing and being seen, MEGA becomes a stage set. Young women can experiment with fashion and gain compliments. In MEGA, young Kazakh women can play with the thin line between looking sexy but not overly provocative, while in other places they might be at least tacitly stigmatized. This is connected with the image of an ideal Kazakh girl who should pay more attention to family values than fashion and money. A perfect daughter-in-law – in the descriptions of my middle-aged and older informants in Aktobe – is first of all intended to care for children and elderly family members, to manage household tasks, and to feed guests. Some of my younger informants had reflected on this public opinion and came to the conclusion that they have to enjoy the time when they are studying, because their life will change significantly after marriage.

Regarding fashionable clothes at MEGA, metrosexual styles that transgress local gender norms can also be observed. While in a highly homophobic environment such as Kazakh-stan showing up in public with unconventional clothing choices could provoke at least verbal critique, walking in MEGA gives visitors an opportunity to view a wider range of fashions and modes of being. Teenagers try out fashions here and are not afraid of showing behaviour that deviates from the commonly accepted norm. MEGA is the only place in the city where girls kissing girls or boys hugging boys can be observed publicly. While open displays of emotion are usually restricted by the Kazakh habitus, here cliques of teenagers and young adults find a public place where the strict age hierarchies are not applied.

During the day, on weekends and holidays, young adults also meet in same-sex groups at MEGA. While young men tend to have a more concrete purpose for their visit, like buying snacks or alcohol in the supermarket, playing air hockey at Happylon or shopping for electronic devices, young women take time to stroll through the corridors and take a look at the clothes in the fashion boutiques. After leaving MEGA, young males either con-tinue towards bars in the streets close by, or they gather in the yards of the *mikrorayons* where masculine behaviour like drinking and smoking is allowed.

In MEGA, women test new commodities and fashion, buy make-up, and sit down at res-taurants and cafes to chat with their friends. Here they can build up social networks, get new information, or just enjoy their time. Knowing people is a powerful resource for getting discounts in cafes, hearing hints of when a sought-after commodity will go on sale, or meeting the right people for future job opportunities. MEGA is 'the place to be'. So being there means participating in avant-garde urban society, being 'cool, and gaining insight into what brings the attention of friends, e.g. knowledge of trends or hot media products. Even if they are often not able to purchase the high-cost fashion articles, young women perceive it as important to be knowledgeable about new trends.

I met one of my informants, 22-year-old Natasha, several times at MEGA. She is a Russian from the regional town of Alga who is studying English and German in Aktobe. Aside from the new Park of the First President in the summer, MEGA is her favourite place to meet with friends. She complains about the high prices there but nevertheless comes back to MEGA again and again. She describes liking to *'posedet' tut, polazit' po magazinam, tam slyuni popuskat', tam na zeny posmotret"* (sit here [in a restaurant], hang around in the shops, drool [meaning being unable to buy the commodities], look at the prices). Because she had to study intensively during the last phase of her study, she was not able to work. The only money she could spend was what she received in support from her parents and from the salary of her betrothed working at an oil station.

The MEGA administration organizes events like fashion parades, for which young women can register and participate. Fashion shows have become popular in Kazakhstan recently and are also conducted at universities and schools. Teenage girls and young women are invited to take part in events like a day of 'living mannequins' when new fashion is presented on the catwalk. They are rewarded with fashion commodities or coupons. The participants I observed – mostly joining together in groups of friends or university classes – take the competition seriously. They tried hard to impress the visitors and compete with each other.

On the day of the 'living mannequins', Saule participated with her fellow student friend Lyassat. They dressed in latest fashions and modelled these in shop windows. The two girls were amused by the event and immediately applied for other shows. Saule moved to Aktobe from the provincial town of Khobda when she was sixteen. For her MEGA is a symbol of urban life. She often comes here with friends or visits acquaintances who work at MEGA and offer her discounts. Some weeks after the fashion event, Saule reported that she had found a job as a wedding entertainer (Kazakh *akyn,* Russian *tomada*). Through this job she could further develop her social network ties and try to meet further employers for the time after her graduation. Her example therefore illustrates how young women can accumulate social capital in MEGA's social space.

MEGA is also a place where someone can look for a romantic partner. Young women appreciate the anonymity of the mall, which allows them to have informal dates with men. The place has turned out to be a hot spot for people using Internet dating sites like Mail.ru or Kiss.kz. The place creates a feeling of security for women. Here spatial conditions appear to have a contrasting character. While corridors with closed shops hurt sales, they are main stages for lovers, meeting and kissing at a place with fewer visitors (especially at noon). The benches in these areas are the most desired in the whole mall, a paradoxical place to have some privacy in public, away from the parental apartment, the school building and the streets. It should also be mentioned that, especially in the 11th *mikrorayon,* many flats can be rented on an hourly or daily basis to serve as a love nest for couples who intensify their relationship after MEGA.

For Kazakh women, meeting in a public place like a park entails the risk of getting kidnapped. The American anthropologist Cynthia Werner (2004, 2009) showed in her works about bride kidnapping that, on the one hand, this ritual could be seen as an operational possibility in the larger process of closing a marriage practised already in the pre-Soviet era. On the other hand, her studies on bride abduction in southern Kazakhstan showed a rising number of non-consensual cases in the years of Kazakhstan's early independence (Werner 2004). While talking about this topic to students in western Kazakhstan, they mainly shared the opinion that the frequency of bride kidnapping in their region had decreased after the 1990s, but they were still aware of its problems.

Aktobe-born Lyassat told me of her own shocking experience of an attempted kidnapping right in front of the university's main entrance. She did not know the groom or anyone in the raiding party. In a panic, she managed to escape from the car that she had been dragged into, but since then she has developed a watchful eye for such situations. She considers bride kidnapping a cultural tradition practised in rural areas but now stays alert in the city as well, and more carefully chooses the places she visits.

Another facet of gendered space is that MEGA also serves as space for Muslim women. In the afternoons, groups of women wearing the *hijab* are a common sight at MEGA. Some women come with children to enjoy MEGA's attractions. Some meet with other women to have a look at the fashion on offer or to have a meal at the food court, where most of the counters sell *halal* meat. Muslim women find MEGA a suitable place to meet and spend their time, as it counts as a safe and clean place.

These observations are in line with the study of Dörhöfer (2007, 67–68). She states that the shopping mall is emphasized as a 'Frauenraum' (German, 'women's space) because consuming household supplies is thought of as a women's task and pleasure. Dörhöfer explains that there are four reasons for this. First, the concentration of a wide assortment of goods is appreciated. Second, women are attracted by the secure, clean and service-oriented environment that the mall offers. Third, the mall offers married women a place for social interaction and a change from their regular family life. Fourth, especially for young women, the mall promises an exciting place to go shopping. Going to the mall should be more than satisfaction of one's needs; in fact it plays with the clients' dreams and expectations.

The shopping mall as a converging space of culture, consumerism and freedom

A multitude of converging spaces exist inside MEGA. It is precisely the possibility of condensing various spaces into one physical place that turns out to be the key to the mall's success. Although some of the shops have had to close due to insufficient customers, MEGA as a whole is 'en vogue in Aktobe. In this perspective, MEGA embodies a place where the capitalist economic order reigns.

Interaction with MEGA can be interpreted as a territorial claim for the younger generation. Other cultural spaces, such as the house of culture (*dom kul'tury*) or the theatres, are dominated by the older generations, which try to incorporate the youth, yet only in the way they predetermine. Groups active at public institutions need an older head to be present to control and lead younger members. A hierarchy based on age is a predominant principle in Kazakhstani society, and it orders social relationships at these institutions. Young people complained that they were used, for example, to give private concerts, or as taxi drivers or maids for their older group leaders. Space for creativity almost doesn't exist there. The house of culture sorts groups by ethnic categories and has the political agenda of fostering friendship and peace between Kazakhstan's people. Minority leaders are too busy struggling behind closed doors with money and resources to offer young people an open ear for their ideas.

The main creative cultural spaces for the youth are music clubs and MEGA. Here other principles of hierarchy function. Instead of age, here money plays the most important role. As long as someone is able to pay, all doors remain open. Nevertheless, the younger generation cannot act completely freely. Most parents tend to restrict their offspring's visits to music clubs because they consider them dangerous, especially for unmarried daughters. In contrast, MEGA is regarded as safe place (at least in the daytime). It is a place in which the younger generation is able to access and construct relations. MEGA functions as a social space where the youth meet with friends or stroll about.

A significant point on social control inside a mall is made by Zhelnina (2011, 67). In her observation, she states that in the reproduction of space, not only the formal administration provides rules of conduct. Visitors also exercise informal control through their imagination of correct and incorrect behaviour. As MEGA is the meeting point of mainly young people, their informal control is much more open to the habits of the younger generation. In my observations I saw a kind of play in two directions. On the one hand, I saw visitors following or resisting the pressure to buy the offered commodities. On the other hand, young visitors in particular played with modes of behaviour which they could not show outside in the street.

Zhelnina sees a new function being created for public space. As public squares formerly were identified as space for conversation, nowadays the public places are connected to 'watching' (Sennett 1992, 1994). She observes a transformation from verbal to visual culture (Zhelnina 2011, 50). Supporting this point, MEGA could be regarded as a kind of stage for visual culture. Fashions change quickly in regard to external trends. The cinema and other events also may be regarded as part of this shift. Saule and her elder sister Makpal regard MEGA as the place where the whole city meets. Because of this they have to be well dressed every time they go. They fear that it could be negative if they were seen in improper clothing here. Once, coming in to MEGA just to work in the mall's administration (where she found a job after her studies), Saule insisted on using the employee entrance.

In contrast to Botoeva's study, in which she sees shopping centres in Bishkek as a fixed factor for polarization in moral discourses, MEGA's meaning is still a topic undergoing negotiation. In opposition to Botoeva's (2006, 48–9) middle-aged, middle-class informants, who reject malls and count them more as a place for the rich, Aktobe's young generation does not emphasize feelings of being excluded or even rejected by the consumerist culture. Instead, they play with the structures of the shopping mall, looking for their own advantages and pathways for participation. For example, even high prices do not put them off. Young women wait for special events to buy the desired commodities at a discount.

Talking with Saule about consumerist culture and moral accusations, I heard that the older generation believe that young people are only interested in money. Saule defends Aktobe'ers of her generation. She explains that money is a tool which is used to buy freedom. Money is needed to stay independent. Economic capital opens possibilities for conversion into social capital in the fast-growing city. In this, MEGA could deliver a stage for establishing social relationships outside the family network that usually gives a structuring frame, especially for young Kazakh women. Economic capital also stays tightly connected to cultural capital in an environment of more and more commercialized education (e.g. private kindergartens, elite schools and sharply rising study fees).

MEGA attracts mainly young people for recreational purposes during their free time and during the holidays. Special events, like those for Nauryz, draw thousands of visitors to MEGA and tie them to the market relations inside. Through offers of special types of entertainment, the visitors find their way into the mall. In this sense it has to be said that MEGA succeeded from the start in entering Aktobe's cultural landscape. In this regard the location next to the city's new memorial axis turns out to be a significant factor.

Thinking about the shopping mall in Central Asia relates to the topic of urbanity. The mall has established its place in the landscape of the city. It offers new social spaces to a city's public space. The mall carries different functions and assuages other needs. It should not be assumed that the mall will replace the bazaar. Rather, it will gain a position parallel to the market, as Ozuduru, Varol, and Ercoskun (2012) suggest in their study of the relationship between malls and shopping streets in Ankara. The mall can be regarded as a gate to global culture via the images transmitted by a mall's shop windows and service offers.

Conclusion

The MEGA shopping mall quickly gained the position of a cultural hot spot in Aktobe. It succeeds in attracting various social groups by offering an ample mix of commerce and entertainment. Although all of my informants came to MEGA for different reasons, they seldom left it unsatisfied. In this lies the strength of the shopping mall concept, which seems to work also in Central Asia. It also pleases the older generation who accompany their family to MEGA, although not to the same extent as the younger generation, who are attuned to the fashion commodities available in the mall.

What can be observed in MEGA is a process of functions being condensed. In the Soviet era, entertainment was dispersed over the city in parks, cinemas and other formal cultural institutions such as theatres or the philharmonic hall. These institutions still exist, but according to my informants, they cannot challenge what MEGA has to offer. Gastronomy and boutiques attract clients from all income groups. The upper class looks for global trademarks in MEGA, while visitors lacking sufficient funds are still able to stroll through the corridors and have a look at the commodities. Hence, MEGA is not uniting visitors within one community, as boundaries between visitors follow this income divide. Desires are created but sometimes stay unrealized for the majority who are unable to acquire the goods in MEGA's fashion boutiques.

MEGA took the first step into the steppe. Until now it has been a unique place in Aktobe that allures and fascinates the inhabitants. If the economic development in oil-rich western Kazakhstan continues, it is to be expected that other malls will open up in the region. The mall offers an open space which attracts in particular the younger generation. They experience it as a stage which they use as a social space in which to (re)produce relationships to other people or goods. My research demonstrates that cultural variation plays a role in this while offering an accessible space for all ethnicities.

MEGA opens up possibilities which would not exist in public space elsewhere in Aktobe, especially for young women. This refers to a broad spectrum from dress code and behaviour to communicative functions and forms of social exchange. For them the shopping mall is more than a market. It is a playground on which social relations can be established, maintained, or transformed. Taking an ethnographic view, the narrative of modernization becomes tangible in its meaning for actors in the field. The mall transcends the level of a mere symbol and becomes a stage of manipulation by local individuals and groups.

Notes

1. Nauryz, the spring festival, is a major holiday shared by many ethnicities along the Silk Road, from the Kurds in the west to the Uighurs in the east. It is celebrated at the spring equinox. In Kazakhstan, Nauryz is recognized as a public holiday on 21–24 March.
2. In Kazakhstan, the anniversary of victory over Nazi Germany is celebrated on 9 May. (When the surrender document was signed at Berlin-Karlshorst, in the evening of 8 May, it was already after midnight in Moscow.) The Central Asian republics maintained Victory Day as a national holiday after their independence.
3. The Commonwealth of Independent States is a regional organization of former Soviet republics.
4. *Dacha* can be translated as 'summer home'. Beginning in the Brezhnev period, workers were given small plots of land for recreation and gardening, which was a tool for backup supply in cases of shortages. In the post-socialist period owners partially began to improve their structure and use *dacha*s as permanent homes.
5. The boom of Kazakhstan's GNP was also reflected in the regions, especially in the oil-rich western parts of the country. As Ursulenko (2010, 4) showed, the regional income spent on consumption (per capita) in Aktobe Province more than tripled between 1999 and 2008, to 12,000 tenge (in 2008, 1 US dollar corresponded to 120 tenge).
6. MEGA official homepage, http://MEGAmall.ru/belaya_dacha/company/, accessed 13 November 2014.
7. Russian RIA-news agency, http://ria.ru/economy/20140918/1024674064.html.
8. http://almaty.megacenter.kz/eng/about_mega, accessed 8 May, 2013.
9. All names of informants changed.
10. Kazakhs continue to trace their descent to clans to the present day. The clans split in the sixteenth to nineteenth century into clan federations (Small, Middle and Large Horde) for political, juristic and security issues. For further information, see Krader (1963).

Disclosure statement

No potential conflict of interest was reported by the author.

References

Alexander, C. 2007. "Almaty: Rethinking the Public Sector." In *Urban Life in Post-Soviet Asia*, edited by Catherine Alexander, Victor Buchli, and Caroline Humphrey, 70–101. London: ULC Press.
Alff, H. 2014. "Post-Soviet Positionalities – Relations, Flows and the Transformation of Bishkek's Dordoy Bazaar." In *Tracing Connections – Explorations of Spaces and Places in Asian Contexts*, edited by Hendryk Alff and Andreas Benz, 71–90. Berlin: WVB.
Appadurai, A. 1990. "Disjuncture and Difference in the Global Cultural Economy." *Theory, Culture & Society* 7: 295–310. doi:10.1177/026327690007002017
Bisembayev, A. A., G. S. Sultangalieva, I. V. Erofeeva, E. I. Medeubaev, and G. I. Kobenova, eds. 2007. *Istoriya Aktyubinskoj oblasti* [History of the Aktobe Province]. Aktobe: Oblastnoj centristorii.
Bodnar, J. 1998. "Art and Commerce as Logics of Budapest's New Public Space." In *City, Space and Globalization. An international perspective*, edited by Hemalata C. Dandekar, 183–192. Ann Arbor: University of Michigan Press.
Botoeva, A. 2006. "Contentious Discourses Surrounding Supermarkets in Post-Soviet Bishkek." *Anthropology of East Europe Review* 24 (2): 44–53.

Carpenter, C.-J. 1978. "Four Contemporary Bazaars in Soviet Central Asia." *Anthropos* 73 (3–4): 584–587.

Crawford, M. 1992. "The World in a Shopping Mall." In *Variations on a Theme Park: The New American City and the End of Public Space*, edited by Michael Sorkin, 3–30. New York: Hill and Wang.

Department statistiki Aktyubinskoj oblasti. 2008. *Dinamicheskie rjady po demograficheskoj Statistike* [Dynamic Rows in Demographic Statistics]. Manuscript. Aktobe: Department statistiki Aktyubinskoj oblasti.

Department statistiki Aktyubinskoj oblasti. 2009. *Demokraficheskij ezhegodnik Aktyubinskoj oblasti* [Demographic Year Book of the Aktobe Province]. Aktobe: Department statistiki Aktyubinskoj oblasti.

Department statistiki Aktyubinskoj oblasti. 2012. *Demokraficheskij ezhegodnik Aktyubinskoj oblasti* [Demographic Year Book of the Aktobe Province]. Aktobe: Department statistiki Aktyubinskoj oblasti.

Dörhöfer, K. 2007. "Passagen und Passanten, Shopping Malls und Konsumentinnen [Passages and Passersby, Shopping Malls and Female Consumers]." In *Shopping Malls. Interdisziplinäre Betrachtungen eines neuen Raumtyps* [Interdisciplinary Perspectives on a New Type of Space], edited by Jan Wehrheim, 55–76. Wiesbaden: VS.

Erkip, F. 2005. "The Rise of the Shopping Mall in Turkey: The Use and Appeal of a Mall in Ankara." *Cities* 22 (2): 89–108. doi:10.1016/j.cities.2004.10.001

French, Antony R. 1995. *Plans, Pragmatism and People. The Legacy of Soviet Planning for Today's Cities.* Pittsburgh: University of Pittsburgh Press.

Goss, J. 1993. "The "Magic of the Mall": An Analysis of Form, Function, and Meaning in the Contemporary Retail Built Environment." *Annals of the Association of American Geographers* 83 (1): 18–47. doi:10.1111/j.1467-8306.1993.tb01921.x

Hahn, B. 2007. "Shopping Center als internationales Phänomen [Shopping Center as International Phenomenon]." In *Shopping Malls. Interdisziplinäre Betrachtungen eines neuen Raumtyps* [Interdisciplinary Perspectives on a New Type of Space], edited by Jan Wehrheim, 15–34. Wiesbaden: VS.

Kostinskiy, G. 2001. "Post-Socialist Cities in Flux." In *Handbook of Urban Studies*, edited by Ronan Peddison, 451–465. London: Sage.

Krader, L. 1963. *Social Organization of the Mongol-Turkic Pastoral Nomads.* The Hague: Mouton.

Manzo, J. 2005. "Social Control and the Management of "Personal" Space in Shopping Malls." *Space & Culture* 8 (1): 83–97. doi:10.1177/1206331204265991

Miller, D., P. Jackson, N. Thrift, Beverley Holbrook, and Michael Rawlands. 1998. *Shopping, Place and Identity.* London: Routledge.

Molodikova, I., and A. Makhrova. 2007. Urbanization Patterns in Russia in the Post-Soviet Era. In *The Post-Socialist City*, edited by Kiril Stanilov, 53–70. Dordrecht: Springer.

Özcan, G. B. 2011. "Basare in Zentralasien [Bazaars in Central Asia]." *Zentralasienanalysen* 38: 2–5.

Ozdemir, A. 2008. "Shopping Malls: Measuring Interpersonal Distance Under Changing Conditions and Across Cultures." *Field Methods* 20 (3): 226–248. doi:10.1177/1525822X08316605

Ozuduru, B. H., C. Varol and O. Y. Ercoskun. 2012. "Do Shopping Centers Abate the Resilience of Shopping Streets? The Co-existence of Both Shopping Venues in Ankara, Turkey." *Cities* 36: 145–157. doi:10.1016/j.cities.2012.10.003

Ryabchuk, A. and N. Onyshchenko. 2012. "From Communism to Capitalism, from Production to Consumption: The Case of the Bilshovyk Plant and Shopping Center in Kyiv." *Radical History Review* 2012: 29–37. doi:10.1215/01636545-1597997

Sennett, R. 1992. *The Fall of Public Man.* New York: W.W. Norton.

Sennett, R. 1994. *Flesh and Stone: The Body and the City in Western Civilization.* New York: W.W. Norton.

Stanilov, K. 2007. The Restructuring of Non-residential Uses in the Post-socialist Metropolis. In *The Post-Socialist City*, edited by Kiril Stanilov, 73–99. Dordrecht: Springer.

Tazhibayev, M. K., A. Utegenov, M. Bapankulov, U. A. Akimov, Zh. S. Bajgurinov, A. K. Kuzdybaev, et al., eds. 2002. *Encyklopediya Aktobe* [Encyclopedia of Aktobe]. Aktobe: Otandastar-Poligrafiya.

Ursulenko, K. 2010. "Regional Development in Kazakhstan." *Kurzanalysen und Information* [Osteuropa-Institut Regensburg] 47: 1–10.

Werner, C. 2004. "Women, Marriage, and the Nation-State: The Rise of Nonconsensual Bride Kidnapping in Post-Soviet Kazakhstan." In *Transformations of Central Asian States: From Soviet Rule to Independence*, edited by Pauline Jones Luong, 59–89. Ithaca: Cornell University Press.

Werner, C. 2009. "Bride Abduction in Post-Soviet Central Asia: Marking a Shift Towards Patriarchy Through Local Discourses of Shame and Tradition." *Journal of the Royal Anthropological Institute* 15: 314–331. doi:10.1111/j.1467-9655.2009.01555.x

Zhelnina, A. 2011. "'It's Like a Museum Here': The Shopping Mall as Public Space." *Laboratorium. Russian Review of Social Research* [Laboratorium. Журнал социальных исследований] 2: 48–69.

The ignoble savage in urban Yerevan

Susanne Fehlings

Department of Social and Cultural Anthropology, Institute for Asian and Oriental Studies, Eberhard Karls University, Tübingen, Germany

ABSTRACT
This article focuses on a recent development in the Armenian capital, Yerevan, described by its urban population as a ruralization process. I explore what it means to call something or someone 'rural' or 'urban', and I compare the social category of 'rural people' with the social category of the (old) urban intelligentsia. This includes an analysis and reconsideration of the traditional 'nature–culture dichotomy' and its meaning for the architecture and urban planning of Yerevan. It also interrogates the classification of people into newcomers from the countryside, urban dwellers, new elites, and young men called *rabiz*.

I am as free as nature first made man,
Ere the base laws of servitude began,
When wild in woods the noble savage ran.
(John Dryden, *The Conquest of Granada*, 1672)

Introduction

My first contact with Armenians was in Crimea in 2007. Back then I attended a commemoration ceremony for the victims of Sumgait,[1] which was organized by the local Armenian community in Simferopol. When I told the participants my intention to conduct fieldwork in Yerevan they were very much surprised. They told me that 'nobody lives in Yerevan anymore' and that 'Yerevan has degenerated into a village'. To them, it did not seem worth going there, and they discouraged me from doing so.

This statement bothered me. Yerevan at that time had a population of approximately 1.3 million, which was one-third of the population of the whole republic. Moreover, the Armenian capital had an impressive city centre, including a central square (Republic Square), an opera house and parks with beautiful fountains, skyscrapers, broad avenues, horrendous traffic, and many satellite suburbs. For me, planning as I was to investigate the urban construction boom and its socio-cultural background, there was no doubt that Yerevan could be termed a city. But during my fieldwork, conducted between February 2009 and March 2010, I heard the argument that Yerevan has fallen to the status of a village quite often. Even if skyscrapers, fast food restaurants, and chain stores have sprouted like mushrooms in the last two decades since Armenian independence, a huge part of the population fears the demise of urban culture, a reversion to 'savagery', 'barbarism', and 'ruralization'. There are two reasons that are cited frequently for this perception of the observed trend: the encompassing *collapse* after the breakdown of the Soviet Union; and the *reorganization of the urban society* due to political and economic change and different migration movements. Both facts had an undeniable effect on urban space, architecture and city planning, and led to a new conflict between different layers of urban society, that is, between the old urban intelligentsia, new elites, and newcomers from rural areas.

Living in an urban neighbourhood in Yerevan for more than a year, I had occasion to share the everyday lives of its inhabitants. By applying classical field methods such as participant observation (Beer 2008), I was able to observe the daily practices, social interactions, and conflicts of my neighbours, who formed a very heterogeneous group. Even if the rural–urban division was not as clear as, for example, in the Kyrgyz neighbourhood in Bishkek described by Schröder (2010, 2011) or in the urban context of Kazakhstan described by Yessenova (2005), the urban–rural classification was a common way to rank individuals and their families, their practices and behaviours, and all kinds of objects, situations, and places in one's environment. These classifications were a topic in many everyday conversations and in the semi-structured and unstructured interviews I conducted with my informants inside and outside the neighbourhood. My informants included individuals of different ages and origins. Most of them were friends of friends or chance acquaintances. Others I chose as interview partners because of their expertise, as in the case of officials of the city administration or representatives of public and semi-public institutions (museums, the association of architects, NGOs). Most of the interviews were conducted in Russian, while everyday conversation took place in Armenian.[2] The data deriving from these observations, interviews, and other methods (archival work, recording of material culture, etc.) were then analysed by applying techniques of 'grounded theory' (Strauss and Corbin 1990).

Starting from this data, I shall explore here what it means, in the context of post-Soviet transition and in the wake of collapse and the reorganization of society, to call something or someone 'rural' or 'urban'. I shall compare the social category of 'rural people', which includes the new local elites, with the social category of the (old) urban intelligentsia, and interrogate the term *rabiz*. I shall thereby explain the ambivalence of these terms and their positive and negative connotations, which are usually linked to concepts of 'modernity' or 'tradition', 'progress' or 'backwardness', 'originality' or 'deracination', and 'rationalism' or 'sacredness/spirituality'. Finally, I shall explain how the 'urban–rural' or 'culture–nature' dichotomy mirrors a specific socio-cultural and cosmological order of the world. This analysis thereby gives insight into the perception of city planning and new trends in urban construction and lifestyle, as well as into contemporary Armenian urban society in general.

The inversion of urbanization

Collapse and city planning

The collapse (Russ.: *raspad soyuza*), which people in Armenia first of all associate with the 'black years' (Russ.: *tshernye gody*) of suffering during the early 1990s, comprises, as in other post-Soviet countries, the collapse of the economic and political system, and the loss of concrete things such as industries, jobs, minimum means of subsistence, health and social security systems, and free access to electricity, heating, and other infrastructure. In addition to the well-known problems of the post-Soviet transition scenario, Armenia, in the years before and after independence, was deeply affected by the Karabakh war,[3] an energy crisis, and the Spitak earthquake,[4] the last of these destroying the city of Giumri. Between 1988 and 1993 the gross national product fell to a fifth or a sixth of its former size, and by 1994, only 30% of the country's industry was working (Platz 2000).

The collapse of the external environment provoked a deep emotional experience. As stated by Platz (2000, 129), 'habitual social action, life, existence and even history seemed to be at an end'. Besides fear, some of this experience is nevertheless remembered in a surprisingly positive way. Thus, many of my friends remembered the 'black years' as a time of solidarity: neighbours helped each other, shared the little they had, and spent their leisure time together, gathering in front of a television, which was plugged into a generator and entertained the whole neighbourhood. Negative memories, of course, speak of the horror and the fear for one's existence. I heard about people who lost everything they had, and who lived selling biscuits on the streets. 'I have no idea how we survived. We wouldn't survive it a second time', the mother of a friend of mine told me (Fehlings 2012, 159).[5]

Collapse is a major topic in the accounts of post-Soviet people. The whole 'transition period' (Russ.: *transformatsia*) – broadly speaking – was (and somehow still is) shaped by the attempt to overcome this trauma. In Armenia, the collapse as an encompassing phenomenon is – according to the interpretation of my informants – mirrored in the decay and demolition of (Soviet) architecture. But people read this decay and demolition of buildings not only as a symbol of material loss but also as a symbol of decay on a spiritual level. The demolition of the urban environment, in their opinion, reflects the state of mind, the morality, and the negligent attitudes of the urban citizens. It thus is a symbol of the now-dominant value system shaped by degeneration, but also of those people who currently have the power to impose their will and their own and often conflicting values on others. At the same time, however, these powerful people, the 'new elites' – a very heterogeneous group of old cadres, the new rich (oligarchs), heroes of the Karabakh war, and the clergy – are accused of being 'rural', and considered to not care about the urban environment in the 'right way', as I shall explain below.

Some parts of Yerevan, its architecture and urban landscape, represent a sad picture indeed. The districts in the industrial south-east and on the periphery of the city in particular look extremely shabby, sometimes even abandoned. TerMinassian (2008, 107), the author of *Erevan: la construction d'une capitale à l'époque soviétique*, compares the once-flourishing industrial sites of the capital to the scenery of Tarkovsky's sombre movie *Stalker*, in which the heroes cross a dangerous, abandoned, and nebulous environment trying to exploit the remains of a lost and mysterious civilization.[6] Fittingly, when I visited the Botanical Garden, I felt as if I were in Stanisław Lem's *Solaris*, as if in a forgotten outpost of humanity inhabited by bewildered remains of the species: the windows of the huge glasshouse were broken; nature had won back the territory; and some elderly women wearing white coats seemed to be living an absurd life in the ruins of their former workplace (Figure 1).

Another example of the observable ravages of time is the former working-class neighbourhood of Errord Mas. It was planned and constructed for the workers of the Kirov

Figure 1. The remains of the botanical garden. The windows of the huge glasshouse are broken. Nature has won back the territory.

chemical factory in the early 1930s and considered a masterpiece of modern urban plan-ning, including residential houses, courtyards, open spaces for parks and fountains, shops, public schools, sports fields, and a 'house of culture' (Russ.: *dom kultura*) for 'cultural activity' (TerMinassian 2008, 107–118, 123–126). Some of my informants grew up here and were very nostalgic about it. Yet today the houses, courtyards and parks are run down, the shops and public buildings closed, and the fountains dry.[7] These are only a few examples of the same phenomenon. To their sorrow, city dwellers observe these kinds of decay in the whole city.

Contemporary Yerevan, the urban configuration as it exists today, is a comparatively new structure. It is based on a master plan designed in 1924 by the Soviet-Armenian archi-tect and urban planner Alexander Tamanyan.[8] This plan was inspired by the English concept of the 'garden city',[9] and especially in the 1950s was implemented with much enthusiasm. The 'garden city' (Russ.: *gorod sad*) concept was based on a circular layout with varied sections, including several so-called 'rural belts' of small forests, parks, gardens, and alleys. These green zones were thought to have a positive impact on the local microclimate and became popular places for residents to spend their free time (Arut-junjan, Astratjan, and Melikjan 1968; Gasparian 2004; TerMinassian 2008). Again and again I heard people complaining that much of these 'rural belts' was destroyed and their trees cut for fuel in the 'black years' of collapse (Platz 2000). The grandparent generation still remembers the erection of the buildings and structures of city planning, which are crum-bling today. They remember when the trees were planted, and they mourned them when they were felled in the years of war and shortages. Thus, the old urban population somehow became witness to the rise and fall of Yerevan, of which the deforestation of the city is the ultimate symbol.

Another development observed by all inhabitants, old and young, was, as in many other post-Soviet cities, the construction boom – especially in the city centre – in recent years. Many writings on post-Soviet cities have described this construction boom, as is visible in collections of essays such as *Representations on the Margins of Europe* (Darieva and Kaschuba 2007) or *Urban Spaces after Socialism* (Darieva, Kaschuba, and Krebs 2011).[10] As noted by Grant (2014, 504),

> the construction industry remains one of the most effective ways to launder money[11] in a post-Soviet world, where complex networks of both government and well-connected private figures have turned to real estate as means of legitimizing less reputable financial gains.

This is why the building activity, though it is an inversion of the described devastation, is perceived equally negatively and serves as a marker for the collapse of old norms and values. In fact, it is perceived as a symbol of the immorality of those people who have abandoned the old values (such as community spirit) and who had the power to initiate and finance current urban planning.

Most of my informants were people who grew up in the city and describe themselves with the attributes of the *intelligentsia* (Russ.) or *mtavorakanuthjun* (Arm.), which means that they identify with Soviet ideals and the moral code of the educated urban population, and – at the same time – with the nationalistic intellectual Armenian avant-garde.[12] These people almost all agree[13] that the new building complexes, especially those built since independence, are ugly and of bad quality and cannot be compared with Soviet architecture and aesthetics.[14] Consequently, architecture originating from the 1990s onwards is constantly under fire. One good example of this is the public debate surrounding the so-called Northern Avenue (Marutyan 2007). Its construction started after independence in the time of Armenia's second president, Robert Kocharyan, and connects two main spots in the urban landscape, the Republic Square and the opera house, both designed by Tamanyan. Yet, while Tamanyan's city planning was also taken as the model for the avenue,[15] its architecture differs from older edifices: the Northern Avenue is a pedestrian zone, edged by skyscrapers that surround the whole centre and hosting private apartments and expensive shopping brands (Figure 2). Most of the buildings still seemed to be empty and uninhabited at the time of my fieldwork in 2010.[16]

My informants usually took grave offence at its conception: 'It's like someone set off a neutron bomb there and all life was snuffed out.' It is from comments like this that we can understand that even the *construction* of houses and the development of *new* infrastructure can be interpreted as devastation and as a marker of collapse. The reason for such a judgement is not only the new architecture itself, but also its symbolic value representing social exclusion and behaviour, habits, and values that are not approved of by a majority of citizens. For the construction of the avenue, many old houses had to be destroyed. Some activists demonstrated against the construction to protect the human rights of the area's residents, who were removed, could no longer afford to live in the area, received very little compensation, and lost a huge part of their quality of life. In some cases my informants even expressed fear that the new architecture would have a negative effect on their health and psychology, and furthermore held it responsible for the huge emigration volume (see below). Yet the most frequent critique concerns the ugliness of the style, which is understood as a metaphor for the encompassing changes.

Figure 2. The Northern Avenue.

Reorganization of urban society

In my introduction I mentioned two factors that are often related to the recent negative developments in Yerevan: *collapse* and the *reorganization of urban society*. The reorganization of urban society had many reasons. While Soviet workers and intellectuals struggled to survive the 'black years', and lost their jobs and positions, newcomers took their place in the young republic. The profiteers of the Soviet collapse were diverse. Some of them began their careers in the Karabakh war. As veterans they gained control over many types of businesses, entered politics after the war, and by the late 1990s dominated the Armenian Parliament. After about 10 years of dominance, the military caste lost its influence, but it was in great part ousted by a new successful business elite. This elite rested upon technocratic skills, personal networks, and economic success. Businessmen – often referred to as 'oligarchs' – managed to cooperate with the government, which – last but not least – led to a monopolization of business and politics (Iskandaryan 2014; Stefes 2006, 2008). If the very first generation of the political elite could be called to some extent 'intellectual',[17] the following generations in contrast had a 'new and alien mentality'. Likewise, the 'New Russians', the so-called 'New Armenians', were 'people who are rapacious, materialist and shockingly economically successful', and 'do not give precedence to various hoary Soviet values, which are still mostly seen in a rosy hue by everyone else' (Humphrey and Mandel 2002, 177). They attract attention because of their swanky style, their preference for certain brands, like Armani, and their mafia-like pretentious behaviour, fulfilling every cliché of a Russian oligarch. 'Belonging to the elite', as in many other post-Soviet countries, is therefore often used as a synonym of 'being corrupt'.

What is interesting in the context of this article is the fact that the 'new elites' and everything they create (such as modern architecture) are often characterized with the term 'rural'. For example, one of my informants, a 40-year-old middle-class man who grew up in Yerevan's centre, railed against the construction site of the Northern Avenue by comparing it to the countryside: 'Look at this; no one would think we are in the heart of Yerevan. It is as if we were somewhere in a village.' I was somewhat perplexed until I understood that to be 'rural' has nothing to do with my conception of the countryside, but is an imaginary category. Thus, 'rural things' do not have to belong to or actually be situated in the countryside. Rather, 'rural' in these contexts is meant as a derogatory term. Here, the accusation of having 'rural roots' equates to labelling something or someone as 'primitive', 'underdeveloped' or 'backward', as being 'of bad taste' or 'ugly'.

On the other hand, this categorization has some basis in reality, to the extent that people from the countryside have in fact become visible as a social group in Yerevan, and have thus contributed to the evolution and definition of the category 'rural', which until then was a term used mainly in Soviet propaganda. The breakdown of the Soviet Union had a deep impact on demography in almost all former Soviet republics – especially in Central Asia and the Caucasus (CAD 2013; Marat 2009). In Armenia demographic changes were directly linked to war, ethnic persecution, drastic poverty, and material shortages, as well as to the earthquake of 1988.[18] In 1993, about one-third of Armenia's population was estimated to be homeless (Platz 2000). There were and still are many different types and directions of migration. According to a rough estimate, about 1 million Armenian citizens left the country between 1990 and 2006.[19] In the first decade after the breakdown of the Soviet Union, this led to a population decline of more than 15% (Mansoor & Quilling 2006, 33).[20] Some of the migrants went to Europe or the United States, where they joined the well-established diaspora communities. But most of the labour migrants left for Russia (CAD 2013), causing a lack of young men in Armenia's rural areas (Menjívar and Agadjanian 2007). It is very difficult to track the movements of Armenian migration in either direction. In its report from 2007 the National Statistical Service noted that 53.1% of migrants who left the country since 1990 had returned at the time of the survey; 55% of them did not go back to their villages but settled in the urban area of Yerevan.[21] One further important population movement could be observed *inside* Armenia. While huge parts of the population, many of them belonging to the Soviet-Armenian intelligentsia, left the country, many families abandoned the countryside and their villages to live in the capital.[22] This rural-to-urban migration is an ongoing process that is observed critically by the urban population.[23]

In total, these movements led to a turnover of the population of Yerevan, changing its composition and structure, which makes especially long-term inhabitants feel that they are losing neighbours, friends, relatives, and their own position in urban life. This impression probably led to the sentiment quoted above, heard in Simferopol long before my arrival in Yerevan. People really sense the loss of their social relations and of their social (urban) environment (compare Schröder 2010). They have the impression that 'nobody is living in Yerevan anymore'. Some people even use the term 'white genocide' (Arm.: *spitak jard*) to describe this situation.

Urban and rural terminology

As one might now understand, the collapse of old things and the appearance of new people, new elites, and new symbols were the main experiences and changes after independence. The 'new elites' mentioned above are, as stated, often associated with the rural population or 'rural migrants'.[24] Their manners, their socio-cultural values, and their understanding of 'modernization', as well as other post-Soviet developments associated with their activity, are thus stigmatized as a ruralization process. To explain the current situation, a young architect told me:

> The powerful only recently became rich. They are still rude and wild. In Europe the powerful gained their fortune several generations ago. These are already different, more cultivated people. In Armenia, there is no law. It is not the president taking decisions but the rich. What can one do if one knows that they have the means to liquidate you? One always has to be careful. Concerning building permission, I have heard of cases when they threatened the chief architect of Yerevan physically. These cases occurred, and what can one do when these rich and strong people are standing in front of you!

The barbarism of the elites hence finds access to the urban landscape. According to the logic of rural–urban categorization, many Yerevantsi (inhabitants of Yerevan) discussed, for example, the social background of Narek Sargsyan. As the city's chief architect he was in charge of the Northern Avenue between 1999 and 2004, and therefore also represented the bad taste, illegal activities, and moral guilt of the new elites. In public discussions his 'bad taste' often was explained with reference to his wild and rural origins and his ignorance of urban life (Marutyan 2007). Similar accusations were made during protests against the demolition of the open-air part of the Cinema Moskva. In this instance, a new church was planned to replace the older, 1960s Soviet cinema building (Abrahamian 2011; Antonyan 2012).[25] This endeavour, initiated by the Armenian Apostolic Church, was quite surprisingly rejected by a broad public. After the breakdown of the Soviet Union, the Armenian Church, which was supported by the Armenian diaspora, gained much influence. Yet, while Christianity is part of Armenian identity, the clergy is often suspected of not representing holiness and purity, as it should, but exploiting its status and behaving like the new rich and *rabiz* (see below). But in this context not only the institution of the Church was criticized by the opponents, but also the former owner of the cinema, who had donated the building plot to the Catholicos (head of the Armenian Apostolic Church) and who was depicted as a 'rural person'. One of Abrahamian's (2011, 149) informants, for example, 'thought that the role of the cinema's owner in this story was preconditioned by his rural origins and hence the lack of a city resident's memory'.

As one might conclude from these examples, quite a large group of people in Yerevan – the new elites, state and church officials, oligarchs, investors, and simply people living in the neighbourhood and not belonging to one's relatives and friends – who could be held responsible for current grievances, social injustices, decadence, and a decline in socio-cultural values – at the same time are stigmatized as 'wild', 'rude', and 'rural'. The categorical use of these terms led me to question in detail what they mean.

Nature, culture, urbanity, and modernity debates

I believe that the term 'rural' cannot be understood without placing it in relation to its opposite, the category of being 'urban'. As we have seen, this may hold not only for material construction and urban planning, but also for particular groups and individuals.

The phenomenon or the awareness of a ruralization process seems to be a common problem in post-Soviet countries and has been described in many articles about post-

Soviet cities (Krebs 2014/15; Kosmarski 2011; Flynn and Kosmarskaya 2012). In their intro-duction to *Urban Life in Post-Soviet Asia,* Alexander and Buchli (2007, 30) summarize the impression of contemporary urban populations in Central Asia and the Caucasus:

> a fear that the road to progress, and the utopian bright future as promised and defined by Soviet development, is now not only impossible, but in fact likely reversed. Urbanity, in many cases, seems to be giving way to 'pre-modern' forms of living and sociality.[26]

This statement implicitly assumes the existence of both a Soviet definition of the term 'rural', and a Soviet perception of 'urbanity'. In my opinion it is worth having a closer look at these definitions. In the Communist Manifesto, Marx and Engels (2012 [1848], 40) describe the city as a bright alternative to the 'idiocy of rural life'. Here, 'rural life' is placed on a level with backwardness and primitivism, while the goal is to develop and pro-gress. This narrative is quite a common one and has been described by ethnographers working in various parts of the world (see e.g. Ferguson 1999 on the Zambian Copperbelt). In the evolutionary theory of historical materialism, 'rural life' belongs to '"pre-modern" forms of living and sociality'. In Soviet ideology, people and peoples had to overcome this stage, join the working class, and become 'urban', which meant 'modern' and 'civilized' (Russ.: *tsivilisovanno*; *kulturno*).

This rural–urban dichotomy is rooted in the nature–culture divide, debated in Western philosophy since antiquity, and was believed by Lévi-Strauss 'to be found among all societies in some form as a cognitive device for understanding the world' (Carrithers 1996, 304; see Lévi-Strauss 1969). According to Tylor (1924 [1871]), culture is 'that complex whole which includes knowledge, belief, art, morals, law, custom and any other capabilities and habits acquired by man as a member of society'.[27] With this descrip-tion the anthropologist summarized the existing understanding of the term as the oppo-site of nature: civilization is a human achievement, which can be interpreted as a consequence of evolution in a Darwinian sense. Man is a product of nature, but thanks to his powers of reason, he is able to overcome biology and position himself above all other species and above creation (compare Carrithers 1996, 395). In the process, man developed from a primate to *homo sapiens*, and from a 'savage being' to 'civilized man'.

Critics, especially the philosophers, writers, and artists of German Romanticism,[28] con-demned this presumed development. In reaction to industrialization and the rationalism of the Enlightenment, they were preoccupied by mystery (*Geheimnis*), emotion (*Gefühl*), and aspiration (*Sehnsucht*), reflected in an enthusiasm for nature, which was charged with a religious and sacred meaning, as illustrated by the writings of Novalis and J. v. Eichendorff and paintings by C. D. Friedrich (Geismeier 1998). The glorification of the 'noble savage', who, especially in the works of Rousseau (1750, 1762a, 1762b), symbo-lizes the 'innate goodness of one not exposed to the corrupting influences of civilisation' (Encyclopaedia Britannica), is an expression of the same longing.

People, cultures, and civilizations, according to evolutionary theories in the humanities, undergo a development similar to humanity as a biological entity. Because of this under-standing, anthropologists such as Frazer, the author of *The Golden Bough* (1950 [1907–1915]), started to explore the development of different aspects of culture in general and in different cultures in particular. The idea was to learn more about one's own history by exploring, for example, the evolution of property (Maine 1959 [1861]), of gender roles (Bachhofen 1980 [1861]), of religion (Tylor 1924 [1871]), or of kinship relations

(Morgan 1964 [1877]) in so-called 'primitive societies'. While anthropologists like Boas and his students emphasized, from the 1880s onwards, the equality of different cultures, there was still a tendency to judge local societies in comparison to Western cultures, which were taken as a model of cultural sophistication and advancement in an evolutionary sense (Carrithers 1996, 394). This was especially true in colonial contexts all over the world, as in the Russian and Soviet context, where this conviction was combined with the Marxist ideology and led to a particular policy and development programme (see Kappeler 2005).

The Soviet manifestation of the above-mentioned debates and their implementation in practice is specific. In this context, 'urbanity' and 'modernity' are used almost as synonyms, and 'modernity' has a specific meaning, which, even if using Western models to some extent, differs from Western perceptions.[29] Bayadyan (2007, 205–219) points out that in Western countries 'modernity' is mostly linked to the notion of nation-state, democracy, and capitalism. In the Soviet understanding, in contrast, 'modernity' was linked to industrialization, urbanization, secularization, and a complete alphabetization (education) of the population (Lewis and Rowland 1969). This second definition, which also defines the values of the urban intelligentsia, is still prevalent in many post-Soviet countries – or at least mingled with the first (Western) definition (compare Yessenova 2005).

The construction of Yerevan, based on the master plan of 1924, served as a model of all aspects of the Soviet definition of 'urbanization/modernization'. In that sense, it was a real success story. The industry that settled in Yerevan attracted many people to the city, and Yerevan grew much faster than anticipated. In 1924 Yerevan had approximately 60,000 inhabitants. Tamanyan was planning a future city for 150,000 people. In 1966 new calculations made it evident that Yerevan would grow to about 900,000 by 1980 (Arutjunjan, Astratjan, and Melikjan 1968). In fact, in the early 1980s a population of more than one million was reached, which was the number that qualified Soviet cities to build a metro system. In Yerevan, the metro, the symbol of achieved urbanity, was officially opened on 7 March 1981 (Ter Minassian 2007, 200–203, 205–211; Arutjunjan, Astratjan, and Melikjan 1968, 268–269).[30] Many of my informants were proud of this fact. They read it as a sign of general progress and as an indicator of moral status – a status which has been reversed in recent times.

The categories of 'urban' and 'rural' people

Simultaneous with the demographic growth in the pre-Soviet and Soviet years, people apparently became acquainted with the conveniences and pleasures of urban life. They got used to the infrastructure, to running water, to concerts, ballets, and their urban environment. The urban intelligentsia, which came into existence during the early stages of city development, was proud of being *urban* (Russ.: *gorodskije*; Arm.: *khaghakhi/khaghakhajin*) and sophisticated (Russ.: *gramatnije, kulturnije, obrazovannije, kulturnije*). Their children were educated in schools, they learned how to play the piano, they knew about classic literature and went for walks in public parks and gardens during their free time.

The social group of intelligentsia is – as mentioned above – difficult to grasp. Almost all of my informants perceived themselves as belonging to this group, while expressing their regret that the intelligentsia as an urban group was dying out after the breakdown of the Soviet Union (Antonyan 2012; for similar observations in Azerbaijan see Fehlings 2014/15).

From this viewpoint, to claim oneself a part of the intelligentsia is a way to distinguish oneself from others, for example corrupt elites, disliked neighbours, and anonymous strangers, who are believed to belong to the category of 'rural'.

Within this 'rural' group there is a special subcategory of people that can be interpreted as the utter opposite of the intelligentsia. This group is known as the *rabiz*. The definition of *rabiz*, which is a result of 'othering' (Fabian 1990) and 'orientalization' (Said [1978]) in the strict sense of the word, may therefore clarify what the urban intelligentsia should not be, and – vice versa – what the term 'rural people' means.

The word *rabiz* apparently derives from an abbreviation of the Russian term for *rab-otniki* or *rab-otschee is-kusstvo* ('art of the working class'; Abrahamian 2006, 98; Hakobyan 2006, 55). Originally, this was the art of Errord Mas, the working-class neighbourhood described earlier. Even if Errord Mas in Soviet times was perceived as a great step towards modernization and urbanization, it still was seen in opposition to the even more developed city centre, and was thus classified as inferior, more 'primitive' and more 'rural'. Since the 1930s the term *rabiz* was used first of all to describe a style of music, nowadays associated with oriental sounds and melodies (Hakobyan 2006, 54–59; Bretèque and Stoichita 2012, 323; Adriaans 2011, 67–88). According to Hakobyan (2006, 59), at the beginning of the 1970s the term began also to be used to designate a group – especially of young men – suspected of listening to and enjoying this music.[31] The characteristics of this category of people were not only a certain taste (for music and other forms of art), but – as I could observe among the young generation in my neighbourhood – comprised a whole lifestyle. *Rabiz* show off with their masculinity. They are proud of their strength, of a mafia-like code of conduct and look, and of their 'brotherhoods' (Arm.: *aperuthjun*). When I talked to some of these young men, they loved to talk about friendship, about their 'brothers' (Arm.: *aperer*), about their own code of honour, about 'business', about fights with other men, and about cars, brands, and women. Hanging around in their courtyards, gathering to discuss car accidents, and wolf-whistling at women, *rabiz* and their brotherhoods belong to contemporary Yeravan's cityscape.

Particularly those people who count themselves among the intelligentsia use the term *rabiz* in a condescending tone. It then contains an evaluation of the person, their 'rural' taste, dress (black clothes), and diction (melodramatic slang), which – not surprisingly – copies the style of the new elites, the 'New Armenians'. It is, I would conclude, a term describing not only 'low culture' but primitivism, barbarism and savagery. Quoting Adriaans (2011, 67):

> Everyone in Yerevan has an opinion on rabiz. The current president Serzh Sargsyan … is 'totally rabiz' primarily because of his poor command of the Armenian language. The new buildings that are being erected in Yerevan … exemplify a rabiz movement, because they 'demonstrate no creative inspiration whatsoever,' and are built for oligarchs who are 'relatively uneducated and have no taste'.

Many in Yerevan see this trend spreading among the young generation, as the following statement from a 30-year-old woman and programmer reveals: 'In the past one would have said that such a person comes from Errord Mas – today, I believe that all these people [in the city] come from Errord Mas.' Interestingly, men are much more vulnerable to this influence. They are considered less progressive than women, which women express in remarks like 'our men are still Asian' or 'they are still wild'.

Generally, the *rabiz* are described as having an uncultivated and rural attitude. *Rabiz*, as per my informants, do not know how to behave in the city. They are *gerghtsi* or *gjughakan* (Arm.: village-like). Due to their (assumed) village background, or because they are 'from the mountains' (Arm.: *lerneric*), they are depicted as 'like savages' (Russ.: *dikij*; Arm.: *vayri*), who 'throw their garbage in the streets and spit on the floor'. Other stereotypes about *rabiz* describe them as *brutal, rude, dirty, backward*, and *oriental/Asian*.[32] The *rabiz* dress like the new rich and love luxury, big cars, and brand-name clothes. But, as suspected by my informants, they are uneducated (Russ.: *njekulturno; njegrammatno*), fatalist, and despondent and do not know what hard work means (compare Adriaans 2011). They love money, but they do not earn it – yet if somehow they get their hands on some, they waste it like fools and use it for unworthy, egoistic, and immoral purposes, such as building the Northern Avenue and thereby chasing away the old population. This is why the *rabiz*'s economic activity and its consequences are also called 'wild capitalism' (Russ.: *dikij kapitalism*) or 'village capitalism' (Arm.: *gerghtsi kapitalism*).

As I could observe during my field research, all these characterizations fit into the description of three categories, which are measured by the same yardstick: 'the new elites' ('New Armenians'), the 'rural newcomers', and the *rabiz*. This is probably why these three categories are mixed up and often cannot be clearly separated. Interestingly, all three groups are also admired, although this may sound surprising, especially as far as the group of 'rural people' is concerned. In my opinion, this admiration can be compared to the perception of nature in Romanticism (see above), and explained with the cultural value that is given to rural life embedded in nature as the sacred environment and the traditional homeland of the Armenian *azg* (kin group).[33]

Sacred mountains and urban gardens

When Armenians talk about their 'sacred homeland', the land of the fathers (Arm.: *Hayastan*), they usually do not refer to Yerevan. First of all the beautiful mountains, Lake Sevan, or other places far away from any urban influences are mentioned. The most sacred places, such as monasteries or so-called pagan sanctuaries, are located near natural springs and rivers, and in remote, mountainous regions that are difficult to reach. For instance, one of my informants, an Armenian from Lebanon, decided to settle in Armenia only after he had experienced the natural Armenian landscape during a touristic journey: 'It was very important to me whether I was attracted by the natural environment or not. I had to feel some kind of mysticism; I had to feel a certain charisma of nature. That is why I visited Armenia.' Finally, this informant settled in Yerevan. When I asked him what he thought about the capital he told me:

> Armenia is not Yerevan. Armenia means something else to us.[34] ... I didn't like Yerevan – all these building constructions, which are difficult to bear. ... Nothing attracts me in Yerevan except the cultural events. I favour the natural environment. ... My spirit is attracted by it. ... It is true, that there are some nice people. No one can doubt that. But I don't feel anything toward them. No affinity. But I feel this affinity when visiting a monastery, or when reaching the top of Mount Aragats. I did it two weeks ago. I climbed Mount Aragats and I felt my heart laughing. I don't know why. It is a mystery.

Mount Aragats, like its twin or opposite, Mount Ararat, is perceived as sacred. According to legends, Grigor the Illuminator, converter and first Catholicos of Armenia, used to pray on its peak (Abrahamian 2007, 180–181). Mount Ararat, which is visible from Yerevan but across the international border, might be of even more importance for Armenian history and folklore. According to Petrosyan (2001a, 35), it influenced Armenian thought and has been a source of Armenian mythology. It is interpreted as the 'mother of the world', and 'was believed to be the place where the sun lay down to rest every night, where Armenian heroes were born, and where "kajs", the mythical protectors of kings, made their home'. It is also taken to be the place where Noah landed with his ark (Genesis 6:1–9:29). If one has a look at the 1889 painting *Descent of Noah from Ararat* by the Armenian painter Aivazovsky, one might find many similarities to Friedrich's paintings and mysticism. However, the impressive mountain also has the reputation of being dangerous and a source of misfortune. In his epic novel *The Legend of Mount Ararat*, Turkish author Yaşar Kemal (2014 [1970]) writes about the wrath of the mountain and its magic power to punish, petrify, and save people. As a place of sacred spirits, it belongs to another world, far from human tangibility. In 1829 the adventurist Parrot (1985 [1834]) reported on the taboo that existed about climbing the mountain, which is why a part of his crew refused to follow him.

These stories reflect well the double nature of the mountain – its holiness and danger – which furthermore seems to be valid for the whole environment: nature carries a sacred meaning, but at the same time it is dangerous, because it is 'wild' and almost impossible to domesticate. 'Nature', as in the accounts of German Romanticism, is 'mystic' and indicates religious meanings. Following this understanding, rural people, who live close to nature, are believed to be closer to the ancestors and the 'innate goodness' (see above). They are supposed to be more knowledgeable about Armenian mythology and traditions, which is extremely valuable after independence, when national topics and the national past becomes a medium to redefine the nation state. Very often, when I asked my informants to explain a certain term or a specific category of kinship relation, they replied that I should ask the villagers, because they might have preserved this knowledge.

Herzfeld uses these kinds of convictions to outline the importance of what he calls 'cultural intimacy' that, according to him, is rooted in local traditions and knowledge and is a breeding ground for nationalism. The significance of 'cultural intimacy' is thus one reason why 'in the romantic folklore of the urban elite, the [backward and marginal groups] embody the national quintessence' (Herzfeld 1997, 7). In this regard even the *rabiz*, in some specific situations, become symbols of heroic manhood, authenticity, indigenous Armenian values, and the real nature of Armenian identity. All stigmas aside, they embody the ideal of the 'noble savage'. Very often I was told about the *rabiz'* 'rural' vitality, their strength (which can turn into brutality), their loyalty towards their friends and kin, and their will to protect their families. Their condition of longing, nostalgia, and regret (Arm.: *karot*), which is a topic in many *rabiz* songs (Adriaans 2011), turns them into romantics. All these features are very much admired and in fact are requirements for being a real and good Armenian man (Arm.: *mi lav hay mard*). This is why *rabiz*-like habits of young men – even of young men with urban origins – are sometimes generously accepted by the older generation and interpreted as a natural stage of an adolescent's development.

Hence, most of my urban informants did not express worries about their lost ties to nature and their lack of knowledge about authentic Armenian traditions and rural behaviour. In her article *Shamans in the City*, Humphrey (1999) stresses the importance of Ulan

Ude's population to maintain connections to the hinterland to keep spiritual ties to the natural environment of the ancestors and spirits. According to my observations, this is not the case for the urban population of Yerevan, where 'to be urban' is a value as such, even for those people who have recently come to live in the capital. Many of my informants maintained relationships with relatives living in the countryside. But these relations, which due to the lack of infrastructure were neglected in times of crisis, did not have an ideological significance bestowed on them, even if they were revitalized and intensified after crisis.

The domestication of nature and its reversion

In comparison to the 'sacred homeland' consisting of the natural environment and sacred places like Mount Ararat or Mount Aragats, the city might be unholy and less authentic. On the other hand, the city – at least since Soviet times – has been a symbol of human achievement and human civilization. Even more, following Kant's (1928 [1784]) conviction that mankind requires culture to develop morality, urban life became a symbol of moral behaviour. It can thus be interpreted as the secular counterpart of the sacred environment. It is one part of a two-part cosmos – the human part. Opposite to nature, the urban environment has become 'domesticated' and therefore is considered predictable and safe (Figure 3).

This domestication of nature in Armenian folklore is symbolized in Noah's first attempt to plant and cultivate a vineyard (Genesis 9:20).[35] After his rescue Noah came down from Mount Ararat and settled at its base. By founding Yerevan, according to the 'father of Armenian history', the historian Movses Chorenatsi (about 410–490 AD), he initiated not only Armenian culture but human culture in general (Samuelian 2000; Shnirelman 2001, 33). This story can of course be compared to many other founding myths recorded by historians or anthropologists. All these myths, as for example, the myths of the conquest of the American *Wild* West, have in common that they describe the emancipation of culture and civilization from nature. One can at least detect the theme of the domestication of nature and 'wild men'.

In the Middle Ages Yerevan was mentioned by travellers like Chardin and Tavernier as a 'city of gardens' (Arutjunjan, Astratjan, and Melikjan 1968; Ter Minassian 2007). The Soviet urban planning of Yerevan, as I have mentioned, replicated that of a 'garden city', with huge parks as a component of the city environment. The term 'garden' evokes a vision of Yerevan as a place of beautiful flora, with blossoming trees, flowers, and vineyards. In the Armenian language there are two words designating garden, *agi* and *partez*; the latter, as I was told, originating in Old Persian and being associated with 'paradise'. But none of its plants are wild. Gardens, like parks, are made and controlled by the human hand. Very often the vineyard is the symbol of this concept. In the Middle Ages planting was considered a cosmic act. Thus Armenian kings, for example King Yervand, who ruled from 220 to 201 BC, and King Khosrov II, who ruled between 330 and 337 AD, planted forests as a model of living for the whole society. Notable for their legendary beauty were the gardens of Queen Shamiram (or Semiramis) of Assyria and Armenia, who also is said to have planted vineyards near Lake Sevan (Petrosyan 2001a; 2001b).[36]

In my opinion, therefore, the medieval 'city of gardens' and the Soviet 'garden city' of Yerevan, just like their historical predecessors, reflect the cosmological order of the city:

Figure 3. The capital, Yerevan, in front of Mount Ararat – human civilization and sacred nature.

the urban cosmos, which has a special place with respect to the rest of the world. Man-made parks and gardens ideally reflect organization and regulation. They are artificial environments – all natural, or in other words 'rural' and 'wild', influences must be harmful to them. This is extremely evident in baroque gardens but is also valid for other types of 'garden art', including 'Russian' and 'Soviet gardening' (Ananieva et al. 2013).

Humphrey (2005, 52) describes the role Soviet ideology gave 'domesticated nature' in the urban environment as follows:

> 'Greening' (ozelenenie) was energetically pursued to promote healthy air, improve the microclimate, decorate the architectural ensemble. And provide a pleasant environment for the leisure of the working masses. Furthermore, it was a process that involved the broad participation of the population (Tsentral'nyi 1967, 245).[37] The inhabitants themselves were to cultivate their collective well-being through voluntary workdays of planting, gardening, and watering.

It is no wonder, then, that if Soviet architecture, the symbol of urbanization and modernization, is falling apart today, and if industrial sites or the botanical garden are abandoned and being overgrown without any human control, this is perceived as 'demodernization' (Platz 2000).

Time, according to some, and as observed by Platz (2000, 115), seemed to have 'ended, ruptured, or begun to go backward', and Armenia, unlike the modern Western world, was no longer taking part in a linear progressive motion: '*het enk gnum*' (Arm.: we are going backward). This was described in terms of a 'ruralization' process, with all its negative aspects: nature has won back what was occupied and cultivated by humans, by society and human civilization; and – at least in the time of crisis – 'existence became "animal" and "inhuman"' (129). The cosmos, the balance between nature and human civilization, is visibly being disturbed and compromised. This also happens, according to my informants, if too many rural people enter the city. They would not care, I was told, about the urban environment; they would destroy the domesticated beauty of parks and gardens, and 'behave like savages' (Russ.: *dikye*), with no understanding of 'cultured behaviour'.

Conclusion

Cities and rural areas, culture and nature, order and disorder have always been conceived of in opposition to each other (see above) – and not only in anthropology and philosophy. Culture and cultivating are usually thereby defined as specifically human ways of surviving. 'Therefore the Lord God sent him out from the garden of Eden to work the ground from which he was taken' (Genesis 3:23). Likewise, the story of the exchange and the replacement of urban populations by animalistic barbarians from rural areas is nothing new. It is part of the myth of the decline of the Roman Empire, and as early as the fourteenth century was described by Ibn Khaldun in his *Muqaddimah* (1967 [1377], 107):

> Since desert life no doubt is the source of bravery, savage groups are braver than others. They are, therefore, better able to achieve superiority and to take over superiority and to take away the things that are in the hands of other nations. The situation of one and the same group changes, in this respect with the change of time. Whenever people settle in fertile plains and amass luxuries and become accustomed to a life of abundance and refinement, their bravery decreases to the degree that their wildness and habits decrease.

With the desert replaced by the harsh countryside and mountains of the Caucasus, this is exactly the myth of Armenia's new (*rabiz-*)elite.

Since its reconstruction in the early 1920s, Yerevan has constantly attracted people from outside and from rural areas, who have renewed its population. It could thus have been accepted as a natural process. Instead, many people in Yerevan argue that the influences of ruralization became more drastic after independence – which is, I guess, first of all a subjective impression.[38] I have made the point in this article that this perception might be linked to the experience of collapse in the 'black years' of the early 1990s, to the overgrowing of the urban parks and landscape (not only metaphorically), and to the loss of a great part of the urban population to labour migration, as well as to the appearance of those new powerful elites that are categorized as 'New Armenians', and their building activity. My informants therefore harboured the feeling that their cosmos has lost its balance and that boundaries have been crossed. *Nature* and *rural* people, in their eyes, have taken the urban sphere. This feeling was very frankly expressed by an old woman (X.), who worked as a university professor in Yerevan. She tried to explain to me the order of things, as they should be:

X.: Of course, a lot changes with the people.
Me: In what sense?
X.: In what sense? Okay, for example … kings live in palaces, you agree?
Me: Yes?
X.: Commoners live in apartments … and peasants should live in the countryside. …
   This is my opinion. … and then, the language …

Me: The language?

X.: The language. Yes. Today, there are very few people speaking grammatically.[39] I don't like this. It harms the image of the city.

This is a final illustration that for many long-term Yerevantsi the fear of ruralization is a fear of living in a chaotic cosmos that has lost its equilibrium. Undomesticated nature, symbolized in the conversation quoted above by undomesticated language,[40] eliminates man-made civilization, and hence urbanization and modernization.

In Armenia, ancestors, traditions, and many things associated with the authenticity of the sacred homeland and environment carry a highly esteemed value. Yet these are values that mostly are separated – or should be separate – from urban life. Each may exist as an ideal, yet as expressed in the quote above preferably should remain in its place in the far-removed background (compare Yessenova 2005). A final conclusion therefore may be: noble savages are noble as long as they live in their natural environment, but they become ignoble – or are perceived as such – once they enter urban Yerevan, as this is not the place for savages but a place created by urban people who perceive themselves as 'civilized' – and are proud of it.

Notes

1. The Armenian–Azerbaijani conflict, which had ceased in Soviet times, restarted in 1988 when Armenia formally claimed the territory of Karabakh. After mass demonstrations in Yerevan, ethnic cleansing took place in both republics. One of the first escalations of violence, known as the 'Sumgait pogroms', took place in Sumgait on 27 February 1988 (Chahmouradian 1995; Swietochowski 1995; Waal 2003; Halbach 2009).
2. Being then more fluent in Russian, I conducted many interviews in that language. Some Russian terms are used in conversations conducted in Armenian as well, however, because they are linked to a very Russian/Soviet context.
3. For further information see Waal (2003) and Halbach and Kappeler (1995).
4. For further information see Libaridian (1989) and Verluise (1995).
5. Platz (2000) gives a comprehensive description of the everyday life of the crisis.
6. Interestingly, fitting into this scenario, I often heard that Yerevan had become a polluted, radioactive zone.
7. Fountains are perceived as a symbol of life. Fountains without water thus really emphasize the metaphor of collapse.
8. Yerevan, according to history books and oral accounts, is an old city which can be traced back to a Bronze Age settlement founded by the Urartian king Argishti I in 782 BC (Shnirelman 2001). Other accounts take up on the Bible (Genesis 6:1–9:29). In the Middle Ages Yerevan was a small oriental city which was repeatedly destroyed by invaders and earthquakes. Tamanyan's master plan was put onto the existing structure of the provincial city of Tsarist times. For further information see Ter Minassian (2007), Hakopian (2003), Astratjan and Melikjan (1968), Fehlings (2014), and Gasparian (2004).
9. City planners like Fournier (1772–1837), Cabet (1788–1856), and Godin (1817–1888) were aware of the problems accompanied by population growth and a rapid growth of cities in the course of industrialization. They are probably the pioneers of socialist city planning (Hotzdan 1994, 41). In 1902 E. Howard published his book *Garden Cities of To-morrow*, where he explained his concept of the 'garden city', which was meant to foster social justice and a balanced social structure. In applying Howard's concept, A. Tamanyan was accused of using a Western and capitalist model in 1928; he defended himself by drawing attention to the fact that the 'garden city' was based on a socialist idea. Indeed, the 'garden city' had already inspired the Russian city planners

M. G. Dikanskij and V. N. Semenov, who both promulgated the model even before the October Revolution (Ter Minassian 2007, 29–40).

10. Both books contain an overview of the most significant literature on Soviet and post-Soviet urban space.

11. As Schneider and Schneider (2003, 298) point out, the link between criminality and the construction industry can be observed worldwide.

12. As with the Soviet intelligentsia in general (see Boym 1994), its Armenian equivalent was a result of the Soviet urbanization campaign and education system. Simultaneously, intellectuals were suspected of being dissidents and – as in the Armenian case (Lehmann 2007) – local nationalists (Antonyan 2012; Fehlings 2015).

13. Grant (2014) describes a totally different perception of post-Soviet architecture in Baku, where the construction boom, representing 'dream images' of a bright future, is seen in a more positive light.

14. Many compared them to the Tsarist architecture of the nineteenth century or to the Soviet buildings of the 1920s–1950s. The result of this comparison was the judgment that the building material of the older constructions was better, that the construction was safer, that living conditions were more comfortable, and that the aesthetic value of the old (Soviet) buildings was higher. These statements are interesting, as one might expect a harsh critique of Soviet rule, for instance in terms of a foreign and colonising power. Yet in Armenia a critique of Soviet rule does not include a critique of Soviet architecture and urban planning. If so, it only includes the critique of buildings from the late Soviet period.

15. That architects claim to follow in the steps of Tamanyan is quite obvious. Besides using the same building materials, Tamanyan's master plan of Yerevan was carved into one of the new buildings of the Northern Avenue, and in public debates the powerful advocates for the avenue (investors, politicians, architects) justify themselves by claiming to accomplish Tamanyan's visions.

16. The emptiness of new buildings has been described by Grant (2014) in Baku, and Pelkmans (2006) in Georgia. Both authors come to the conclusion that the emphasis is on the construction rather than the use of the buildings. I was told that diaspora members, who use them on their holidays, bought most of the flats in the new skyscrapers. When I visited Armenia in 2014, most of them looked much more inhabited.

17. The first political elite was rooted in the dissident intelligentsia, which supported the nationalist movement of 1988–1991. The movement was therefore called the 'revolution of mathematicians' (Iskandaryan 2014).

18. The TASS and UPI in 1993 talked about more than 300,000 refugees from the Karabakh war and about 500,000 people who lost their homes in the earthquake (Platz 2000, 124).

19. National Statistical Service of the Republic of Armenia, *Labour Migration in Armenia: The Results of a Pilot Sample Survey* (2007), http://www.armstat.am/file/article/mig_rep_07e.pdf.

20. According to the United Nations and World Bank data from 2010/11 the emigration stock remains at 28% of the population of Armenia (CAD 2013, 11; Makaryan 2013, 2).

21. See note 19.

22. I was not able to track the rural–urban migration in the population statistics.

23. An additional phenomenon after the breakdown of the Soviet Union was the inward migration of ethnic Armenians from the Middle East or from Western countries *to* Armenia. Motivations included rediscovering their sacred homeland and joining their ethnic brothers in the Karabakh war. Other Armenians became victims of persecution during the Armenian–Azerbaijani conflict: while Azerbaijanis fled from Armenia to Azerbaijan, Armenians fled from Baku and other places to the Republic of Armenia. Quite often, these Armenian families did not stay in Armenia long, but joined the migration toward Russia. One reason for this direction of migration was that in most cases there were family ties.

24. Indeed, many politicians, who gained power within the so-called Karabakh Movement and because of coming from the Karabakh Mountains, do have rural origins. Armenians even talk about a 'Karabakhization' of policy.

25. The Armenian Apostolic Church argued that there was a church named St Poghos-Petros next to this place until it was destroyed by the Soviets in 1931. To demolish the cinema and replace it

with the reconstruction of the 'old' church can be interpreted as an act of revenge for the former demolition (Abrahamian 2011).

26. In many post-Soviet countries this trend goes along with a homogenization of the population. As Yerevan was almost a mono-ethnic city in the late Soviet period, this trend was less visible.

27. This definition can be seen as a description of the subject of anthropology, and was the starting point for a huge number of definitions stressing different aspects of culture, for example the 175 definitions given by Kroeber and Kluckhohn (1978).

28. Romanticism was an artistic, literary, and intellectual movement between the end of the eighteenth and middle of the nineteenth century. Representatives were philosophers like Fichte, Schelling, Hegel, and Schlegel; writers like Schiller, Hauff, Eichendorff, Novalis, Brentano, Hoffmann, and Uhland; and artists like Friedrich, Runge, Blechen, Overbeck, and Koch (Kammerlohr 1997).

29. For the debate on 'Western modernity' and its relation to other interpretations and implementations of the notion of 'modernity' see Eisenstadt (2000), Englund and Leach (2000), Gaonkar (2001), and Sahlins (1999).

30. In 1920 about 80% of the Armenian population lived in the countryside. In the last years before Stalin's death this was only 50%; in 1960, 35%; and in 1975, 20% (Suny 1997, 372–373).

31. The classification of social groups according to the music they listen to seems to work also for Baku (Fehlings 2014/15) and for the Turkish context, where 'urban decay', 'ruralization', and rural migrants are associated with a music style called 'arabesque' (Kandiyoti and Skatanber 2002; Stokes 1992).

32. The rural–urban dichotomy correlates with other dichotomies used in a similar way, for example, Oriental/Asian–European and East–West. These dichotomies match with evolutionary stages in Marxist theory.

33. Usually, the diaspora communities trace back their origin to places in eastern Turkey. These 'lost lands' are perceived by them as 'homeland', which is an emotionally loaded term linked to nostalgia, grievance, and longing. Because of this situation of loss, the Republic of Armenia, the successor state of Soviet Armenia, being the only country under Armenians' control, became an important meaning, not only for those living on its territory, but also for those living in exile.

34. When my informant says 'us' he means the people of the Armenian diaspora, who did not grow up in Armenia.

35. The term 'culture' apparently stems from the Latin *colere* – to cultivate, to maintain, to plough (Haller 2005, 29).

36. Queen Shamiram/Semiramis is also associated with the myth of the Hanging Gardens of Babylon (Roscher 1909–1915, 678–702). To the ancient imagination, especially in the Middle Ages as described by Petrosyan, the 'world as a garden' concept was widespread in Armenia. This concept of the world apparently originated in pre-Christian cultures of the Near East and was adopted in the Bible narration of the Garden of Eden (Petrosyan 2001a; 2001b).

37. Tsentral'nyi Nauchno-Issledovatel'skii i Proektnyi Institut po Gradostroitel'stvu Gosudarstvenno Komiteta po Grazhdanskomu Stroitel'stvu i Arkitekture pro Gosstroe SSR, *Osnovy Sovetskogo grado-stroitel'stva* (Moscow: Stroiizdat, 1967) – see Humphrey (2005).

38. In Soviet times there were restrictions on internal migration, which made it more difficult for rural people to move to urban centres (Krebs 2014/15).

39. 'Grammatically' in this context means 'in a cultivated and educated way', which includes the correct use of grammatical forms, the avoidance of slang terms, and the preference for a distinguished diction in Russian and in Armenian. X. used the German term *literarisch*, which Germans would not use in this context. I think she was trying to translate the Russian term *literaturno* or *gramatno*.

40. Unrefined Russian and Armenian slang.

Disclosure statement

No potential conflict of interest was reported by the authors.

Funding

This work was supported by the Deutscher Akademischer Austausch Dienst (German Academic Exchange Service).

References

Abrahamian, L. 2006. *Armenian Identity in a Changing World*. Costa Mesa: Mazda Publishers.

Abrahamian, L. 2007. "Dancing Around the Mountain: Armenian Identity through Rites of Solidarity." In *Caucasus Paradigms: Anthropologies, Histories and the Making of a World Area*, edited by B. Grant & L. Yalçin-Heckmann, 167–188. Berlin: Lit Verlag.

Abrahamian, L. 2011. "Yerevan Sacra: Old and New Sacred Centers in the Urban Space." In *Urban Spaces After Socialism: Ethnographies of Public Spaces in Eurasian Cities*, edited by D. Tsypylma, W. Kaschuba, and M. Krebs, 131–151. Frankfurt a.M. & New York: Campus Verlag.

Adriaans, R. 2011. *Sonorous Borders: National Cosmology and the Mediation of Collective Memory in Armenian Ethnopop Music*. Accessed October 15, 2015. http://dare.uva.nl/cgi/arno/show.cgi?fid=224083.

Alexander, C., and V. Buchli. 2007. "Introduction." In *Urban Life in Post-Soviet Asia*, edited by C. Alexander and V. Buchli, 1–38. Oxon & New York: University College London Press.

Ananieva, A., A. Bauer, D. Leis, K. Steyer, and B. Morlag-Schardon. 2013. *Räume der Macht: Metamorphosen von Stadt und Garten im Europa der Neuzeit*. Bielefeld: Transcript.

Antonyan, Y. 2011. "Religiosity and Religious Identity in Armenia: Some Current Models and Developments." *Acta Ethnographica Hungarica* 56 (2): 315-332. doi:10.1556/AEthn.56.2011.2.4

Antonyan, Y. 2012. "The Armenian Intelligentsia Today: Discourses of Self-Identification and Self-Perception." *Laboratorium* 4 (1): 76–100.

Arutjunjan, V. M., M. M. Astratjan, and A. A. Melikjan. 1968. *Jerevan*. Moskva: Isdatjelstvo Literatury po Stroitjelstvu.

Bachhofen, J. J. 1980 (1861). *Das Mutterrecht: Eine Untersuchung über die Gynaikokratie der Alten Welt Nach Ihrer Religiösen und Rechtlichen Natur*. Frankfurt a.M.: Suhrkamp Verlag.

Bayadyan, H. 2007. "Soviet Armenian Identity and Cultural Representation." In *Representations on the Margins of Europe: Politics and Identities in the Baltic and South Caucasus States*, edited by T. Darieva, and W. Kaschuba, 205–219. Frankfurt a.M. & New York: Campus Verlag.

Beer, B. 2008. *Methoden Ethnologischer Feldforschung*. Berlin: Reimer Verlag.

Boym, S. 1994. *Common Places: Mythologies of Everyday Life in Russia*. Cambridge and London: Havard University Press.

Braux, A. 2013. Azerbaijani Migrants in Russia. *Caucasus Analytical Digest* 57 (3): 5–7.

Bretèque, E. Amy de la, and V. Stoichita. 2012. "Musics of the New Times: Romanian *Manele* and Armenian *Rabiz* as Icons of Post-Communist Changes." In *The Balkans and Caucasus: Parallel Processes on the Opposite Sides of the Black Sea*, edited by I. Biliarsky, O. Cristea, and A. Oroveanu, 321–335. Newcastle upon Tyne: Cambridge Scholars Publishing.

CAD. 2013. "Migration." *Caucasus Analytical Digest* 57: 1–17.

Carrithers, M. 1996. "Nature and Culture." In *Encyclopedia of Social and Cultural Anthropology*, edited by A. Barnard, and J. Spencer, 393–396. London & New York: Routledge.

Chahmouradian, S. 1995. *La Tragédie de Soumgaït : un Pogrom D'Arméniens en Union Soviétique*. Paris: Seuil.

Darieva, T., and W. Kaschuba. 2007. *Representations on the Margins of Europe: Politics and Identities in the Baltic and South Caucasus States*. Frankfurt a.M. & New York: Campus Verlag.

Darieva, T., W. Kaschuba, and M. Krebs. 2011. *Urban Spaces after Socialism: Ethnographies of Public Places in Eurasian Cities*. Frankfurt a.M.: Campus Verlag.

Eisenstadt, S. N. 2000. "Multiple Modernities." *Daedalus* 129 (1): 1–29.

Encyclopaedia Britannica. 2015. 'Noble Savage'. *Encyclopædia Britannica Online*. Accessed September 29, 2015 http://www.britannica.com/art/noble-savage.

Englund, H., and J. Leach. 2000. "Ethnography and the Meta-Narrative of Modernity." *Current Anthropology* 41 (2): 225–248. doi:10.1086/300126

Fabian, J. 1990. "Presence and Representation: The Other and Anthropological Writing." *Critical Inquiry* 16 (4): 753–772. doi:10.1086/448558

Fehlings, S. 2012. "Auf der Suche nach der verlorenen Zeit." In *Die Postsowjetische Stadt: Aushandlungsprozesse im Südkaukasus*, edited by W. Kaschuba, M. Krebs, and M. Pilz, 150–167. Berlin: Panama Verlag.

Fehlings, S. 2014. *Jerewan: Urbanes Chaos und Soziale Ordnung*. Berlin: LIT Verlag.

Fehlings, S. 2015. "Intimacy and Exposure – Yerevan's Private and Public Space." *International Journal of Sociology and Social Policy* 35 (7/8): 513–532. doi:10.1108/IJSSP-02-2015-0028

Ferguson, J. 1999. *Expectations of Modernity: Myths and Meanings of Urban Life on the Zambian Copperbelt*. Berkeley: University of California Press.

Ferry, M. 2013. "Female Migrants From Georgia: Profiles and Migratory Projects." *Caucasus Analytical Digest* 57: 8–10.

Flynn, M., and N. Kosmarskaya. 2012. "Exploring "North" and "South" in Post-Soviet Bishkek: Discourses and Perceptions of Rural-Urban Migration." *Nationalities Papers: The Journal of Nationalism and Ethnicity* 40: 453–471. doi:10.1080/00905992.2012.685061

Frazer, James G. 1950 (1907–1915). *The Golden Bough: A Study in Magic and Religion*. London: Macmillan.

Gaonkar, D. P. 2001. *Alternative Modernities*. Durham, NC and London: Duke University Press.

Gasparian, M. 2004. "Stadtentwicklung in Yerevan." *Trialog* 83: 13–19.

Geismeier, W. 1998. *Caspar David Friedrich*. Leipzig: E.A. Seemann Verlag.

Grant, B. 2010. "Cosmopolitan Baku." *Ethnos* 75 (2): 123–147. doi:10.1080/00141841003753222

Grant, B. 2014. "The Edifice Complex: Architecture and Political Life of Surplus in the New Baku." *Public Culture* 26 (3): 501–528. doi:10.1215/08992363-2683648

Hakopian, T. Kh. 2003. "The History of Yerevan." In *Old Yerevan*, edited by Y. Shahaziz, 10–39. Yerevan: Murni Hratarakdjutiun.

Hakobyan, H. 2006. "Njekotoryje Charakteristiki Rasvitija Rok-Dvishjenija v Armenii." In *Jushnyj Kavkas: Terrirorii. Istorii. Ljudi*, edited by Regionalnaja Stipendiatskaja Programma Fonda im. Genricha Bjollja, 38–61. Tbilisi: Heinrich Böll Stiftung.

Halbach, U., and A. Kapeller. 1995. *Krisenherd Kaukasus*. Baden-Baden: Nomos Verlagsgesellschaft.

Halbach, U. 2009. "Der Konflikt um Bergkarabach." In *Der Krieg um Bergkarabach*, edited by E. Reiter, 15–34. Wien & Köln & Weimar: Böhlau Verlag.

Haller, D. 2005. *Dtv-Atlas Ethnologie*. München: Dtv.

Hann, C. 1994. "After Communism: Reflections on East European Anthropology and the "Transition"." *Social Anthropology* 2/3: 229–249.

Herzfeld, M. 1997. *Cultural Intimacy: Social Poetics in the Nation State*. New York & London: Routledge.

Hotzdan, J. 1994. *dtv-Atlas zur Stadt: Von den Ersten Gründungen bis zur Modernen Stadtplanung*. München: Deutscher Taschenbuch Verlag.

Howard, E. 1946 [1902]. *Garden Cities of To-Morrow*. London: Faber and Faber.

Humphrey, C. 1995. "Introduction." *Cambridge Anthropology* 18 (2): 1–12 (special issue).

Humphrey, C. 1999. "Shamans in the City." *Anthropology Today* 15 (3): 3–10. doi:10.2307/2678275

Humphrey, C. 2005. "Ideology in Infrastructure: Architecture and Soviet Imagination." *The Journal of the Royal Anthropological Institute* 11 (1): 39–58. doi:10.1111/j.1467-9655.2005.00225.x

Humphrey, C., and R. Mandel. 2002. "The Market in Everyday Life: Ethnographies of Postsocialism." In *Market and Moralities: Ethnographies of Postsocialism*, edited by C. Humphrey, and R. Mandel, 1–19. Oxford and New York: Berg.

Ibn, Khaldun. 1967 [1377]. *The Muqaddimah: An Introduction to History*. London: Routledge & Kenan Paul.

Iskandaryan, A. 2014. "Formalization of the Informal: Statebuilding in Armenia." In *Informality in Eastern Europe: Structures, Political Cultures and Social Practices*, edited by C. Giordano and N. Hayoz, 451–484. Bern: Peter Lang.

Kammerlohr, O. 1997. *Epochen der Kunst: Vom Klassizismus zu den Wegbereitern der Moderne*. München & Wien: Oldenbourg Verlag.

Kandiyoti, D., and A. Skatanber. 2002. *Fragments of Culture: The Everyday of Modern Turkey*. London & New York: I.B. Tauris & Co Publishers.

Kant, E. ca. 1928 (1784). *Idee zu Einer Allgemeinen Geschichte in Weltbürgerlicher Absicht*. Leipzig: Meiner Verlag.

Kappeler, A. 2005. "Von ethno-nationalen Laboratorien zu selbständigen Staaten: Die Konstruktion von Nationen in der Sowjetunion und ihr Erbe." In *Kulturelle Dynamik der Globalisierung: Ost- und Westeuropäische Transformationsprozesse aus Sozialanthropologischer Perspektive*, edited by J. Riegler, 235–257. Wien: Verlag der Österreichischen Akademie der Wissenschaften.

Kemal, Y. 2014. *Die Ararat-Legende*. Zürich: Unionsverlag Taschenbuch.

Kharatyan, H. 2007. *Life is Very Sad: Poverty in Armenia*. Yerevan: The 'Hazarashen' Armenian Center for Ethnological Studies NGO.

Kosmarski, A. 2011. "Grandeur and decay of the "Soviet Byzantium": Spaces, People and Memories of Tashkent, Uzbekistan." In *Urban Spaces After Socialism: Ethnographies of Public Places in Eurasian Cities*, edited by T. Darieva, W. Kaschuba, and M. Krebs, 33–56. Frankfurt a.M. & New York: Campus Verlag.

Krebs, M. 2014/15. "The Right to Live in the City." *International Journal of Sociology and Social Policy* 35 (7/8): 550–564.

Kroeber, A. L., and C. Kluckhohn. 1978. *Culture: A Critical Review of Concepts and Definitions*. Millwood & New York: Kraus.

Lehmann, M. 2007. "Bargaining Armenian-ness: National Politics of Identity in the Soviet Union after 1945." In *Representations on the Margins of Europe: Politics and Identities in the Baltic and South Caucasus States*, edited by T. Darieva, and W. Kaschuba, 166–189. Frankfurt a.M. & New York: Campus Verlag.

Lem, Stanislaw. 2006 (1868). *Solaris*. Berlin: List Taschenbuch.

Lewis, H. M. 1964 (1877). *Ancient Society or Researches in the Lines of Human Progress From Savagery Through Barbarism to Civilization*. Cambridge: Belknap Press of Havard University.

Lewis, R. A., and R. H. Rowland. 1969. "Urbanization in Russia and the USSR: 1897–1966." *Annals of the Association of American Geographers* 59 (4): 776–796. doi:10.1111/j.1467-8306.1969.tb01811.x

Lévi-Strauss, C. 1969. *The Elementary Structures of Kinship*. Boston: Beacon Press.

Libaridian, G. J. 1989. "Armenian Earthquakes and Soviet Tremors." *Society* 26 (3): 59–63. doi:10.1007/BF02699249

Maine, H. S. 1959 (1861). *Ancient Law: its Connection with the Early History of Society and its Relation to Modern Ideas*. London: Oxford University Press.

Makaryan, Sh. 2013. "Challenges of Migration Policy-Making in Armenia, Azerbaijan and Georgia." *Caucasus Analytical Digest* 57: 2–4.

Mansoor, A., and B. Quilling. 2006. *Migration and Remittances: Eastern Europe and the Former Soviet Union*. Washington, D.C.: The World Bank.

Marat, E. 2009. *Labor Migration in Central Asia: Implications of the Global Economic Crisis (Silk Road Paper 2009)*. Washington, D.C.: Central Asia-Caucasus Institute & Silk Road Studies Program.

Marutyan, H. 2007. "Armenia-Diaspora: Meeting in the Yerevan Center." *Handes Amsorya*: 363–428. (Armenian; Russian script).

Marx, K., and F. Engels. 2012 (1848). *The Communist Manifesto: A Modern Edition*. London: Vero.

Menjívar, C., and V. Agadjanian. 2007. "Men's Migration and Women's Lives: Views From Rural Armenia and Guatemala." *Social Science Quarterly* 88 (5): 1243–1262. doi:10.1111/j.1540-6237.2007.00501.x

Morgan, L. H. 1964 (1877). *Ancient Society*. Cambridge: Belknap Press of Havard University.

Parrot, F. 1985 (1834). *Reise zum Ararat*. Leipzig: Brockhaus Verlag.

Pelkmans, M. 2006. *Defending the Border : Identity, Religion, and Modernity in the Republic of Georgia*. Ithaca: Cornell University Press.

Petrosyan, H. 2001a. "The Sacred Mountain." In *Armenian Folk Arts, Culture, and Identity*, edited by L. Abrahamian and N. Sweezy, 33–39. Bloomington: Indiana University Press.

Petrosyan, H. 2001b. "The World as a Garden." In *Armenian Folk Arts, Culture, and Identity*, edited by L. Abrahamian and N. Sweezy, 52–59. Bloomington: Indiana University Press.

Platz, S. 2000. "The Shape of National Time: Daily Life, Historym and Identity during Armenia's Transition to Independence, 1991." In *Altering States: Ethnographies of Transition in Eastern*

Europe and the Former Soviet Union, edited by D. Berdahl, M. Bunzl, and M. Lampland, 114–138. Ann Arbor: University of Michigan Press.

Roscher, W. H. 1909–1915. *Ausführliches Lexikon der Griechischen und Römischen Mythologie (Vierter Band, Qu-S)*. Leipzig: B.G. Teubner Verlag.

Rousseau, J.-J. (F. Bouchardy). 1996 (1750). *Discours sur les Sciences et les Arts*. Paris: Gallimard.

Rousseau, J.-J. (H. Denhardt). 2010 (1762). *Émile Oder über die Erziehung (Émile ou de L'education)*. Köln: Anaconda Verlag.

Rousseau, J.-J. (E. Pietzcker & H. Brockard). 2010 (1762b). *Du Contrat Social ou Principes du Droit Politique/ Vom Gesellschaftsvertrag Oder Grundsätze des Staatsrechts)*. Französisch/Deutsch. Stuttgart: Philipp Reclam.

Sahlins, M. 1999. "What is Anthropological Enlightenment? Some Lessons of the Twentieth Century." *Annual Review of Anthropology* 28: i–xxiii. doi:10.1146/annurev.anthro.28.1.0

Said, E. W. 2009 (1978). *Orientalismus*. Franfurt a.M.: Fischer Verlag.

Samuelian, T. J. 2000. *Armenian Origins: An Overview of Ancient and Modern Sources and Theories*. Yerevan. Accessed June 15, 2012. www.arak29.am.

Schneider, J., and P. Schneider. 2003. "Wounded Palermo." In *Wounded Cities: Destruction and Reconstruction in A Globalized World*, edited by J. Schneider and I. Susser, 291–309. Oxford & New York: Berg Publishers.

Schröder, P. 2010. "'Urbanizing' Bishkek: Interrelations of Boundaries, Migration, Group Size and Opportunity Structure." *Central Asian Survey* 29 (4): 453-467. doi:10.1080/02634937.2010. 537143

Schröder, P. 2011. *From Shanghai to Iug-2: Integration and Identification among and beyond the Male Youth of a Bishkek Neighbourhood*. Halle-Wittenberg: Dissertation, Martin-Luther-Universität Halle-Wittenberg.

Shnirelman, V. A. 2001. *The Value of the Past: Myths, Identity and Politics in Transcaucasia*. Osaka: National Museum of Ethnology.

Stefes, C. H. 2006. *Understanding Post-Soviet Transitions. Corruption, Collusion and Clientelism*. Hampshire & New York: Palgrave Macmillan.

Stefes, C. H. 2008. "Governance, the State, and Systemic Corruption: Armenia and Georgia in Comparison." *Caucasian Review of International Affaires* 2 (2): 73–83.

Stokes, M. 1992. *The Arabesk Debate: Music and Musicians in Modern Turkey*. Oxford: Clarendon Press.

Strauss, A. L., and J. Corbin. 1990. *Basics of Qualitative Research: Grounded Theory Procedures and Techniques*. London: Sage Publications.

Suny, R. G. 1997. "Soviet Armenia." In *The Armenian People From Ancient to Modern Times (Volume II) – Foreign Domination to Statehood: The Fifteenth Century to the Twentieth Century*, edited by R. G. Hovannisian, 347–387. New York: St. Martin's Press.

Swietochowski, T. 1995. "Der Streit um Berg-Karabach: Geographie, ethnische Gliederung und Kolonialismus." In *Krisenherd Kaukasus*, edited by U. Halbach and A. Kappeler, 161–178. Baden-Baden: Nomos Verlag.

Ter Minassian, T. 2007. *Erevan: la Construction D'une Capitale à l'Époque Soviétique*. Rennes: Presses Universitaires de Rennes.

Tylor, E. B. 1924 (1871). *Primitive Culture: Researches Into the Development of Mythology, Philosophy, Religion, Language, Art, and Custom*. New York: Brentano's.

Verluise, P. 1995. *Armenia in Crisis: The 1988 Earthquake*. Detroit: Wayne State University Press.

Waal, T. de. 2003. *Black Garden: Armenia and Azerbaijan Through Peace and War*. New York & London: New York University Press.

Yessenova, S. 2005. "'Routes and Roots' of Kazakh Identity: Urban Migration in Postsocialist Kazakhstan." *Russian Review* 64 (4): 661–679. doi:10.1111/j.1467-9434.2005.00380.x

Avoidance and appropriation in Bishkek: dealing with time, space and urbanity in Kyrgyzstan's capital

Philipp Schröder

Institute for Asian and African Studies, Humboldt-Universität zu Berlin, Germany

ABSTRACT

Much has changed since Frunze was renamed Bishkek in 1991 and became the capital of independent Kyrgyzstan. Though it was once considered to be among the 'greenest' and most 'orderly' cities of the Soviet Union, today many of its long-term residents complain about the new settlements (*novostroiki*) that have emerged during the last two decades. To Bishkek's urbanites, the recent arrival of migrants is not associated with an escape from rural poverty and a rightful struggle for civic rights, but indicates a massive cultural and aesthetic degradation of familiar urban life. In this article, beyond contesting narratives of cosmopolitan nostalgia vs. legitimate belonging, I investigate how urban practitioners in fact produce and deal with different spaces in the city. My ethnographic accounts not only identify social avoidance as an essential pulse of Bishkek's current rhythm, but also illustrate that after a period of post-rural socialization previously stigmatized migrants may manage to smoothly blend into urban spatial flows and lifestyles.

Introduction: beyond 'green Frunze' and 'Bishkek chaos'

In Soviet times Frunze enjoyed a reputation as among the greenest cities that the USSR had to offer. On a clear day, its location just north of the snow-capped Ala Too mountain range made for exceptionally picturesque scenery. From these mountains also came the water that was channelled through the city to provide much-desired cooling during the hot Central Asian summers. And in the original gridiron street plan, introduced in the late nineteenth century by the Tsarist administration, there was ample space for tree-lined streets and public parks.

Almost all accounts that reflect on the days of Soviet Kyrgyzstan – be these personal memories, popular songs or newspaper clippings – evoke this image of Frunze as an urban landscape abundant in fresh air, fountains and recreational areas. Local historian Petrov (2008, 4) traces this motive even to the city's eponym, the Bolshevik Military Commander Mikhail Vasilyevich Frunze:

> Later it turned out that in the translation from Moldovan [language], and a Moldovan was the father of the general, 'Frunze' means 'green', and this epithet then just perfectly matched this small city drowning in greenery.

Furthermore, the pride of Frunze rested on its being a project of 'European type', which in terms of urban planning was realized in a clear-cut, chessboard layout oriented along major avenues. This, as the *Frunze Encyclopaedia* of 1984 noted, 'comfortably distinguished it from the old Eastern cities with their crooked and narrow bystreets' (Oruzbaeva 1984, 18). From this viewpoint, Frunze was green and neat; plus it was not as densely populated as other Central Asian capitals, such as Tashkent in Uzbekistan or Almaty in Kazakhstan. At the time, for its residents these characteristics of Frunze's cityscape and demography merged into a particular urban order(liness), which most essentially was cosy and predictable.

Nowadays, few people would not qualify such a perception as Soviet nostalgia. Much has changed since Frunze was renamed Bishkek in 1991 and became the capital of independent Kyrgyzstan. As movement in the country is de facto no longer regulated by the earlier *propiska* system of state-issued residency permits, within just over two post-Soviet decades the population of Bishkek has almost doubled, to more than 1.3 million.

Along with this, the city area has widely expanded, and new types of settlement have emerged. Back in Frunze, besides the remaining courtyard houses of the early twentieth century, the city's material environment was dominated by Socialist apartment blocks, of which the first were built in the late 1950s. Until 2014, Bishkek has added new housing opportunities in the very rich and VIP price range, as well as at the economically precarious end, where mud bricks and plastic wrap are the main building stocks. Among many of the long-term residents of Bishkek, as of other post-Soviet urban settlements, such recent migration and building trends have generated anxiety about 'disorder' (*bardak*) and the 'ruralization' of their city (Nazpary 2002; Alexander, Buchli, and Humphrey 2007; Schröder 2010; Flynn and Kosmarskaya 2012).

In this article, I want to move beyond dissecting the nostalgic discourses of loss and deprivation among established Bishkekians (*Bishkekchany*) or simply juxtaposing these with the opposite claims of rural newcomers about their well-deserved belonging to this city. Rather, my aim is to expand on these competing notions of dis/order by focusing on how urban residents of different provenance in fact navigate and deal with Bishkek's urban environment.

In the following sections, I will first outline how a Socialist-era neighbourhood (known as Iug-2) came to serve as a durable social and symbolic resource for its long-time inhabitants. I will then contrast this established (Soviet-Frunze) form of urban dwelling with the everyday struggles for social rights and urban citizenship among the inhabitants of Bishkek's so-called new settlements (*novostroiki*). Having identified the 'urbanites' (*gorodskie*) and the 'rurals' (*selskie*) as two of Bishkek's main urban practitioners, I will use the example of Dzerzhinka Park to illustrate how alternating strategies of appropriation and avoidance shape the imaginaries of the city's public space. To oppose an oversimplified image of a 'divided city', I will then move on to introduce the category of 'newcomers' (*priezzhie*). This evidences that after a period of post-rural socialization in the city, recent migrants may in fact leave behind the stigma of 'village backwardness' and smoothly blend into Bishkek's urban flows. Eventually, from the ethnographic vignettes gathered here will emerge not only an urban landscape with spatial routines and intangible boundaries, but also an understanding of Bishkek's everyday rhythms – and thus an insight into the question, 'What is the right time to be in the right place?'[1]

A socialist neighbourhood as a resource: Iug-2 and Almaz's 'own yard'

Iug-2 (South-2) is a so-called micro-region settlement just south of the railway tracks that cut through Bishkek's centre in the east–west direction. Built from the 1970s onwards, the neighbourhood consists of 19 apartment buildings in the classic Socialist grey-panel style, each nine storeys high. In between these buildings, there are yards with benches for socializing, playgrounds, a small bazaar and other shops, as well as the 69th Middle School (Figure 1).

The original inhabitants of Iug-2 – who were assigned apartments through their workplaces or other Soviet administrative agencies – had all sorts of backgrounds. Some were teachers, some worked in local factories, others were artists or writers, policemen or KGB employees (who, interestingly, received apartments on the top two floors exclusively). Corresponding to the city's demographic situation during most of the Socialist era – until 1989 the ethnic Kyrgyz made up only 23% of its population – the majority of Iug-2's inhabitants were of 'European origin', i.e. they were ethnic Russians, Ukrainians, Belorussians or Germans.

Almaz is a young Kyrgyz resident of Iug-2, who I first met there during my fieldwork in Bishkek in 2007. One April day, as we sat on a bench in the neighbourhood, he explained to me:

> I was practically born into this quarter. Where we are sitting right now, this has been my yard since I could walk. Everything started here for me: I found my best friends and I learned many life lessons. Shanghai is our brotherhood.

Figure 1. The Iug-2 neighbourhood in Bishkek (picture by Philipp Schröder).

This quote addresses multiple aspects that will be of interest for this article. To begin with, Shanghai is the local nickname of Iug-2. Its origin dates back to the days before the micro-region was built, when – according to the urban legend – this part of town was still covered in tiny and low-built houses with narrow, dirty passages between them. Evidently, among local residents this evoked associations of the more traditional neighbourhoods in the Chinese metropolis of Shanghai. Other similar epithets for Frunze/Bishkek quarters at the time were Boston, Paris, London, Zapad (West), and Vostok (East) (Nasritdinov and Schröder 2016).

To be aware of such informal designations, but even more to hold personal memories of these neighbourhoods' local histories, qualifies as an essential building block of Bishkek urban knowledge. Among those who considered themselves 'true urban boys' (*nastoiashie gorodskie patsany*), their key memories usually referred to the violent fights between some of these neighbourhoods, which they had been involved in during their youth. Back in the 1990s and early 2000s, according to Almaz and his peers, mass brawls involving several hundred young men regularly occurred between Shanghai and Zhiloi, the main rival neighbourhood, across the street.

At this juncture, the geographical entwines with the social. The Shanghai boys claim that they engaged in these fights mostly to protect their 'territory' and to secure their quarter's outer border. At the same time, the presence of a common enemy such as Zhiloi furthered social integration within Shanghai. When they rallied around the larger spatial marker of their Shanghai neighbourhood, other differences among them, such as those of age and ethnicity, faded into the background. Multiple decades later and a continent apart, this confirms Evans-Pritchard's (1940, 293) classic insight that the 'latent hostility between local communities … allows also their fusion in a larger group'.

In his observations on the dynamics of a 'balanced opposition' among the Nuer of Southern Sudan, Evans-Pritchard noted further that 'fission' is the complement to 'fusion'. In Shanghai, such temporary separation, which occurred whenever the feud with Zhiloi rested, was institutionalized in the form of belonging to one particular yard of the neighbourhood. In the comment above, Almaz pointed to this, claiming that the bench where I was sitting with him was located in 'his yard'. That fact remained unchallenged by other neighbours, because Almaz's parents' apartment happened to be in the building right next to that shared inner space.

This briefly describes the pattern of territorial appropriation in Shanghai. Back in the day, for the fights against Zhiloi, all of Shanghai came out and united to defend the honour and borders of their neighbourhood. In times of peace, however, a young man's primary belonging was with his 'native yard' (*rodnoi dvor*), where he usually found his closest friends and would 'hang out' most of the time.

One's 'own yard' was thus a particular urban space. It was neither fully private, like for instance the inside of a family's apartment, nor completely public, because its users were rather exclusively Iug-2 residents, some of whom, like Almaz, would go as far as to use violence to 'defend' their yard against unknown trespassers. With Lofland (1998, 9–10), we could therefore describe such a yard as belonging to a 'parochial realm', a place that for a certain group is associated with intimate ties and senses of community.

In his comment, Almaz condensed all this into the term 'brotherhood'. Beyond the social institution of friendship, such collective male camaraderie found expression in graffiti art on buildings in the neighbourhood, with slogans such as 'Shanghai rules'.

Furthermore, in the popular (Russian-language) social network Odnoklassniki there existed a Shanghai online community, where current and former neighbourhood brothers shared photos and exchanged news on their ongoing lives. Taken together, these indications may qualify to depict the territorial entity called Iug-2 or Shanghai as a resource for the symbolic expression of belonging and social integration among long-term inhabitants like Almaz.

Change has come: VIP communities and Bishkek's new settlements

In independent Kyrgyzstan, the cityscape of its capital, Bishkek, has undergone quite a change as compared to the one of its predecessor, Frunze. Nowadays, we can notice new types of urban living next to the ever-fewer historic courtyard houses from the early twentieth century and the Socialist-era micro-regions like Iug-2.

What has forcefully materialized in these new types, on first glance, is the novel upper and lower social strata of Kyrgyzstan's post-Soviet society. On the way there, shock-therapy economic reforms and *privatisatsiia* mingled with a new 'democratic'-style polity. As in other Central Asian countries, this withdrawal of socialism's paternalistic care has lastingly altered the social contract between citizens and their new states (Alexander and Buchli 2007). When reflecting upon their nation's unique transformation, many in Kyrgyzstan point to the blend of exceptionally weak governments – notorious for their chronic instability and two 'revolutions' in 2005 and 2010 – and a highly commercialized economy. A prime example of the latter is Bishkek's Dordoi Bazaar. As one of the region's prime trade hubs for the re-export of Chinese goods, it is estimated to provide employment for up to 20% of Kyrgyzstan's labour force and account for one-third of the national GDP (Payaz 2014).

As in neighbouring Kazakhstan and Uzbekistan, Kyrgyzstan's version of post-socialist capitalism has produced a thin layer of so-called 'new rich' (*novye bogatye*). In Bishkek's privatized urban space, they occupy gated communities, just south of the city centre, which offer a close-up mountain view and have fitting names such as Tsarist Village and VIP Town. Also, in recent years Bishkek has been experiencing a real estate boom, with about 200 simultaneous projects that developed new apartment complexes all over the city. At prices that in 2014 ranged from $500 to $1500 per square metre, and with local banks offering annual interest rates as high as 20%, certainly not everyone can afford such an 'elite apartment'. Still, the busy remodelling of Bishkek's cityscape generally is taken to signify the emergence of an upper-middle class (*vyshe srednii klass*) and the expansion of prosperity beyond the super-wealthy few. The inflow of remittances from abroad has a significant impact on this dynamic construction business in Bishkek. Kyrgyzstan's labour migrants, the majority of them earning their money in Kazakhstan or Russia, are estimated to transfer back home more than $2 billion annually (equalling about 30% of the GDP). As of 2013, in a time before Russia's economic crisis was in full force, to reinvest migration earnings in Bishkek's real estate market to prepare for one's homecoming seemed a promising option for many.

On the other hand, in Kyrgyzstan transnational migration as a widespread and routine source of livelihood is a fairly recent phenomenon that has set in only since the millennium (e.g. Reeves 2012). Before that, during the 'wild' (*lihie*) 1990s, the retreat of the now independent state from crucial life domains – such as social welfare, health, transportation and education – had been especially felt in the remoter areas. This caused a rural exodus towards the country's major cities, with the capital, Bishkek, as the main destination.

In fact, unemployment in the countryside and Frunze's severe housing shortages had already been prevailing concerns during the late Soviet era. Despite the resistance of the Kyrgyz Communist leadership to Gorbachev's ambitions for reforms and public debate, at that time the first social movements appeared to address these issues. As Anderson (1999, 19) notes:

> In the summer [of 1989] the settlers formed 'Ashar' (Mutual Help), the first significant indepen-
> dent social organization to be created in the republic, and under its auspices they began to
> seize land and build shanty towns on the outskirts of the city.

This marked the introduction of yet another type of dwelling in Bishkek's urban environ-
ment, the *novostroiki*. Unlike the VIP communities and elite apartment complexes, which are protected by high walls, private security, and the social leverage of their inhabitants, the *novostroiki* are not out of reach. On the contrary, it is exactly the fact that they are not secluded and commonly associated with precarious living conditions, which makes them a tangible and contested element in the cityscape (Figure 2).

Official data currently list 48 such new settlements, with a total population of about 400,000 (Nasritdinov 2013). These numbers have been challenged by recent ethnographic research, which instead speaks of only 29 *novostroiki*, hosting less than 200,000 people (Fryer, Nasritdinov, and Satybaldieva 2014, 186). Yet even these lower

Figure 2. View of a *novostroika* (new settlement) in Bishkek (picture by Philipp Schröder).

estimates give a striking impression of the rapid and massive urban change that Bishkek has witnessed in the last two decades.

Much about the outside perception of the *novostroiki*, and of their inhabitants' life-worlds, hinges on the quandary of illegality. To begin with, most of the plots where such newcomers to Bishkek have built their houses were squatted. At different times since Kyrgyzstan's independence, this informal appropriation occurred for different reasons. Fryer, Nasritdinov, and Satybaldieva (2014, 183–184) note a first wave in 1989–1991, when land squatting was mostly a form of social protest against the late Communist regime's unjust land allocation. This was followed by a longer 'economic wave', in 1992–2005, as large numbers of ethnic Kyrgyz from rural areas relocated to Bishkek to find new post-Soviet employment. After 2005, the authors highlight the commercial-political aspect, pointing out that during the tenure of President Kurmanbek Bakiev land-grabbing and reselling was turned into a profitable business, captured in quotes such as 'Vote for Bakiev and get a plot of land!' (184; see also Alymbaeva 2013, 136–143).

According to the city's urban development plan, most areas where we now find *novostroiki* were not originally designated for residential purposes. The settlement of Altyn Kazyk, for example, is close to the city's waste disposal site. Furthermore, it has municipal gas pipelines passing just beneath the surface, which adds a constant risk of explosion to the pressing health hazards emanating from the waste site (Zhumakadyr kyzy 2012, 13–14). Such conditions may again prove to be extreme hurdles when it comes to advocating for a new settlement's formal incorporation into the Bishkek municipality.

A major negative repercussion for the inhabitants of such *novostroiki* commonly is the lack of an official residency permit (*propiska*), which complicates access to basic health care, social services and education. It is thus often the question of a settlement's legal status that shapes its residents' rights as citizens or advances their social exclusion. In a recent article, Isabaeva (2014) has pointed to the actual complexity of this situation in contemporary Bishkek. Taking the example of the Kyzyl Zher neighbourhood, she characterizes its residents as 'denizens', which (in contrast to 'citizens') 'denotes permanent settlers or long-term immigrants who enjoy a range of civil and social rights (but not political [rights])' (252). Her ethnographic descriptions tell how in Kyzyl Zher people strategize towards being acknowledged as regular Bishkek citizens, for instance by staging road-blocks at politically opportune times to coerce decision-makers into promises of resolving everyday *novostroika* struggles with the supply of electricity or drinking water.

Until the state attends to these issues, the residents of new settlements in Bishkek, often in cooperation with local NGOs, have to take matters into their own hands. In some cases collective funds are set up to pave roads or organize sewerage, while individually families need to resort to paying bribes, for example to obtain medical treatment or to secure their children's admission to school (see also Zhumakadyr kyzy 2012, 9).

In these ways, the post-Soviet migrants to Bishkek's outskirts appropriate urban space and aim to reassign previously uninhabited lands to a parochial domain. Particularly in the capital's first *novostroiki*, which currently are in their third decade, such community features have long emerged. Besides local hairdressing salons, car washes and informal bodies of self-governance, this also includes new socio-economic hierarchies. In the Kelechek settlement, for example, Aida Alymbaeva (2008, 74) observed that over time the pioneering migrants of the early 1990s, who mostly originated from the northern districts of Kyrgyzstan closer to Bishkek, have begun to serve as landlords. In special housing compounds, set up around shared water access and toilet facilities, they offer single rooms with electricity and separate access doors to the very recent newcomers (most of whom are from the country's southern region).[2]

Regardless of their uncertain living arrangements in Bishkek, many residents of *novostroiki* remark that more importantly they have left behind the arduous conditions in their rural homes and now can demand their rightful share of the city. To elucidate the blend of necessity and resilience that she discovered among her Kyzyl Zher respondents, Isabaeva (2013) employs the notion of 'quiet encroachment'. Introduced by Bayat (2000) to examine the activism of the urban subaltern in Third World cities, 'quiet encroachment' aims to capture 'the silent, protracted but pervasive advancement of the ordinary people on the propertied and powerful in order to survive and improve their lives' (545).

As regards Bishkek's cityscape, this marks a parallel to Almaz and his peers in Iug-2. Similarly to how these urbanites in a socialist neighbourhood made 'their yard' into a meaningful place, so also the newcomers to the capital have charged the (expanding) urban landscape with their personal memories, communal relations and imaginaries of urbanity. Here, the notion of encroachment serves quite well to illustrate how such processes of urban appropriation relate to lines of conflict between the rural migrants to Bishkek and the city's 'indigenous residents' (*korennye zhiteli*).

Bishkek's rurals and urbanites in a 'divided city'

Beyond matters of law and of infrastructure development, there is also socio-cultural marginalization to overcome for the residents of *novostroiki* like Kyzyl Zher. Their claim of belonging to Bishkek tends to be contested by those who perceive themselves as the 'real urbanites', because they were born in the capital or already lived there in Soviet times. The tensions between such 'rural newcomers' and the *Bishkekchany* have been a recurrent theme in Kyrgyzstani media and popular culture.

The antagonism towards the rurals in the city was well captured in an interview with Kyrgyz filmmaker Emil Jumabaev, (Ayjigitov 2013; Ibraev 2013) a self-proclaimed 'authentic' and third-generation resident of the capital. His words reflect distress about how the invasion of a 'barbaric mass' of rurals has turned a progressing city into a 'dirty, ugly and dismal' settlement, washing away the delicate plants of 'modern urban culture' that Frunze had so onerously developed during the Soviet project:

> The urban civilization did not enter into their [the rural migrants] flesh and blood. … The catastrophe at the end of the century quickly demonstrated that their tough burden is not to be nomads anymore, but also not yet to be modern townspeople. And the increasing milieu of [other] migrants from the villages coerced them to drop even those few outward urban features that were present in them.

From that perspective, the encroachment of Bishkek's newcomers onto urban turf does not proceed silently at all, but appears more like a rampant and noisy assault on the familiar urban fabric. The numbers game between public media, city officials and scientists about the 'real' numbers of *novostroiki* (48 vs. 29) and newcomers (0.4 million vs. 0.2 million) in Bishkek adds fuel to the urbanites' phobia about a 'ruralization' of their city. Similar concerns about the reversal of urban civilizational achievements to 'pre-modern forms of living and sociality' (Alexander and Buchli 2007, 30) have been documented in many other post-Socialist contexts as well (e.g. Nazpary 2002; Darieva 2011; Kosmarski 2011).

In contemporary Bishkek, the key term to capture the cultural degradation of city life is *myrk* (Schröder 2010, 455–456; Kuehnast 1998, 647). Taken as embodying the antipode of any long-term urban dweller, the *myrki* (plural) are commonly denied to possess the qualities that used to shape civilized urban life. Here it is in particular the *myrki*'s village socialization that is understood as the root cause of their problematic role in the city. The *myrki* are portrayed as not speaking Russian properly, because while growing up in the periphery their primary language of everyday communication in school and among kin and friends was Kyrgyz. Being distant from Bishkek is also considered a reason why no *myrk* could ever have developed as fine-grained a taste for appearance and clothing as their urban contemporaries. For the most part, to urbanites such as Almaz and his peers from Iug-2, the *myrki*'s inadequacies of language and style were simply amusing.

A rather serious concern was the urbanites' conviction that due to their village past the *myrki* are poor at resolving conflict with words. From that vantage point the *myrki* were portrayed as overly aggressive and easily turning to violence. Taken to Bishkek's urban arena, this was not worrisome as long as a particular space was appropriated without inviting competing claims. In fact, such was the case for the private and parochial domains within the respective neighbourhoods. Given their image of the *novostroiki* as a raw wilderness or 'jungle', Almaz and other urbanites saw no reason to risk exploring these unknown lands. In contrast, they would have been ready to defend their Iug-2 neighbourhood against any intruders. Such bravery, however, was hardly required, because it remained a rare occasion that an inhabitant of Iug-2 was bothered in his own neighbourhood (but see Schröder 2010, 456).

From these observations, the social and imaginary geography of contemporary Bishkek invites the notion of a 'divided city' (Low 1996, 388–390). Beyond the well-protected VIP communities and post-Soviet economic segregation, this comprises also the various non-elite residents of the city, such as the established urbanites and the new *myrki*. Their perceptions of the capital are contradictory: what for the urbanites presents itself as a familiar, 'cultured' core of the city, which is being suffocated by an ever-tightening, uncivilized belt, for the *novostroiki* residents seems part of their rightful participation in the continuous urbanization of the Kyrgyz Republic's capital.

The intimate environments of their neighbourhoods aside, Bishkek's distinct urban practitioners have also formed zones of predominance in the public domain. One example of this is Dzerzhinskiy Boulevard, which is a park that stretches like a green ribbon through the city in the north–south direction. Originally named after Felix Edmundovich Dzerzhinskiy, the first director of the Bolshevik secret police, this boulevard of more than 100 metres' width and two kilometres' length has long had been the pride of Frunze. Usubaliev (1971, 231), for example, enthusiastically notes that Dzerzhinskiy Boulevard is even wider than Leningrad's Nevsky Prospekt (43 metres) and New York's Broadway (47 metres). In Soviet times, the apartment buildings along Dzerzhinka were reserved first and foremost for the republic's prime artists, scientists and administrators. Today, the boulevard officially goes by the name of Erkindik (Freedom), and several recent construction projects demonstrate the efforts to revive this quarter for elite residential purposes (Figure 3).

Figure 3. Dzerzhinka/Erkindik Boulevard in Bishkek (picture by Philipp Schröder).

At the southern end of Dzerzhinka is Bishkek's main train station, from which many of Kyrgyzstan's labour migrants embark on their trips to Kazakhstan or Russia. It is only a three-minute walk from there, over a bridge and across the railway tracks, to Iug-2. Thus, Almaz and his peers often strolled over to the train station and then continued for a short walk 'down' Dzerzhinka. After about 500 metres to the north, at the second major intersection, they usually stopped, claiming that this marked the border of an area informally known as upper Dzerzhinka. Everything further north, until the boulevard met Bishkek's major east–west avenue, Chui, Almaz identified as the lower part of Dzerzhinka, which already belonged to the city centre.

Yet, in the eyes of many urbanites, its proximity to the very central parts of Bishkek did not at all make lower Dzerzhinka a particularly urbanized space. The reason for this was quite simply that due to its exceptional prominence this area usually attracted exactly those who did not know the city well. Tourists or random visitors to the capital aside, lower Dzerzhinka and its vicinity were therefore also known as the most desired destination to stroll and be out for the recent migrants to Bishkek, including the inhabitants of the *novostroiki*.

The urbanites, in contrast, cherished the upper part of Dzerzhinka as a space to which they could escape from these 'noisy and unpleasant crowds, creating a village atmosphere'. Such descriptions again exposed the rurals of the city as strangers to the commonly expected public behaviour. Hannerz (1980, 105) has suggested the term 'traffic relations' to capture those fleeting interactions that remain 'minimal' and 'unfocused', precisely because the participants are proficient in going with the regular urban flows and thus do not raise each other's attention. To emphasize that exactly the opposite was true for the *myrki,* the urbanites employed the expression 'without limits' (*bez predel*).

'If you want to see the real Myrkystan', a friend of Almaz told me, 'then go to the square on a holiday. This is without limits.' The 'square' here referred to Bishkek's main square, Ala-Too, which is not far from lower Dzerzhinka and Chui Avenue, in the city centre. Close to Ala-Too are also the Parliament Building, the White House and Panfilov Park, an amusement park with all kinds of games, rides, swings and other attractions. On major holidays, especially on Kyrgyzstan's Day of Independence, 31 August, the area around Ala-Too Square was lined with all kinds of kiosks offering beverages and food. Most of those who crowded Bishkek's centre on such a holiday to enjoy a good time and stroll through the city were either recent migrants to the capital or visitors from close-by villages. Almaz's friend, like many of his urban peers, was nothing short of disgusted by that scene:

> 'These *myrki* go crazy in the city. First they get drunk and then they start fighting. On the holidays, believe me, it is better not to be in the centre.'

In fact, this was the strategy that most urbanites employed. Whenever a red number on their calendars marked a holiday, they avoided or bypassed the downtown areas. Instead of joining the crowd and proudly challenging the *myrki* for the 'symbolic control of the streets' (Low 1996, 391), the urbanites stayed behind in their neighbourhoods, or met in 'safe' places, such as those cafes and establishments which they knew would not be frequented by their rural antipodes.

Eventually, these brief ethnographic accounts illustrate that divisions in Bishkek's public space were created not only along geographic lines or mental maps, but also in reference to time. In the case of Dzerzhinka Boulevard, where the appropriation of an urban area occurred simultaneously, this led to the establishment of boundaries that separated the urbanites (upper part) from the *myrki* (lower part). On major holidays, however, the capture of Bishkek's centre by the recent migrants and rural visitors coincided with the urbanites' withdrawal into uncontested areas (of their neighbourhood or a particular cafe). Then again, there was no alternative occasion during which the urbanites gathered on a larger scale to symbolically reject the *myrki*'s aspiration of belonging to the capital. The urbanites, as Flynn, Kosmarskaya, and Sabirova (2014, 1514) have recently asserted, would rather travel down memory lane and reminisce about formerly 'wonderful Frunze'.

Violent encounters and the urbanization of *myrki*

As one would expect, the tides of expanding and contracting claims on different corners of Bishkek's cityscape do not always proceed harmoniously and without ruptures. Sometimes when actual encounters between urbanites and recent migrants are unavoidable, dis-agreement about the proper way of conduct can turn from a verbal into a violent altercation.

Talant, another inhabitant of the Iug-2 neighbourhood, shared the following story with me, which occurred during a birthday celebration in a cafe in central Bishkek.[3]

> I was already quite drunk. All of a sudden I felt something in my back. It was as if some shoes or hands were moving along my shirt. I turned around to see whether someone was behind me. I spotted this guy, who was just sitting down with a group at a table close by. They were *myrki*, you could see that right away. They were loud and vulgar. In short, they just did not behave in the right way. I knew two of the girls in that group from university. Usually they were all right. I couldn't get why they would be at a cafe with such guys. So I went over there to talk to this guy. I said: 'Look, you just have to apologize, nothing more. You can do it very quietly, so that none of your friends will hear anything. Afterwards we shake hands, and that's it.'

The other young man seemed to agree. Yet just when they were shaking hands, Talant heard a sound. He turned around and looked towards the restrooms.

> There, I saw two or three of this guy's friends beating up someone from our group. So the fight started. But we really had no chance. We were fewer than them and also in our group there were some guys who never had fought before in their lives. You couldn't count on them. At one moment I was lying on the floor. With one hand I protected my head, with the other one I grabbed my phone to call Semetei [a friend]. I felt something warm on my back and turned my head. It was blood! [Talant rolls up his shirt and shows me his back.] Do you see these marks? Believe it or not, this guy was stabbing me with a fork!

Referring to incidents like this, the urbanites accused the *myrki* of applying violence inap-propriately. Not at all did this mean that the young men who had grown up in the city condemned physical violence as such, because in their understanding it was integral to Kyrgyz masculinity. Rather, they argued that the *myrki* do not constrain their violent urges in accordance with the informal rules that the urbanites considered to give the right measure. For the case at hand, they claimed that another urbanite would have accepted Talant's offer to settle this issue calmly instead of turning to violence as a first response.

Other elements in the urbanites' code outlined when violence should be halted. Since their youth, when Almaz and his peers had fought against their enemy neighbourhoods, they had learned not to continue a fight 'after the first blood' (*pozle pervoi krovi*). In Talant's story this was not the case, and he and his friends were quite sure that the *myrki* had let go of Talant only because they could not be sure when his help would arrive. Also, there should be no violence when females are present. But in the eyes of many urbanites, such as these young men from Iug-2, these common-sense orientations have become null and void with the arrival of the *myrki* in the city. Another long-term neighbour of Almaz from lug-2 expressed his personal disenchantment like this:

> With these *myrki* you never know. They don't care about this [the code of appropriate vio-lence]. They beat their girls anyway, so why should they not beat up another guy in front of females? All of this is simply without limits [*bez predel*].

The anthropology of conflict teaches us that incompatible interests and intentions may either contribute to destabilizing a society or bring about new ways of social organization and integration (e.g. Elwert 2002; Eckert 2004). In dealing with conflict, social actors gen-erally have three options: they may turn to violence (as happened inside the Bishkek cafe); they may try to avoid altercation and sidestep an open conflict (as exemplified by the different zones of predominance along Dzerzhinka park); or they may develop ways of resolving conflicts by procedure, i.e. through legal or informal institutionalization.

As the incidents presented here vividly show, the urbanites and the *myrki* have not established ways of harmonizing their respective normative codes on how to behave 'properly' (*akkuratno*) in Bishkek's cityscape. Instead, they oscillate between (violent) appropriation and avoidance. Again in the words of filmmaker Emil Jumabaev, such instances show the lack of 'a cultural base that unites us as a nation'. On the other hand, Jumabaev thinks that such common ground could be provided 'by the city itself, [the City] with a capital letter'.

But is there in fact a 'civilizing' force of Bishkek, which enables both recent migrants and long-established urbanites to have their encounters in the urban domain progress beyond confronting or evading each other? Emil Jumabaev reflects on this convincingly:

> *Myrk* – this is an intermediate state between the lost, maternal and traditional organics and the inability or unwillingness to adapt, to become a part of the modern city in all its complexity and contradictions. *Myrk* – this is a condition, a temporary, fluid, surmountable one, there is nothing fatal to it. This is like a diagnosis, but not a verdict.

This observation indicates that the term *myrk* most of all captures an ambiguous and tem-porary state. A *myrk* therefore resembles quite strongly what Turner (1969) has called 'liminal personae', literally 'threshold people'. Caught in the process of initiation into city life, the *myrk* find themselves in a delicate position 'betwixt and between' rural and urban social status. At the other end of this adaptation, which above all entails polishing one's Russian speaking and internalizing urban public behaviour and appearance, a former *myrk* tran-sitions to what is locally known as a newcomer (*priezzhyi*). This label, in the eyes of urbanites such as Almaz or Talant, granted a recent migrant a 'sufficient' degree of urbanity and hence spared them from further public stigmatization (see also Schröder 2010, 456).

Aiperi is a young Kyrgyz woman who qualifies as such a newcomer.[4] In 2003 she had moved to Bishkek from the rural Issyk-Kul area to become a student. In hindsight, Aiperi smiles about the time-consuming efforts it took her 'to learn how the city and its people move'. Along the way, Aiperi engaged in a (critical) examination and practice of the urban 'habitus', which according to Bourdieu (1990, 69–70) also entails individuals' unconscious and embodied ways of carrying themselves, i.e. 'of standing, speaking, walking, and thereby of feeling and thinking'.

When I first met Aiperi in 2007, these were no longer concerns for her; she had already passed through her post-rural, urban socialization. At that time Aiperi moved between different Bishkek neighbourhoods all the time and frequently changed from one rented apartment to the next. Sometimes this was due to a disagreement with a landlord, other times she found a 'better and cheaper place somewhere else'. Whenever Aiperi showed up at the real estate agency to get a new list of suitable rentals, this resembled an audition on her achievements in urbanity. The decisive moment came when the real estate agent called a landlord on behalf of Aiperi to set up a meeting. These phone conversations were meant to provide a first orientation as to whether a tenant could be considered reliable (in terms of payment) and civilized (in terms of treating the furniture appropriately and obeying the house rules). Although Aiperi was profiled as an 'Asian' by the agent, i.e. an ethnic Kyrgyz and thus a potential *myrk,* in all other domains she was highly recommended to the landlords as a young woman who was 'intelligent', 'beautiful', 'working', and – most importantly – 'already urban'. With such clear evidence of her integration success, not only could Aiperi manage her everyday encounters with urbanites in other social situations, but also it has opened up opportunities for her to appropriate urban space through the prism of the many Bishkek neighbourhoods that she has inhabited in recent years. When based on this story Aiperi further elaborated that she was now 'urban enough', this went deeper than being a claim of belonging to Bishkek. It was at the same time a self-confident statement about her rural background, which she did not at all aim to fully extinguish. Similarly, in her study on urban narratives in Kazakhstan, Yessenova (2003, 147) takes the example of a recent migrant to Almaty to argue that 'his rural identity, built upon an imaginary link with ancestry and locality at its core, emerges from this assessment as a self-confirmation of being uncorrupted by the urban environment'. In quite the same way, many of Bishkek's newcomers emphasize being adapted to city life, yet still resisting its most dubious laissez-faire temptations and even their bringing to the city a hard-working village attitude (see Schröder 2013).

To illustrate how nevertheless the contrasting urban and rural virtues correlate, Yessenova's interlocutor from above presents us with an intriguing metaphor: 'The city is the "heart" of the nation, inspiring to follow [its dynamics.] But the village is its "soul"' (2003, 148). Although this juxtaposition of urban-modern-dynamic vs. rural-traditional-pure is a popular one in Kyrgyzstan as well, the last paragraphs have demonstrated that a Bishkek newcomer like Aiperi clearly escapes this rigid dichotomy. Therefore, Aiperi may also serve to put the urbanites' phobia into perspective: what they understand as the ruralization of Bishkek by the *myrki,* from the other vantage point may be taken as the urbanizing alteration of rural migrants into newcomers.

After all, Aiperi ended up living very close to the Iug-2 neighbourhood that Almaz calls home. And when she passed by the yard of Almaz and his peers almost daily, it was not her village background that these young urbanites noticed, but rather her 'elegance' and 'good style'.[5]

Conclusion: the urban rhythm of Bishkek

In this article, I have assembled ethnographic vignettes on different forms of urban dwelling in Kyrgyzstan's capital. Iug-2, the neighbourhood of Almaz and his friends, has been part of the cityscape since the 1970s. Pervaded by the memories, networks and symbolic associations of its long-term inhabitants, Iug-2 thus transcends the epochal turn from socialist Frunze to post-socialist Bishkek. Yet also, as an earmark of Soviet urban aesthetics and sociality, this neighbourhood time contrasts sharply with the extensive changes that the city has experienced from the late 1980s onwards.

Bishkek's new settlements were set up in the outskirts to absorb the many incoming migrants who escaped rural poverty. Regardless of their precarious state, the *novostroiki* therefore encapsulate their inhabitants' struggle for urban citizenship. On the other hand, many established residents of Bishkek see an urban antipode emerging from these new settlements. To them, what is stigmatized as *myrk* (or 'rural in the city') embodies the ruin of urban culturedness, i.e. the disregard of established norms of conduct and a disturbing intrusion into the urban environment. Here especially the example of Dzerzhinka Park has shown how the urbanites' and the *myrki*'s alternating strategies of appropriating and avoiding public spaces may affect the social and imaginary geography of the city. At the same time, and especially for those who recall Soviet life in Frunze, the *myrki* may constitute only the very latest episode and most personal symbolization of a larger, civilizational decline. Often, the baseline for the moral-aesthetic judgments of these long-term urbanites had already been established before the rural migration to Bishkek set in. Aside from embodiments and changing urban landscapes, these judgments critically drew on contrasting two historical epochs, as part of which, for instance, the loss of socialist-era, 'honest' factory jobs was juxtaposed with the emerging 'capitalist exploitation' in the post-1991 trading bazaars.

Much about the conflict involving Bishkek's rurals and urbanites runs in parallels. While the rurals' active presence in the city manifests as a hands-on insistence on their rightful participation, the urbanites' rather passive response is to convey their aversion through city nostalgia. Similarly, the urbanites and the rurals draw on quite incompatible repertoires to validate their respective demands. The Bishkekians, behind a notion of urbanity as a multi-ethnic and Russian-speaking community, refer to the cosmopolitan ambitions of Soviet and early post-Soviet ideology, as captured in slogans such as the 'friendship of peoples' or 'Kyrgyzstan – our common home' (see Schröder 2010, 454–455; Gullette 2010).

In contrast, many recent migrants to Bishkek base their entitlement to urban well-being on notions of ethnic nationalism. In this view, the post-Soviet predominance of the country's titular 'nationality' in politics, economy and administration logically must include the capital. This undermines the legitimacy of any aspirations that non-ethnic Kyrgyz residents might want to declare (for an example, see Flynn and Kosmarskaya 2012, 457). For the case of Kyrgyzstan's so-called 'second city' of Osh, Megoran (2013) has recently framed the violent struggles that occurred there in 1990 and 2010 between ethnic Kyrgyz and Uzbeks in light of these groups' competing narratives regarding their (historical) belonging to that urban territory. Although this differs from the situation in Bishkek, where predominantly ethnic Kyrgyz are separating along the lines of their either urban or rural provenance, we can still notice how in a similar way urban conflict links with 'nationalism as a geographical phenomenon' (892) to inform the rhythms of both these Kyrgyz cities in regard to dividing and sharing spaces.

Regardless of their different content and form of articulation, the opposing claims of Bishkek's urbanites and rurals eventually address the very same entity: the Kyrgyz state. By extension, it is understood to be the duty of municipal and other government agencies to reach binding decisions on the legal status of particular new settlements and to serve as the guarantor of social and moral order. From this vantage point, it seems premature to classify long-term Bishkekians as an affluent elite that sits above the poor *novostroiki*-rurals in the city's hierarchy. Essentially, this would neglect that the majority of both these groups share belonging to what Nazpary (2002) has called the 'dispossessed', i.e. citizens who were stripped of vital social and economic rights when socialism dissolved.

The fact, therefore, that in Bishkek social avoidance between ordinary city residents – both urbanites and rurals – remains a viable practice to deal with conflict situations is not because an obvious supremacy of one civic group would force the other into 'everyday forms of resistance' – as for example Scott (1985) and Alber (2004) have shown for the interaction between native peasant populations and colonial regimes. Rather, it seems that in Kyrgyzstan's capital similarly marginalized groups opt to avoid each other because the weak performance of state agencies results in insufficient institutionalization and unreliable mediation of their competing interests (Eckert 2004, 16). Avoidance, in that regard, is not only an element in Bishkek's current rhythm, i.e. an everyday practice that impacts, to speak with Lefebvre (2004, 89), the social construction and experience of a particularly 'localised time' or 'temporalised place'. Beyond the urban domain, avoidance may qualify to be conceived of as a more encompassing modality for further theorizing about the connectedness of space, time and society in Kyrgyzstan, for instance when investigating the government's ambition for materializing its territorial integrity in rural border areas (Reeves 2014).

Finally, I introduced the case of Aiperi, a young woman who had relocated to Bishkek from a remote village some years prior to my fieldwork. This demonstrated that there is (literally) more between the urbanites and the *myrki* than retreating into comfort zones, some sporadic violent encounters, or contentions between civic and ethnic nationalism. In fact, Aiperi's case revealed that over time a former villager can acquire the sensory identifiers of urbanity – parlance and phenotype mostly – to transform into a so-called newcomer. Beyond pacifying the urbanites' horrors of a relentless ruralization of their city, the potential for post-rural socialization promises to such newcomers that they could blend into Bishkek's routines and spaces without much constraint.

Aiperi's case thus resonates well with Lefebvre's (2004, 39–45) further observation that urban rhythms work towards the social disciplining of the body, which through repetitive training – 'dressage' – over time attunes to the beats of a city. Taken to another Central Asian context, again the southern Kyrgyz city of Osh, Liu (2012, 146) highlights a similar association between the traditional *mahalla* neighbourhoods of ethnic Uzbeks as a particular socio-spatial field for urban dwelling and the 'cultivation' of proper personhood:

> Indeed, the mahalla as an idiom of tarbiya [social training] should be interpreted as an instance of bodily imagination, a mode of 'carnal knowledge', an embodied subject's total engagement with the world that is both cognitive and corporeal.

Following such 'social training', aside from avoiding conflict and blending in, the emergent urban habitus of a newcomer, and his or her knowledge about 'what is the right time to be in the right place' in Bishkek, may also be utilized to express identity. Then, someone's presence in a particular place, such as the newest glittery shopping mall or a cinema that screens only English-language movies, reflects attachment to urban lifestyles and patterns of consumption. Aiperi, for example, designates the rather expensive gym that she regularly visits as a 'safe and fun place', where she can enjoy her spare free time during a spin class and without being exposed to 'primitive' and '*myrk*-like' male advances. With access to this gym, Aiperi thus presents herself as a Bishkek newcomer, who also is 'successful' (able to afford), 'busy' (managing time) and 'connected to the world' (in terms of global fitness trends).

Building on Lefebvre's ideas about the effects of pervasive commodification on everyday life, Edensor (2010, 3) notes that 'the rhythms of space also change with the acceleration of the rhythms of consumption, fashion and innovation under an intensified consumer capitalism'. For the residents of formerly socialist cities, we could expect that this is an exceptionally rapid change: one, for example, in which only a few years came between 'vanilla as the [only] flavor of Communism' in Soviet Frunze and a choice among 31 flavours of ice-cream on the streets of Bishkek (see Kuehnast 1998, 640–644).[6]

In conclusion, this highlights that next to classic Socialist neighbourhoods, new settlements, urbanites, *myrki* and newcomers there are yet many more pulses of Bishkek's rhythm to be explored. Here, future research on urban stops and flows, such as public transportation, bazaar trading or local fashion production, promises further insights into the emergent properties of places and the stabilizing routines within Bishkek's landscape.

Notes

1. The data for this article were gathered during multiple long-term ethnographic fieldwork stays in Bishkek between 2007 and 2015.
2. Flynn and Kosmarskaya (2012, 459–462) explore in some detail the antagonistic discourse surrounding Kyrgyzstan's intra-ethnic north–south divide. See also Schröder (2010, 462).
3. This excerpt is based on Schröder (2012, 257–258).
4. See also Schröder (2012, 264–278).
5. Although the choice to present Aiperi's case at this point may invite reflections about a gendered nature within these urban–rural dynamics, this does not correspond to my fieldwork data. Quite unrelated to gender, long-term urban dwellers of both sexes assigned the label of *myrk* to males and females of rural appearance or behaviour, or on the contrary acknowledged their 'achievements' in urbanity. In that sense the urban standards varied in particular contents, yet not in their general form – e.g. appropriate dress codes for men and women, which made it easier or more difficult for men or women to pass as newcomers.
6. Taking the example of ethnic Uzbeks in Osh, Liu (2012, Ch.6) skilfully reconstructs their changing perceptions of economic and other developments in Kyrgyzstan and neighbouring Uzbekistan since the mid-1990s. Here, the expression 'order before development' is taken to represent the continuing strong influence of the state in Uzbekistan, whereas Kyrgyzstan has rather embraced 'Western-style' market liberalization and democracy. Among others, this vividly illustrates the different speeds at which the 'unmaking of Soviet life' (Humphrey 2002) proceeded in Central Asian republics.

Acknowledgements

I am grateful to the participants in the workshop Tracing Migration and Global Connectedness: Urban Contexts in Central Asia and Beyond (Berlin, May 2013), where I first presented my thoughts on this topic. I also want to thank Manja Stephan-Emmrich and two anonymous reviewers for their insightful comments.

Disclosure statement

No potential conflict of interest was reported by the author.

Funding

Research for this article was supported by the Max Planck Institute for Social Anthropology (Halle/Saale), the Humboldt-Universität zu Berlin and the VolkswagenStiftung.

References

Alber, E. 2004. "Meidung als Modus des Umgangs mit Konflikten." In *Anthropologie der Konflikte. Georg Elwerts konflikttheoretische Thesen in der Diskussion*, edited by J. Eckert, 169–185. Bielefeld: transcript.

Alexander, C., and V. Buchli. 2007. "Introduction." In *Urban Life in Post-Soviet Asia*, edited by C. Alexander, V. Buchli, and C. Humphrey, 1–39. London: UCL.

Alexander, C., V. Buchli, and C. Humphrey, eds. 2007. *Urban Life in Post-Soviet Asia.* London: UCL.

Alymbaeva, A. A. 2008. "K voprosu ob urbanizacii [To the Question of Urbanization]." *The Academic Review: The Journal of the History Institute of the Kyrgyz Academy of Sciences* 1: 65–77.

Alymbaeva, A. A. 2013. "Internal Migration in Kyrgyzstan: A Geographical and Sociological Study of Rural Migration." In *Migration and Social Upheaval in the Face of Globalization in Central Asia*, edited by M. Laruelle, 117–148. Leiden: Brill.

Anderson, J. 1999. *Kyrgyzstan: Central Asia' s Island of Democracy.* Amsterdam: Harwood Academic Publishers.

Ayjigitov, M. 2013. "V Bishkeke reshayut, kak obedinit jiteley novostroek i korennih frunzentsev." *Vecherniy Bishkek*, July 22. Accessed November 27, 2014. http://www.vb.kg/doc/236842_v_bishkeke_reshaut_kak_obedinit_jiteley_novostroek_i_korennyh_frynzencev.html.

Bayat, A. 2000. "From 'Dangerous Classes' to 'Quiet Rebels': Politics of the Urban Subaltern in the Global South." *International Sociology* 15 (3): 533–557. doi:10.1177/026858000015003005.

Bourdieu, P. 1990. *The Logic of Practice.* Cambridge: Polity Press.

Darieva, T. 2011. "A 'Remarkable Gift' in a Postcolonial City." In *Urban Spaces After Socialism: Ethnographies of Public Spaces in Eurasian Cities*, edited by T. Darieva, W. Kaschuba, and M. Krebs, 153–180. Frankfurt: Campus Verlag.

Eckert, J. 2004. "Gewalt, Meidung und Verfahren: Zur Konfliktethnologie Georg Elwerts." In *Anthropologie der Konflikte. Georg Elwerts konflikttheoretische Thesen in der Diskussion*, edited by J. Eckert, 7–25. Bielefeld: transcript.

Edensor, T. 2010. "Introduction: Thinking about Rhythm and Space." In *Geographies of Rhythm. Nature, Place, Mobilities and Bodies*, edited by T. Endesor, 1–18. Aldershot: Ashgate.

Elwert, G. 2002. "Sozialanthropologisch erklärte Gewalt." In *Internationales Handbuch der Gewaltforschung*, edited by W. Heitmeyer and J. Hagan, 330–367. Wiesbaden: Westdeutscher Verlag.

Evans-Pritchard, E. E. 1970 [1940]. "The Nuer of the Southern Sudan." In *African Political Systems*, edited by M. Fortes and E.E. Evans-Pritchard, 272–296. London: Oxford University Press.

Flynn, M., and N. Kosmarskaya. 2012. "Exploring 'North' and 'South' in Post-Soviet Bishkek: Discourses and Perceptions of Rural-Urban Migration." *Nationalities Papers: The Journal of Nationalism and Ethnicity* 40 (3): 453–471. doi:10.1080/00905992.2012.685061.

Flynn, M., N. Kosmarskaya, and G. Sabirova. 2014. "The Place of Memory in Understanding Urban Change in Central Asia: The Cities of Bishkek and Ferghana." *Europe-Asia Studies* 66 (9): 1501–1524. doi:10.1080/09668136.2014.957926.

Fryer, P., E. Nasritdinov, and E. Satybaldieva. 2014. "Moving Toward the Brink? Migration in the Kyrgyz Republic." *Central Asian Affairs* 1: 171–198. doi:10.1163/22142290-00102002.

Gullette, D. 2010. *The Genealogical Construction of the Kyrgyz Republic.* Folkestone: Global Oriental.

Hannerz, U. 1980. *Exploring the City. Inquiries toward an Urban Anthropology.* New York: Columbia University Press.

Humphrey, C. 2002. *The Unmaking of Soviet Life. Everyday Economies after Socialism.* Ithaca: Cornell University Press.

Ibraev, K. 2013. "Po gorodu sonnomu pechal saksofonnaya..." *Slovo Kyrgyzstana*, July 3. Accessed November 27, 2014. http://slovo.kg/?p=23510.

Isabaeva, E. 2013. "Migration into the 'Illegality' and Coping with Difficulties in a Squatter Settlement in Bishkek." *Zeitschrift für Ethnologie* 138: 1–16.

Isabaeva, E. 2014. "From Denizens to Citizens in Bishkek: Informal Squatter-Settlement Residents in Urban Kyrgyzstan." *The Journal of Social Policy Studies* 12 (2): 249–260.

Kosmarski, A. 2011. "Grandeur and Decay of the 'Soviet Byzantium'. Spaces, Peoples and Memories of Tashkent, Uzbekistan." In *Urban Spaces After Socialism. Ethnographies of Public Places in Eurasian Cities*, edited by T. Darieva, W. Kaschuba, and M. Krebs, 33–56. Frankfurt: Campus.

Kuehnast, K. 1998. "From Pioneers to Entrepreneurs: Young Women, Consumerism, and the 'World Picture' in Kyrgyzstan." *Central Asian Survey* 17 (4): 639–654. doi:10.1080/02634939808401061.

Lefebvre, H. 2004. *Rhythmanalysis: Space, Time and Everyday Life*. London: Continuum.

Liu, M. 2012. *Under Solomon's Throne: Uzbek Visions of Renewal in Osh*. Pittsburgh, PA: University of Pittsburgh Press.

Lofland, L. 1998. *The Public Realm: Exploring the City's Quintessential Social Territory*. New York: Aldine de Gruyter.

Low, S. M. 1996. "The Anthropology of Cities: Imagining and Theorizing the City." *Annual Review of Anthropology* 25: 383–409. doi:10.1146/annurev.anthro.25.1.383.

Megoran, N. 2013. "Shared Space, Divided Space: Narrating Ethnic Histories of Osh." *Environment and Planning* 45: 892–907. doi:10.1068/a44505.

Nasritdinov, E. 2013. "Myths and Realities of Bishkek novostroikas." TEDx Bishkek, May 12. https://www.youtube.com/watch?v=7gySTS2D77g.

Nasritdinov, E., and P. Schröder 2016. "From Frunze to Bishkek. Soviet Territorial Youth Formations and Their Decline in the 1990-s and 2000-s." *Central Asian Affairs* 3 (1): 1–28. doi:10.1163/22142290-00301001

Nazpary, J. 2002. *Post-Soviet Chaos. Violence and Dispossession in Kazakhstan*. London: Pluto Press.

Oruzbaeva, B. 1984. *Frunze. Entsiklopdia [Frunze. Encyclopedia]*. Frunze.

Payaz, J. 2014. "Kyrgyzstan Wants to Keep Its Wholesale Markets in the Customs Union." *The Central Asia-Caucasus Analyst*, February 5. Accessed November 28 2014. http://www.cacianalyst.org/publications/analytical-articles/item/12907-kyrgyzstan-wants-to-keep-its-wholesale-markets-in-the-customs-union.html.

Petrov, V. G. 2008. *Frunze Sovetskiy, 1926–1991 [Soviet Frunze, 1926–1991]*. Bishkek: Literaturnyi Kyrgyzstan.

Reeves, M. 2012. "Black Work, Green Money: Remittances, Ritual, and Domestic Economies in Southern Kyrgyzstan." *Slavic Review* 71 (1): 108–134. doi:10.5612/slavicreview.71.1.0108.

Reeves, M. 2014. *Border Work. Spatial Lives of the State in Rural Central Asia*. New York, NY: Cornell University Press.

Schröder, P. 2010. "'Urbanizing' Bishkek: Interrelations of Boundaries, Migration, Group Size and Opportunity Structure." *Central Asian Survey* 29 (4): 453–467. doi:10.1080/02634937.2010.537143.

Schröder, P. 2012. "From Shangai to Iug-2: Integration and Identification Among and Beyond the Male Youth of a Bishkek Neighbourhood." PhD diss., Martin-Luther-Universität Halle-Wittenberg.

Schröder, P. 2013. "Ainuras Amerikanische Karriere. Räumliche und Soziale Mobilität einer jungen Kirgisin." *Zeitschrift für Ethnologie* 138: 235–258.

Scott, J. C. 1985. *Weapons of the Weak: Everyday Forms of Peasant Resistance*. New Haven: Yale University Press.

Turner, V. W. 1995 [1969]. *The Ritual Process: Structure and Anti-Structure*. New Jersey: Transaction Publishers.

Usubaliev, T. U. 1971. *Frunze – Stolitsa Sovetskogo Kirgizstana [Frunze – The Capital of Soviet Kyrgyzstan]*. Moscow: Mysl.

Yessenova, S. B. 2003. "The Politics and Poetics of the Nation: Urban Narratives of Kazakh Identity." PhD diss., Mc Gill University.

Zhumakadyr kyzy, B. 2012. "Development in Urbanized Settings: A Study of Novostroikas in Bishkek." *Bachelor thesis*, American University of Central Asia.

Experiencing liminality: housing, renting and informal tenants in Astana

Kishimjan Osmonova

Institute for Asian and African Studies, Humboldt-Universität zu Berlin, Germany

ABSTRACT

This article is intended to contribute broadly to research in post-socialist urban studies. Based on ethnographic fieldwork and interviews with 'newcomers' to the capital, Astana, from different parts of Kazakhstan, I examine the renting practices of newcomers. I analyse the experiences of newcomers in their new urban milieu of Astana, and try to answer the question of what it means to live in the city for various groups of individuals on a daily basis. I examine the Soviet and post-Soviet housing and the continuities of the Soviet legacy when it comes to the institution of *propiska* (city registration). I show that living in shared flats is a coping strategy to deal with expensive rents and meant to be a transitory step towards homeownership. For this reason many accept high rents and crowded housing as 'normal'. Furthermore, I argue that informal renting practices are acceptable mostly for young and single people, who are free to experiment with city life, and are on their way to establishing careers and personal lives. However, elderly newcomers and young families with children who do not wish to live in shared flats, but have to rent, feel 'homeless' and trapped in 'liminal housing'. For them, renting is undesirable, and they feel a sense of incarceration if they fail to secure housing.

Renting in shared flats and informal tenants in Astana

To understand housing and accommodation issues for many 'newcomers' (*priezzhie*) in Astana, one has to live like one of them – that is, in shared flats with multiple sub-tenants. Here I give some examples and a general characterization of life in this temporary housing. Upon my arrival to Astana in 2010, I found accommodation in a shared flat through newspaper advertisements. Newspapers offered quite a variety of accommodation opportunities, ranging from the most expensive, newly built elite apartments in the Left Bank to shared rooms in the old town in old Soviet *krushchevka* flats. After making several phone calls, I arranged to see one flat that same day, and agreed to move in on the following day. This is the most usual and fastest way to find affordable accommodations. My new shared flat was a new one-bedroom apartment in an almost-finished brick housing compound in the old town, which is considered the centre of town. Many of these new housing compounds have a triangular form. In the case of my compound (Figure 1) the left wing was still incomplete, and it remained 'frozen' during my stay, like many other housing projects that had run into trouble during the financial crisis. My flat was on the top (11th) floor, and there was no functioning elevator. My flat-mates and I had to manage the stairs every day, because up to the time of my departure, three months later, the elevator was still not functioning. This was my entry point into the intimate lives of my respondents, who during my fieldwork shared many stories of their arrival and lives in Astana.

Our flat was a fairly spacious one-bedroom apartment, with a big kitchen and a balcony. My flat-mate Dilnaz, 27 years old, worked as a chief of staff at the local criminal court. She was also the main tenant. I would share my room with her. Two other sub-tenants slept in the other room, which was actually the living room, with a large sofa bed in one corner. But soon an additional person moved in. Alima, our new flat-mate, slept on an air mattress in the other corner of the living room. During the day, everyone was allowed to use the couch in the living room, and when everyone was at home in the evening we would gather in this room to watch TV. This was a communal mode of living, where everything was shared. There was no private space, except the space that was allocated for sleeping. In total, it was five women sharing a one-bedroom flat, each paying about 14,000 Kazakh tenge (about US$ 100) monthly (later two more people joined us). To rent a one-room old *khrushchevka* flat cost at least US$ 250 at that time, equal to a typical salary for teachers in Astana. There are no statistics available on the percentage of the population that rents or shares flats in this manner, since most people are not registered officially (through *propiska*, or city registration) and thus are not included in the official statistics. Nevertheless, 70–80% of the people I interviewed (60 in total) were renting, usually with several other

Figure 1. A newly built housing compound from brick where my flat-mates and I lived in Astana (photo by author, 2010).

people in shared flats. Many of them also stated that although they paid higher rents, their present housing situation in Astana was worse than it had been in their home towns or villages. Despite the vast, empty, and seemingly uninhabited urban space, especially in the Left Bank, the renters enjoyed very little actual living space in Astana. The whole economy of rented flats operates outside the control and regulation of the state, leaving regulation to market forces. Neither landlords nor tenants are protected, since most of the time they do not have written agreements, which leaves a lot of room for all kinds of ad hoc and informal negotiations in the rental market.

The above-described temporary and transient renting practice is common not only among the very poor, marginalized, or ethnically diverse newcomers, but also among those with stable salaries working for the public sector. For example, Dilnaz, the main tenant, worked for the court, and enjoyed a favourable salary, paying only 20% of her salary for rent. Meanwhile, other renters paid 60–70% of their income for the rent in our shared flat. Those employed in the private service sector usually had unstable and temporary jobs. All of the tenants were in their twenties, had some higher education, and had come to Astana in search of career prospects. Other sub-tenants in our shared flat included two female medical students, who studied together and were friends. One of them was a Russian from northern Kazakhstan, while the other had an Uzbek and Kazakh ethnic background and came from the south of the country. These girls were taking their final exams and moved out right after exams, just a few weeks after I had moved in. They returned to their home towns during the summer holiday. Dilnaz immediately sought replacements and took in three more sub-tenants. The two young women were in their mid-twenties and worked in the administration of a local university in Astana. However, they too left, after staying for only about a month, opting to spend their holiday in their home region and avoid paying any rent during their absence. Dilnaz's choice of sub-tenants was quick, and seemed to be based on the principle of 'first come, first served'. She relied on her judgment about who would fit in, and in cases of conflict she would just ask them to leave. During the more than three months that I stayed in this flat, her sub-tenants included a Kyrgyz (myself), a Russian, a Tatar, and three Kazakhs: from Taraz (to the south), Karaganda (north) and Aktau (west). It was an ethnically and socially mixed group. In this way, the next three months proved to be very hectic and exhausting, as new flat-mates were moving in while old ones were moving out; complete strangers joined us and shared our lives, sometimes for a month or even less.

The findings of this research are based on participant observation and in-depth interviews collected in Astana during four months in 2009 and three months in 2010. The methodology is based on the methods of qualitative research, which include ethnographic descriptions that produce detailed accounts of respondents' experiences and personal stories. The data collected are not meant to be a representative sample of Astana's population. I interviewed 27 males and 33 females. Most of the respondents (43 out of 60) came from smaller towns and from the vicinity of Astana. The majority of them were ethnic Kazakhs; only 13 were ethnic Russians. Half were rather young people, 20 to 35 years old. Ten of the respondents were pre-capital native residents, who had inhabited the old Tselinograd before it became the capital, Astana. My six flat-mates were young single women, mostly in their mid-twenties, who had moved to Astana in recent years. One of them, Dilnaz, was a local. Through participant observation I got an insight into the everyday lives of my flat-mates and their mode of living in shared flats. My six flat-mates were typical 'newcomers' who did not own housing and could not afford the high rents of single apartments in Astana. Here, thousands of newcomers solved their housing problem by renting shared flats. Most renters in Astana cannot imagine renting for the rest of their lives, because the rents swallow a large part of their salaries, sometimes up to 80%.

It is important to mention that most internal migrants in Kazakhstan perceive themselves not as migrants but as *priezzhie* ('newcomers' in Russian). When my respondents said that every second person in Astana is a *priezzhiy* they meant mostly Kazakhstanis who came to Astana from different parts of Kazakhstan. They are all citizens of Kazakhstan, as opposed to *migranty* (a Russified label for labour migrants from other Central Asian countries, such as Kyrgyzstan or Uzbekistan). Thus, because Kazakhstani newcomers in Astana almost never refer to themselves as *migranty*, I will use the terms 'newcomers' and *priezzhie* instead of 'migrants'.

In analysing the housing situation and renters in Astana I apply the concept of liminality, similarly to the way Bjorn Thomassen has applied it in his recent book *Liminality and the Modern: Living through the In-Between* (2014) regarding contemporary times under the influence of consumerist and globalized culture. He asks how we can employ this concept to understand the social, cultural and political processes in modernity. Since the postmodern turn in the 1980s, liminality has come to be seen in an especially positive light, where freedom and innovation are welcomed, while sacred norms are mocked and authority questioned (1). 'At its broadest, liminality refers to any "betwixt and between" situation or object, any in-between place or moment, a state of suspense, a moment of freedom between two structured world-views or institutional arrangements' (7). Here Thomassen goes beyond the narrow definition of the term, which means a middle stage during a concrete rite of passage. Seen in this light, renting is an appropriate temporary solution during a transition, which in the long term is undesirable. I show that mobile tenants who are rather young find themselves in a transitional stage of 'neither here nor there' (Turner 1967, 96–97). This transformation becomes all too apparent when the elderly and young families with children have to rent. It is not a viable solution for them; for the younger generation who are single renting is seen as acceptable, but for the elderly it is a sign of failure.

Soviet and post-Soviet housing

A shortage of adequate housing in major cities, especially in the capitals, was all too familiar in Soviet times, and thus does not surprise many Kazakhstanis at present. Soviet cities, despite being considered the 'cradle of civilization', had a problem of chronic housing shortages (Alexander, Buchli, and Humphrey 2007). In Central Asia one important reason for this was the inflow of immigrants, especially from the European parts of the Soviet Union, during times of rapid industrialization (Alexander, Buchli, and Humphrey 2007). Soviet housing was seen as a public service, and the state was supposed to provide housing to all of its citizens, but in reality the housing shortage was manipulated and was used as 'punishment, incentive and reward' (Attwood 2010, 5). Due to higher wages and better services and goods, cities were more attractive than villages. However, access to the big cities was mostly restricted, through the institution of *propiska*.

The children of the privileged could secure jobs in the cities or the capital city through bribery, while the children of the poor would be sent to remote areas, at least for a few years (Rigi 2003, 38). In cities and towns one had to wait years to be entitled to receive an apartment, which usually was allocated through the workplace or the local municipality (Attwood 2010).

After the fall of the Soviet Union and the post-1991 privatization, most flats were privatized by their long-term tenants, for little money, based on their *propiska*. Discussing the role of *propiska*, Hatcher and Thieme (2015, 11) argue that during the early privatization period *propiska* holders became entitled to ownership rights, which made *propiska* an important instrument in the transition towards capitalist logic. The major change since independence is that Kazakhstan's housing policy changed from state-driven to market-driven, to encourage homeownership through market economy mechanisms, such as attracting foreign investments and development of banks and financial institutions (Rolnik 2011). Western governments and international organizations also played a role, by encouraging the growth of private ownership in the developing world globally (Hatcher 2015). However, this shows an inherent negative bias towards forms of renting as an alternative to homeownership, which is promoted by many governments as a way to foster individual autonomy and responsibility (UN-Habitat 2003; Gilbert 2008). Renting is thus seen as undesirable and negative, in comparison to homeownership. In this light, the Kazakh government has also ignored the rental market, as mentioned earlier, leaving regulation to the private sector.

In the background of Astana's spectacular architecture, homeownership is part of the 'Astana dream' lifestyle. The practical realities, however, significantly diverge from this dream, as homeownership is the single most desired commodity, as well as the hardest one to attain. As Bissenova (2012, 121) has showed, purchasing or upgrading one's housing has become the number-one priority for the aspiring middle class in Astana: 'New apartment buildings become part of the image and picture of a "beautiful life" and a "must have".' Many newcomers to Astana, impressed by the construction boom and the building of residential housing, hope to obtain new apartments. Nevertheless, the real prospects of buying an apartment in a newly built housing compound prove to be unrealistic for many.

At their inception, the grand monumental construction projects of Astana left the residential housing sector neglected, which resulted in a shortage of adequate housing for many newcomers (Köppen 2013, 14). Astana's newest part of town, the Left Bank (Figure 2), mostly became a sanctuary for the affluent upper classes and government employees. The latter were fortunate enough to get subsidized flats through a government housing programme. In Kazakhstan, selected categories of civil servants are eligible for state housing. The state housing programme (*gosudarstvennaia zhilishnaia programma*), similar to the socialist type of redistribution, allows government workers (*gosslujashije*) and public-sector employees (*budjetniki*) access to low-interest mortgages to buy subsidized housing for US$ 350 per square metre (Bissenova 2012, 147). This is far below the market value, enabling even low-ranking government workers to apply for the programme. Many bureaucrats have indeed received subsidized housing. However, public officials and civil servants are not the low-income or socially vulnerable group in urgent need of housing. In this regard, the United Nations Report of the Special Rapporteur on the right to adequate housing in Kazakhstan correctly notes that the country's

Figure 2. Elite housing condominiums built mainly for government employees in the Left Bank of Astana (photo by author, 2010).

current Housing Relations Act supports this already advantaged group, giving civil servants the same rights to subsidized housing as disadvantaged groups such as the disabled (Rolnik 2011). Indeed, between 2005 and 2007 more than 35,000 priority citizens (e.g. civil servants) gained access to housing, in comparison to only 10,000 persons from socially protected groups such as low-income families (Rolnik 2011).

Other individuals who are not eligible for state housing have to rely on mortgages from banks. *Ipoteka* is short for the Russian term *ipotech'noe kreditovanie*, meaning a home loan or credit, which became very popular starting in early 2000 and reached its peak in the pre-crisis financial years of 2006–2008. The Kazakh state encouraged national banks to promote the local credit market, which led to a situation where obtaining a bank loan was easier than getting a passport (Yessenova 2010, 20–21). Consequently, the desire for homeownership, as well as easily available home loans, led to the inflation of housing prices and to a housing bubble. Many entrepreneurs wished to capitalize on the subsequent construction boom, which also led to speculative housing. In the aftermath of the financial crisis, many suffered because they could not pay their mortgages; those who were included in the government bailout praised President Nazarbayev, who took care of their bad investments. The state had to get involved to solve the credit crisis, as the scene of unfinished construction could undermine Kazakhstan's promise of modernization, which Astana was supposed to epitomize (Bissenova 2012, 146). Although the homeowners are not the very rich of Kazakhstan, many are members of the aspiring middle class, who back the state in its modernization quest. Bissenova rightly argues that the rising propertied middle class in Kazakhstan supports the status quo because they feel protected by the regime. In this way the state supports those who are already affluent, while the poor (e.g. renters) receive no help with their housing situation.

Renting, gaining independence and self-reliance

Aside from the emergent new group of distinctive upper-middle-class homeowners, another group, the renters, constitutes the vast majority of newcomers in Astana who struggle with housing. The stories of renters in Astana are not included in the public discourse, and therefore remain marginalized. Here I argue that, despite complaining about the lack of affordable housing and high rents, renters reproduce the discourse of homeownership attached to the modernization discourse of Astana. Moreover, renters feel powerless to change anything and push even harder to buy their homes even though they feel excluded from the state provision of modern housing. They wait many years, renting in the hope that they too can buy an apartment in Astana some day. Indeed, some of my respondents worked at two or three jobs, hoping to save up to buy their own apartment.

This is how Alima, my flat-mate, described her initial housing experience in Astana:

Shocking! Nightmare!! [laughs] It was a three-room flat, and each room was rented out. In one room there were three people living, in the second one four, and the third I was renting with another girl. So all in all it was nine people sharing an old three-room *khrushchevka* flat. It was on the fifth floor. The kitchen was so small, I felt like I was living in a dormitory. Of course, I was shocked! Well, I stayed three months there – the owner decided to kick us all out and rent to families rather than to singles. We were all singles. Then I had only one day to find myself a new place. … So I found a place in a two-room flat, I was sharing a room with three other girls and the owner of the flat lived with his family in the other room. I lived there for two years. And now when I think about it after these years, the four of us could have just rented a one-room flat on our own. It seems so terrible now when I think about how we lived then.

Since she did not know the city well enough back then, Alima took the first flat that was available upon her arrival. In this way she changed flats and flat-mates many times in Astana. Finding suitable flat-mates, as well as a reliable landlord, was not at all easy. Despite this experience, Alima justified this mode of living for newcomers:

Yes, you have to rent here, but I don't think it is a big minus. I had no other choice. It is just part of living in Astana, because it is the capital and therefore acceptable until you have your housing. So I find it acceptable.

Such communal living is widespread and is largely accepted in Astana as a legitimate way to cope with the expensive housing in the capital. Many renters accept high rental prices as 'normal' despite the fact that they continue to struggle to make ends meet. The majority of them are single people like Alima or married couples in their twenties and thirties. The couples opt to rent a room for themselves in a shared flat. Initially, after her arrival in 2008 Alima worked for two years in the flourishing banking sector. This was her dream job. She was already considering getting a loan and buying an apartment, but then she was laid off during the financial crisis. When I met Alima, she did not see herself as exactly living the 'Astana lifestyle'. Her salary was barely enough to cover her rent; she could not afford to go shopping in the new shopping malls, or go out to socialize in bars and cafes. She felt disconnected from the 'Astana dream', but nonetheless she was proud to have moved to the new capital.

Many renters agreed that in their hometowns or villages such living conditions would be unacceptable. This attitude of tolerating the unacceptable can be linked with the condition of liminality. In the transitional phase there is a temporary suspension of social norms and rules (Turner 1967; Thomassen 2014). Since Alima also believes that eventually she can achieve the 'Astana dream', which includes homeownership, she is ready to wait and cope with temporary difficulties. In the meantime, the utopia of Astana is effective in the present and serves to justify the negative aspects such as the high rents and lack of well-paid jobs as 'normal'. Here the crowded conditions become readily accepted and even justified in Astana's liminal urban space.

It is true that similar shared flats existed during Soviet times. The communal apartment (*kommunalka*) was a particular type of Soviet housing, where several unrelated families were put together in one apartment (appropriated by the state from the rich aristocratic owners), with shared kitchens, bathrooms and hallways (Gerasimova 2002, 207). This policy was called 'compression' (*uplotnenie*) (Attwood 2010). However, the nature of such communal apartments was forced, and it was families (up to 20 of them) who lived in private rooms in such big communal apartments for decades, under the system where private property was abolished (Gerasimova 2002, 212–215). The communal apartments functioned like a 'social institution with its rules, arrangements and hierarchical system of power', where the state 'intruded into the domestic life of citizens' through rules and mutual control (212). It was a kind of community, but one where there was no choice but to tolerate other tenants and social life was represented by a 'constant battle for privacy' (Attwood 2010). The crucial difference is that now the citizens can enjoy their privacy without the watchful eyes of the state in their privately owned apartments. As I experienced in shared flats in Astana, there is also a complete lack of privacy, since private rooms and sometimes even beds are shared by unrelated persons. Still, it is a voluntary arrangement.

As can be seen, there is a hierarchy of renting options, ranging from the elite flats in the Left Bank, as the most prestigious, to the least desired and respected old *khrushchevka* flats, *vremiankas*, and old dormitories. The flats have an advantage in amenities such as hot water, gas and heating, while the *vremianka* represents a 'village' mode of life, with outdoor toilets. *Khrushchevka* flats (Figure 3) are five-storey apartment blocks constructed under the leadership of Nikita Khrushchev in his campaign to provide inexpensive mass housing, starting in the 1950s, with standardized designs, usually having small bathrooms and kitchens. From the early 1960s these types of housing blocks represented the modernization of the urban landscape (Crowley and Reid 2002, 14). The *vremianka* (Figure 4) is a substandard private dwelling that people have built with poor-quality construction materials such as mud bricks. This is the cheapest renting option, and poorer *priezzhie* such as manual workers in the construction sector live in *vremiankas*, without basic amenities. Subsistence farming in urban garden plots is usually situated next to such *vremiankas*. There is a stigma of poverty associated with these dwellings, and thus in Astana it is illegal to keep livestock in these city-centre properties (Alexander, Buchli, and Humphrey 2007). There are also informal settlements, ignored by officials and mostly located on the edges of Astana, with similar housing of mud brick. One of the goals of the city municipality is to get rid of these types of private dwellings, which are the antithesis of what constitutes modern and world standards. In fact, the city administration has put a two-metre-high wall along the streets in front of such dwellings located in the centre. These walls are covered in pictures depicting future construction projects to replace the old *vremiankas*.

Figure 3. Khrushchevka type flats in the 'old town' of Astana built during Khrushchev's mass housing campaign (photo by author, 2009).

Figure 4. A vremianka dwelling offering rooms for rent. Poorer newcomers usually stayed in them (photo by author, 2009).

In the beginning, newcomers prefer to share flats with friends and relatives, but later they usually become confident enough to move out and live with strangers. Collective renting allows newcomers to integrate quickly into the city, since many find themselves in a similar situation. New friendships can allow the formation of important social networks, which can be used to gain employment. In this regard, my flat-mates sought help from new friends rather than from their relatives in Astana. Some did not even inform relatives of their arrival. As one woman from a nearby village said, 'We haven't told relatives that we are here; first we need to stand on our own feet, and then we'll tell them. But nobody has even bothered to ask.' On several occasions Dilnaz helped me renew my migration card in Astana, and her work contacts were very helpful. Likewise, she helped other flat-mates get a *propiska*. These were often short-term, small favours for fees, without the need of reciprocity or future commitment. Astana has such a mixture of newcomers that new friendship and alliances form as quickly as they dissolve again. This instability of social relations was not seen as negative as such, but was attributed to Astana's flow and urban dynamics. Although socializing among tenants took place, it was rather superficial and temporary. Still, friendships were made, and mutual support often developed. My flat-mates borrowed money from each other when needed. Sometimes they went to socialize together in cafes or bars.

Like Alima, Raima, a young Kazakh woman in her twenties, was trying hard to find a way to establish her life anew in Astana. She managed to find a job there with a stable salary despite numerous unsuccessful efforts and initial hardships. She lived together with five others in a shared three-room *khrushchevka* in the old part of town. Although she could not afford better housing, her salary was enough to cover her basic living expenses. She could afford to go out with friends to bars and restaurants from time to time. Crucially, Raima appreciated her freedom to date and socialize with no control or pressure from her parents. For instance, her boyfriend was a Russian man in his late thirties who was a divorcé with two children, and likewise was a newcomer in Astana. She had also experienced personal growth and valued her experience. She came from the northern part of Kazakhstan, and spoke only Russian, but in Astana her best friend was from Chimkent, in southern Kazakhstan. Reflecting on her life in Astana, Raima said:

> Here in Astana you are on your own. I have such a feeling sometimes that no one cares about you or what you do, really. You come here and you must organize your life, and no one will hinder you, nor will anyone help you.

Not anticipating the hardships upon her arrival to their full extent, she learned to solve her problems alone. She said that one needs to adapt new circumstances. Raima recalled that she had wanted to try something new and test her skills three years before when she had arrived in Astana. Her goals were radically different back then, but Raima claimed that she still achieved what she had now by relying on herself. She concluded:

> Salaries are higher here of course. And I think in Astana I was able for the first time in my life to fully be independent and take care of myself. And in addition to that, I could help out my parents money-wise like many others do here. So it really was independence from parents.

It was a valuable experience about independence. Clearly, Raima's early expectations were not fully realized, but she claimed that her 'initial hopes and dreams were replaced by new ones'. Likewise, Alima was not ready to give up her aspirations easily, as she concluded about moving to Astana:

> I do not regret it at all. On the contrary, I made a good decision and feel very proud. Before, if someone told me that I would move away from my parents, and start over again in a new city, renting a shared flat with total strangers, I would never believe it! My friends also thought that it was wishful thinking.

Thus, shared flats were cheaper and also offered freedom and independence to many in Astana. Moreover, there was a temporary community feeling with other tenants who found themselves in a similar situation. As Alima stated, sharing was tolerated, and if there was a conflict with other tenants she could change flats any time. In this process, those like Alima learned to be flexible and integrate discrepancies as 'normal', which characterizes the liminal experiences of newcomers.

In this sense, in the end, despite complaining about the unaffordable housing, many renters reproduce the homeownership discourse. Saule, a single mother in her late thirties, wished that not only state employees were eligible for state housing but at the same time did not expect any assistance or support from the state:

> I never heard of any help with rental housing from the state, to be honest. I did not hear, I do not rely on the state. I am on my own, I am telling you I never depend on anyone, I only count on my efforts. For example, I am not going to blame the government or someone else, because everything depends on a person. ... But I am telling you, if something does not work, I blame myself. I look for reasons and mistakes that I did, that's why I think it all depends on you. ... Yes, housing is expensive everywhere. But there are people who earn enough and buy houses. So we can do it too, I suppose. We can! ... My salary is enough for me. If people spent their money wisely they would have enough. People manage to live for 30,000 tenge, and even for 15,000 tenge [US$ 100]. ... I think I will manage, in five years, maybe, to get a flat, hopefully.

She guesses it will be five years before she achieves the dream of owning a house. Her suggestion that people should spend money wisely means that one needs to save up and be ready to sacrifice personal material comfort, as she does at the moment, living in crowded flats sharing a rented room with four people. Saule could afford better housing conditions but she chose not to and was saving money. Furthermore, powered with self-reliance, she was thinking she wanted to find a second job when I met her at a job fair in Astana. With the second job she could afford to take out a home loan and bring her son from the village, where her mother was taking care of him. Convinced that possibilities to earn more money exist in Astana, she told her story of how three years before she had left her job as a village teacher and worked her way up from a cleaning lady to an engineer in Astana. She mentioned that her relatives helped her find a job, but without her hard work it would not have been possible. She had practically no free time. In this context, those who complained about high rents or other difficulties did not find a great deal of empathy, and simply were seen as unfit to adapt and cope.

This attitude of self-reliance becomes apparent in the over-identification of many newcomers with the Astana discourse of modernization while trying to realize their goals and ambitions. Astana's discourse of the 'city of the future' supports a neoliberal subjectivity where one can succeed primarily based on individual risk taking and self-reliance, as seen in Saule's example. Bissenova (2012, 118) also notes that:

Much as in the United States, Kazakhstan has acquired a neo-liberal social vision and a set of personal dream worlds (not unlike 'the American Dream') that, together, have been a culprit in, and have significantly contributed to, the creation of the housing bubble and the ensuing meltdown.

In this connection, the image of Astana produced and circulated by the media (hyper-real Astana) denies the actual material conditions and diversity (Laszczkowski 2011, 85). Therefore, when encountering a discrepancy between the hyper-real Astana and the lived reality as seen in renting conditions, many newcomers are disenchanted. But as Laszczkowski (2012) also argues, in the end these critical views do not transcend the modernization project of the state. For instance, the renting situation only increases the desire for ownership of spacious new apartments.

Landlords and *propiska*

In Kazakhstan one is legally allowed to sublet his or her apartment as a private landlord, and the revenue is taxed at 10% as additional earnings. However, if the revenue exceeds a certain amount, or if additional persons are hired on a permanent basis, the landlords must legally register themselves as private entrepreneurs, and pay 2–3% of the profit gained by tenancy agreements (E.gov 2015). The final option is to register as a legal entity or corporation and pay a 20% revenue tax. Landlords who fail to declare revenues and pay taxes are subject to administrative punishments such as fines. Since regulation and enforcement are weak, most rental housing remains in the shadows, and there are no accurate data on the extent of the rental market. This situation creates a highly profitable, unregulated market, as in many post-Soviet countries, where the legislation and regulation of rental housing are slow and weak and only starting to develop. Therefore, the private rental sector largely remains informal and undocumented because of ease of tax evasion and lack of hard rent controls (Dübel, Brzeski, and Hamilton 2006). As in mature Western market economies, the demand for private rentals is especially high for the young and mobile. Higher incomes have driven up rents in the attractive cities such as capitals and major post-socialist cities. Rental supply in these countries is usually much smaller than in Western economies, but rental housing is growing (Dübel, Brzeski, and Hamilton 2006). In Kazakhstan, too, the rental market is mostly in the hands of private homeowners.

In the cases of shared flats, tenants usually do not have written tenancy agreements, and all matters are settled by informal negotiations and agreements. Dilnaz, my flatmate, who was the main tenant, had no written contract with the owner of the apartment. The landlord trusted Dilnaz, and their relations were based on verbal agreement only. The same was true for the relationship between Dilnaz and us, her sub-tenants. We never actually met our landlord. Dilnaz herself was a local, but she did not wish to live with her mother and chose to rent instead. She was a native of Tselinograd, a so-called *mestnyi* (local). This status gave her a number of advantages over newcomers, such as having a real local registration (*propiska*), and with that she gained the local landlord's trust more easily. At the beginning of each month Dilnaz collected money from us and paid the rent. Dilnaz exercised almost unlimited authority in our flat, as she could ask any of us to leave the flat at any time. Such arrangements are very risky for tenants as well as landlords, since neither have legal protection of rights or obligations. Landlords are not protected with the stability and security of rental payments. The payments may be delayed, or damage could be done to the property; no deposits are paid as security measures. On the other hand, tenants do not always get high-quality housing for the high rents they pay, and they can be asked to leave suddenly, without prior notice. Landlords do not always undertake maintenance repairs and do not promise stability of prices or duration of the renting period. My flat-mates complained about previous landlords who had cheated them by taking payment of rent in advance, then renting the promised apartments to other tenants. Meanwhile, the government has started to pay more attention to the rental sector to better protect landlords as well as tenants. At present, evictions take place based on court rules, and the process lasts up to three months, during which the tenant stays in the flat without paying rent (Vermenichev 2014). These conflicts between tenants and landlords happen quite often.

Propiska, an administrative system of registration, was introduced in 1932 in the Soviet Union to control internal migration, which permitted a holder of a *propiska* to work in a given town and reside at the specific address (Hatcher and Thieme 2015). It was part of the internal passport system, which also guaranteed that the citizen had rights and benefits (Hatcher and Thieme 2015). Every person was registered at a particular address, and in accordance with registered residency he or she had access to employment, primary and secondary education, health care and other social benefits. Several reasons seem to lie behind the logic of *propiska*. It was to keep rural dwellers 'tied' to the land and keep them from moving to cities – and it was a repression instrument to keep unwanted individuals under control and away from the cities (Morton 1980). Only later was *propiska* directly linked with payment of social benefits and access to health care. With time, in the light of differences between urban spaces and the countryside in terms of living conditions, the city *propiska* became a privilege and hard to attain, and depended on getting a job in the city.

Post-Soviet independent Kazakhstan formally declared the institution of *propiska* unconstitutional and infringing on citizens' rights to move and reside freely within the country, and replaced it with mandatory registration of place of residence (*registratsiya po mestu prozhivania*). Explaining the difference between the Soviet *propiska* system and the current registration system, the vice-chairman of the Migration Police Department, Sainov, said that the Soviet *propiska* had an authorizing nature (*razreshitelniy kharakter*) while the present registration has a notificatory nature (*uvedomitelniy kharakter*) (Akkyly 2012). This measure was meant to change the restrictive nature of *propiska* to that of a citizen-friendly registration seen primarily as a person's legal address for contact and planning purposes. Similar changes followed in other former Soviet republics; as Hatcher (2011, 8–9) says, 'The former *propiska* system was altered to conform to international best practice (and human rights legislation) on internal freedom of movement.' Hence, there is a difference between registration systems that are notificatory, in comparison with those that directly restrict internal movement.

Despite the abolishment of the *propiska* in Kazakhstan as such, the new administrative system of registration is nothing less than an uncanny reinstatement, keeping most of its old functions. Free movement is allowed, but one still has to be registered at a temporary or permanent address. Thus, it is not surprising that most people continue to call it *propiska*. All my respondents in Astana referred to it as *propiska* as well. When they move, citizens must unregister from the previous place of residence, and within 10 days register themselves at the new address. The Population Service Centre (Tsentr Obsluzhivania

Naselenia) is the responsible local institution (under the Internal Affairs Agency) where citizens must be registered in a book of registration and renew their registration accordingly. Moreover, the process of registration itself is bureaucratically overburdened. Applicants have to unregister from the previous address and collect the needed papers for the new address. There are up to 10 required documents, including the original documents proving ownership of the property of the applicant or the agreement of tenancy if rented. In addition, the landlord must be present at the registration office with the applicant and provide his or her identity documents (Edilet 2014). Many landlords feel discouraged by such time-consuming procedures and refuse to register their tenants, and also to avoid paying more utility costs and taxes. In Astana the landlords and employers do not offer their tenants or employees any assistance with registration. Based on his research in Kyrgyzstan on *propiska* Hatcher (2015) argues that landlords avoid the formal tenancy agreements to protect their own property rights by making sure tenants remain invisible. Because of the legacy of *propiska*, homeowners are afraid that tenants could claim partial ownership of the property in addition to paying taxes. Under Soviet law it was hard to evict tenants who were registered in apartments, so many treated the apartments as theirs (Attwood 2010, 161).

But, crucially, those who lack this formal *propiska* are cut off from social security and must pay higher prices for social services in the private sector. When they were sick my flat-mates would go to private clinics and pay higher rates than in a state hospital. Recent work on the impact of the registration system on access to basic services concludes that 'In Kazakhstan's registration system, there is a direct link between a citizen's registration status and his or her access to basic public services, to the extent that lack of registration often makes this access impossible' (Kotova, Ishmukhambetova, and Asanova 2010). Concretely, the report lists barriers in gaining access to 'free emergency medical service, daycare and secondary education, welfare benefits, eligibility for civil status documents (passports, identification cards, driving licenses, etc.) employment issues, social and political life'. Thus *propiska* itself becomes a commodity, promising the holder access to jobs, security, medical insurance, and other provisions guaranteed by the state.

Since there are no restrictions on registrations being issued in cities in post-Soviet Kazakhstan, the influx of internal migrants in Astana is not restricted or regulated. Almaty is an exception. There, restrictions on registration were introduced in 2010 on the basis of sanitation concerns (Akkyly 2012). Since many were sceptical about the transfer of the capital, officials were worried that the new capital would not appeal to new residents, and hence encouraged people to move to get higher salaries, a promising career in state bureaucracy, and housing subsidies for government and the public sector. This proved to be a successful strategy, and with the construction boom, the new capital attracted not only skilled professionals but also thousands of unskilled workers from all over Kazakhstan and beyond – particularly from the neighbouring Central Asian states. However, most of the *priezzhie* living in shared rented flats in Astana are not registered. They have to face this problem from the time of their arrival and need to address it throughout their stay, if they have not managed to find a solution for long-term registration. Almost all of my respondents mentioned facing difficulties obtaining a local *propiska*. As, Nurzhan, one of my respondents, eloquently put it, 'Without *propiska* and your own flat you cannot do anything here, these two issues decide everything.' Newcomers are frustrated when they cannot get a *propiska*, because without it many face restrictions and difficulties initially finding employment and getting access to social benefits. Saule, a young woman, explained that at first she could not work because she had no *propiska*. 'Nobody [landlords] wants to give you *propiska*. Last year when I lost my passport I had to buy a *propiska* for three days for 15,000 tenge (US$ 100) just to apply for a new passport. We bought a *propiska* from a private person through the newspaper ads.' In this way most *priezzhie* find a temporary solution, which is to buy a temporary *propiska* from a third party when needed.

In connection with fake and real *propiska,* Reeves, in her research on Central Asian labour migrants in Russia, notes that the trouble begins when migrants buy a presumably real *propiska* but it turns out to be a fake when checked by the police. It is extremely hard to differentiate between 'clean' and 'fake' registration when the fake usually looks exactly the same (Reeves 2013). In Astana I did not hear of a similar problem, as the price of a real *propiska* is much higher than a false one. However, it is possible that some newcomers who are new and have no experience get cheated and buy *propiska* which turn out to be forged. A false *propiska* is needed at the beginning to show to potential employers, who cannot judge easily whether it is real. Prices on the open market for *propiska* depend on authenticity. For 5000 tenge (US$ 33) one can buy a fake *propiska*. This type of outright fake *propiska* is a forged one, which does not correspond to any real address or is based on falsified documents. The real *propiska* is more expensive, as seen in the above example with Saule, who bought a *propiska* with a valid address for three days for 15, 000 tenge (US$ 100). But even with a valid registration there is very little guarantee; for example, a person might be no longer registered at the given address after buying a registration. In Astana one sees numerous ads for *propiska*; these leaflets sometimes occupy the whole advertisement board at bus stops, promising all sorts of arrangements. Their visual omnipresence is a vital reminder of the demand for *propiska* on the market.

The authorities are aware of the problem, and efforts to eradicate the illegal *propiska* market are also under way. In 2007 the Kazakh authorities attempted to simplify the process of registration by broadening the range of options for registration to include additional types of housing such as dormitories, resort housing, hotels, *dacha*s (summer houses), and most significantly a place of employment (Uchet Online Directory 2007). Previously, citizens were to be strictly registered at residential dwellings such as private houses or flats. Moreover, since 2011 those who fail to register within 10 days and live without registration for longer than three months are subject to administrative fines of 10,000 tenge (US$ 66); before three months one gets a warning (Akkyly 2012). In 2010 about 140,000 citizens were fined in Kazakhstan for violating registration rules, according to the Ministry of Internal Affairs (Akkyly 2012). The latest addition to the law on *propiska,* in effect as of 1 January 2015, stipulates that not only will residents living without registration be fined, but also homeowners who agree to register multiple people at their property (Akkyly 2012). Officials recognize that a large proportion of the internal migrants in big cities do not live where they are registered.

Elderly and renting: becoming 'homeless'

Thomassen (2014, 7) argues that liminality explains nothing in itself; it just happens. What differs is the way individuals react to these experiences. The outcomes are open to multiple directions. As mentioned, there is a risky tendency to romanticize and celebrate liminal experiences in postmodern consumer societies; such interpretations are far removed from the original meaning of liminality for individuals and society, argues Thomassen (8). Liminality in itself, he argues, is not something to be wished for, as the cases of marginalized renters in Astana seem to confirm. Viewed from this perspective, it is a mistake to romanticize collective renting as a desired end, since newcomers hope to own their own housing and live with their family, enjoying stability, not having to move constantly. Concretely, for renters protracted renting means being stuck in a transitional phase, with no prospect of buying a house and not being able to return to their home towns. In this light, the experiences of migrants and refugees have been identified as liminal where 'in-between-ness' is not a liberation but a constraint, because they are in 'suspension, limbo, transit, non-places, and marginality' (Andrews and Roberts 2012, 4).

This transitory state becomes apparent when we look at the similar renting experiences for the elderly in Astana, as the following case with Ainagul shows. If renting is tolerable for the younger generation who are unstable in their social status, it becomes a stigma for the elderly newcomers. Ainagul, a woman in her fifties who had come from the small town of Arkalyk to Astana four years earlier with her husband and four grown children, still struggled with paying high rents:

> We thought that we would get a flat, *propiska*, that we will have housing. We have lived here for four years now and still rent a place. We can't even dare to dream about getting a flat because none of us works for the government or public sector. My children were not able to get higher education. I am already in my pre-retirement age, no chance. ... All the flats are expensive. I rent a place here not far from work, I walk to work. ... But we are paying a huge amount of money for rent. Too expensive, just too expensive here! Our salary is small. ... We came because of the construction. We thought there is work here and there will be housing since they [government] are building houses. But not everyone can afford them. People thought: 'Wow, construction! And we will also get something' – young people and young families had high hopes. But it is not easy. Those who had money bought houses, or took flats on *ipoteka*. ... We are now just surviving here, what can you do?! We eat up what we earn and still I cannot afford to eat meat, very rarely that I eat meat. ... And my situation now – I have no home, nothing, I am homeless, in short. At the age of 52 I am left without a home.

Her situation was very precarious, as she was often short of money, paying more than 60% of her salary for rent. She belongs to a new, marginalized group who consider themselves 'homeless'. The move to Astana for this elderly woman was traumatic since she had endured a complicated surgery, during which her husband left her for a much younger woman who had her own flat. The husband could not take all the difficulties with moving in and out of multiple apartments. They had had four children together and had lived together for 35 years. Ainagul was renting a room with other sub-tenants in a shared flat, but despite sharing a common kitchen, toilet and bathroom, they were strangers to each other and had little communication. The other sub-tenants were young families, and they had little in common with Ainagul. This starkly contrasted with the social life of my flat-mates in our shared flat. The relatives of Ainagul's husband kept in contact with her ex-husband, but they never visited Ainagul. Furthermore, the elderly like Ainagul are unable to invite guests or relatives and feel left out of their extended family support network. Often they cannot invite guests over because there is not enough space to host them, making them feel ashamed of their housing situation. In this light, homeownership becomes the basis of security and social acceptance. As Bissenova (2012, 134) also points out, housing is crucial 'to maintain one's identity, privacy, and social status' in Kazakhstan. This means that the elderly and middle-aged newcomers who want to start a new life in Astana face prejudice if they fail to obtain housing. In the case of Ainagul, she faced double marginalization: first as a divorced woman and second as a 'homeless' person who had to rent. Thus, while the younger generation is embracing the 'uniqueness' and freedoms that Astana offers, the older generation feels lost and unable to manage the stress of constantly moving. Against this background, where private property defines whether a person is rich or poor, renting increases not only the feeling of material deprivation but also symbolic status deprivation.

Similar to the elderly, those who move to Astana with families and especially young children cannot accept renting as a long-term solution. And those who want to start a family are likewise constrained by the absence of housing. Some of the single women in their late twenties I met were under pressure to get married and have children, but they complained that in order to give birth they needed an apartment. If the couple secure housing, they can stay in Astana, and if not they have to go back to their home towns or other regions where housing is more affordable. Therefore, renting offers only a temporary solution and is accepted by society as a necessary stage for mostly the young and unmarried while they are studying or early in their careers. No one wishes to stay in 'transition' forever, as the ultimate goal is stability and immobility rather being in constant movement. Without proper reintegration, liminality is dangerous since it can lead to feelings of alienation and loss of being at home. As Thomassen (2014, 17) succinctly put it:

> If moving into liminality can best be captured as a loss of home and a ritualized rupture with the world as we know it, any movement out of liminality must somehow relate to a sort of home-coming, a feeling at home *in* the world and *with* the world, at the levels of both thought and practice.

Conclusion: the liminality of renting in Astana

In Astana newcomers were searching for their share of luck in the new capital of Kazakhstan. For many it was an obvious choice in the light of Kazakhstan's booming economy and flourishing new capital, which promised a jump into a future full of hope and economic opportunities in the 'city of the future'. Indeed, the sight of constant construction, glimmering hotels and shopping malls, and the sound of bulldozers and cranes, communicated a message of progress and prosperity. Newcomers made up an army of renters, unstable, vulnerable and dissolving, but also coming together again. Mostly occupying the unstable private and service sectors, their livelihoods were insecure. Many had been living in Astana for several years, but their mode of living made them neither permanent residents nor newcomers. They had no registration, no proper accommodation, and also were constantly searching for better jobs and higher salaries. Refusing to leave when difficulties arose, many remained in the city and tried harder to succeed. The desire to live in the capital and find a well-paid job united them. A few did succeed and were able to realize their goals and ambitions, while many others were struggling to live up to the 'Astana lifestyle', as was the case with my flat-mates. Astana still remained an enchanting city, even if their dreams had not been realized so far. They hoped that one day they would manage to buy a flat. In the meantime, they had to cope with renting in shared flats. Certainly, the dream of homeownership and the reality of renting are quite apart from each other, so that no one is pleased to pay high rents for a prolonged period of time.

In this article, I have showed that renting is a highly unstable and transitory (liminal) mode of living, which nonetheless has become accepted as a part of living in the capital and as a part of urban living. The liminal experiences of renters in Astana contain both aspects: the positive qualities such as the freedom to move, gain independence and experiment with new life modes; and the negative side such as instability, uncertainty, ambiguity, being in limbo, and coping with disappointments. The younger generation accepts renting because it is perceived as only a temporary stage until one settles down and can renew one's social networks after gaining more stability. For the time being, renting allows tenants flexible participation in the 'city of the future' since they can leave and come back any time they want. The liminal stage might be quite long for some, and even longer for those with no prospects of getting a house. For my flat-mates this meant that their transition into adulthood and starting a family was postponed. For the elderly, liminal housing has disrupted their entire social status. For them, Astana's urban space is 'foreign', where old social norms and values are becoming less observed. Consequently, housing becomes vital for a person to feel like a worthy member of society. Some can become stuck in a permanent transition, like the divorced Ainagul, with no prospects at all of buying a house. Inability to secure housing becomes a sign of failure and draws social stigma as an unreliable person. Thus, despite the stories of independence and freedom, the dark side of liminality in shared flats becomes prevalent as renters increasingly feel trapped and frustrated.

In many cities in developing countries, a great proportion of the urban population rely on renting as a preferred tenure choice since it allows them to move to cities temporarily in search of work or better prospects; and it is not only low-income groups that benefit from renting (Dübel, Brzeski, and Hamilton 2006). Similarly, newcomers in Astana – especially the young and mobile – who cannot purchase housing depend on the rental market, a fact that allows them to be flexible while pursuing their study or career goals. But Kazakhstan still lacks a comprehensive national housing policy, and relies too much on market institutions such as home loans to encourage homeownership. Moreover, as mentioned, the state housing policy supports the already privileged group of civil servants, putting them on the same level as low-income and vulnerable groups, who are in greater need of adequate housing. Finally, the rental market and tenants are ignored to a large extent by the government, though most of the newcomers in Astana rely on renting to cope with the shortage of affordable housing. Instead of demanding affordable rents with better quality and tenancy agreements, the renters just work harder and hope to purchase housing in the future. The rental market is seen as benefiting private landlords, who are only interested in making a profit, while offering as little protection as possible to tenants. Renters feel powerless to influence or change the rental market. In this article, I have paid attention to both the liberating and the dark sides of the liminal state in the context of housing. The negative side becomes dominant when the dream of obtaining housing becomes even more distant.

Acknowledgments

I thank Philipp Schröder for invaluable feedback and comments. This work is based on fieldwork material conducted during 2009–2010 for my dissertation project on Astana. I am grateful for an Erasmus Mundus Scholarship from CASIA (Central Asia Student International Academic exchange with EU).

Disclosure statement

No potential conflict of interest was reported by the author.

References

Akkyly, S. 2012. "V Kazakhstane vosobnovili institut Propiski." [Kazakhstan has re-Established the Institute of Propiska Control]. Accessed August 2, 2012. http://rus.azattyq.org/content/propiska_mvd_sainov_ergalieva_nazkhanov_baiseitova/24474434.html

Alexander, C., V. Buchli, and C. Humphrey, eds. 2007. *Urban Life in Post-Soviet Asia*. London: CRC Press.

Andrews, H., and L. Roberts, eds. 2012. *Liminal Landscapes: Travel, Experience and Spaces in-between*. London and New York: Routledge.

Attwood, L. 2010. *Gender and Housing in Soviet Russia Private Life in a Public Space*. Manchester: Manchester University Press.

Bissenova, A. 2012. "Post-Socialist Dreamworlds: Housing Boom and Urban Development in Kazakhstan." PhD diss., Cornell University.

Crowley, D., and S. E. Reid, eds. 2002. *Socialist Spaces: Sites of Everyday Life in the Eastern Bloc*. Oxford: Berg.

Dübel, H. J., W. J. Brzeski and E. Hamilton. 2006. "Rental Choice and Housing Policy Realignment in Transition: Post-Privatization Challenges in the Europe and Central Asia Region." Working Paper, 3884. World Bank Policy Research.

Edilet (Republican Center of Legal Information). 2014. "О некоторых вопросах документирования и регистрации населения Республики Казахстан." [Clarifying a few issues with documenting and registering the population]. Accessed February 1, 2014. http://adilet.zan.kz/rus/docs/V1100007324#z504

E.gov (Electronic Government of the Republic of Kazakhstan). 2015. "Nalogi pri sdache nedvijimosti v arendu." 2015. [Taxes for leasing private property]. Accessed June 1, 2015. http://egov.kz/wps/portal/ContentcontentPath=/egovcontent/citizens/tax_finance/taxation/article/nalogi_za_arendu&lang=ru#

Gerasimova, K. 2002. "Public Privacy in the Soviet Communal Apartment." *In Socialist Spaces: Sites of Everyday Life in the Eastern Bloc*, edited by D. Crowley and S. E. Reid, 207–230. Oxford: Berg.

Gilbert, A. 2008. "Slums, Tenants and Home-ownership: On Blindness to the Obvious." *International Development Planning Review* 30, i–x.

Hatcher, C. 2011. "Making Citizens Legible: Legacies of Population Registration Systems in Post-Socialist Cities." Working Paper. October. Switzerland, Social Research Centre, University of Zürich.

Hatcher, C. 2015. "Globalising homeownership: housing privatisation schemes and the private rental sector in post-socialist Bishkek, Kyrgyzstan." *International Development Planning Review* 37 (4): 467–486.

Hatcher, C., and S. Thieme. 2015. "Institutional Transition: Internal Migration, The Propiska, and Post-Socialist Urban Change in Bishkek, Kyrgyzstan." *Urban Studies* doi:10.1177/0042098015587252.

Köppen, B. 2013. "The Production of a New Eurasian Capital on the Kazakh Steppe: Architecture, Urban Design, and Identity in Astana." *Nationalities Papers* 41 (4): 590–605. doi:10.1080/00905992.2013.767791

Kotova, T., L. Ishmukhambetova, and J. Asanova. 2010. "The Impact of the Registration System on Access To Basic Services in Kazakhstan". Executive Summary. Danish Church Aid.

Laszczkowski, M. 2011. "Building the Future: Construction, Temporality, and Politics in Astana." *Focaal* 60: 77–92. doi:10.3167/fcl.2011.600107

Laszczkowski, M. 2012. "" City of the Future": Built Space and Social Change in Astana, Kazakhstan." PhD diss., Philos. Fak. I, Martin-Luther-Univ. Halle-Wittenberg Halle/Saale.

Morton, H. 1980. "Who Gets What, When and How? Housing in the Soviet Union." *Soviet Studies* 32 (2): 235–259.

Reeves, M. 2013. "Clean Fake: Authenticating Documents and Persons in Migrant Moscow." *American Ethnologist* 40 (3): 508–524. doi:10.1111/amet.12036

Rigi, J. 2003. "The Conditions of Post-Soviet Dispossessed Youth and Work in Almaty, Kazakhstan." *Critique of Anthropology* 23 (1): 35–49. doi:10.1177/0308275X03023001811

Rolnik, R. 2011. "Report of the Special Rapparteur on Adequate Housing as a Component of the Right to an adequate standart of living, and on the right to non-discrimination in this context." United Nations General Assembly, 19 January. Accessed April 8, 2015. http://www.un.kz/en/articles/1/15.jsp

Thomassen, B. 2014. *Liminality and the Modern: Living through the In-between*. Farnham: Ashgate.

Turner, V. 1967. *The Forest of Symbols: Aspects of Ndembu Ritual*. Ithaca: Cornell University Press.

Uchet Online Directory. 2007. "Soglasno Postanovleniu Pravitel'stva KR, grazhdane Kazakshtana ne imeushie propiski, mogut zaregistrirovatsia po mestu raboty, v svoem office." [According to the New Rule, Citizens of Kazakhstan, Who Do Not Have propiska Can Register at the Place of Work, at their Office]. Accessed February 15, 2015. http://www.uchet.kz/news/detail.php?EID = 10965

UN-Habitat. 2003. *Rental Housing: An Essential Option for the Urban Poor in Developing Countries*. Nairobi: UN-Habitat.

Vermenichev, A. 2014. "Metry-prokaty. Rynok arendnogo jilya v Kazakhstane ne reshaet socialnyh zadach I nujdaetsia v 'perezagruzke." [Meters and rents. Renting Market in Kazakhstan Cannot Solve Social Issues and Needs 'Recharging']. Retrieved June 3, 2015. https://sk.kz/mobile/read_news/4562010

Yessenova, S. 2010. "Borrowed Places: Eviction Wars and Property Rights Formalization in Kazakhstan." *Research in Economic Anthropology* 30: 11–45. doi:10.1108/S0190-1281(2010)0000030005

'Only by learning how to live together differently can we live together at all': readability and legibility of Central Asian migrants' presence in urban Russia

Emil Nasritdinov

Anthropology Department, American University of Central Asia, Bishkek, Kyrgyzstan

ABSTRACT
This paper questions the effectiveness and usefulness of the Russian government's policies of migrant integration. Using a unique combination of ethnographic research methods (observations, interviews and survey) with methods from psychology (cognitive mapping) and urban studies (GIS mapping), I depict the presence of Central Asian migrants and their interaction with local long-term residents in two cities of the Russian Federation: Kazan and Saint Petersburg. On the basis of my findings, I argue that the readability (defined as the ease with which the city can be 'read' and understood) and legibility (defined as the degree to which individual components of an urban environment are recognizable by their appearance) of urban space in Kazan have positive effects on the relationship between these two communities, while the ambiguity and uncertainty of urban identity in Saint Petersburg make the life of migrants very vulnerable and unpredictable, and result in the growth of xenophobic views among the local residents. This allows me to argue that the policy of migrant integration will be more successful if it is built on learning to live with differences, instead of trying to 'Russify' migrants or create various forms of supra-ethnic identity.

Introduction

Riding the late-evening metro train in Saint Petersburg one day, I was astonished to see two very contrasting posters next to each other. The one on top depicted a chalkboard drawing of a schoolboy, a labyrinth of streets in Saint Petersburg and the boy's home. The text suggested: 'A proper route home can help avoid danger. Think it through with your child.' The image below included a smiling girl in a traditional costume, with the text: 'Welcome! Kazan is a place of special hospitality.' The girl was inviting metro riders to attend the University Olympic Games held in Kazan in the summer of 2013. My astonishment emerged from the realization of how well these two images, accidentally posted next to each other, represented the main idea of my research: that senses of security and hospitality are embedded in the urban experience and mutual perception of two distinct groups – the local residents of two Russian cities, Kazan and Saint Petersburg, and the Central Asian traders who also work and live there (Figure 1).

Figure 1. Photo taken on the metro train in Saint Petersburg, June 2012.

Nearly 5 million migrant workers from Central Asia work in Russia today (Dmitriev and Pyaduhov 2011; Abashin, 2012). Most of them are concentrated in large Russian cities, such as Moscow, Saint Petersburg and Yekaterinburg. In its scale, labour migration to Russia currently is second to the United States (Laruelle 2013). A declining Russian population and the demand for labour on the one hand, and poverty and unemployment in Central Asia on the other, has resulted in a significant Central Asian presence in urban Russia. This phenomenon is attracting attention from experts, policy analysts, state officials and academic scholars. Laruelle (2013) points out that today most of the academic research on migration from Central Asia to Russia is done within the field of sociology and anthropology and studied either at the macro level (quantitative studies) or at the micro level (ethnographies of everyday life of migrants). Meso-level studies are missing. I would add that there are many economic studies of Central Asian migration, but very few contributions from other fields. This research attempts to partially fill in these gaps. On the one hand it brings in methodologies from psychology and urban studies, such as cognitive and GIS (geographic information systems) mapping, respectively, thus expanding the traditional palette of migration research instruments; on the other hand, its main object of study becomes an urban neighbourhood – a meso-level unit that is smaller than the national macro level or that of urban statistics, but larger than an individual migrant's life narrative.

Abashin (2012) proposes that what it means to be a migrant is shaped differently in different parts of Russia and that putting everything under one denominator is a big mistake. Therefore, in this contribution, I draw my main analytical insights from a rigorous comparison of two cities in order to see how contextual differences affect migration experiences.

The conceptual inspiration for this paper is drawn partly from Reeves's (2013) concept of the 'space of uncertainty' – the product of a specific 'mode of governance in urban Russia that thrives less on rendering subjects legible than on working the space of ambiguity between life and law' (p. 508). Reeves examines how a 'boundary between being legible and illegible to the state is blurred and fraught with social and moral uncertainty' (p. 509), and how the uncertainty and ambiguity of Central Asian migrant workers' legal status breeds suspicion, racist thinking and everyday humiliation. Abashin (2012) develops a similar discourse on the ambiguity of the term 'migrant' in contemporary Russian legislation and public discourse. He shows that there is no one agreed-on definition of who is a migrant, that different competing classifications are used interchangeably depending on who uses them, and that such ambiguity eventually results in associating 'migrants' with ethnically or racially different 'others' and with various 'threats' and 'dangers' for Russian society (Abashin 2012; Mukomel 2013).

What I take from these studies is the detrimental character of uncertainty and ambiguity that characterize the interaction between migrants and locals, between migrants and the state, and among migrants themselves. I apply these categories (uncertainty and ambiguity) to the analysis of urban space and I contrast them with readability and legibility as positive and beneficial features of the urban environment. Readability is the ease with which the city can be 'read' and understood, while legibility means the degree to which individual components of an urban environment are recognizable by their appearance. For example, in the same study mentioned above, Reeves shows that familiarity with urban space narrows the gap between 'documentary' and 'real' legality for migrant workers and reduces their exposure to certain risks. On the basis of my research findings, I argue that indistinctness and ambiguity in the socio-spatial organization of a city only reinforce the uncertainty and fear of the 'other', while clarity and legibility can make it easier for communities 'in conflict' to successfully navigate urban space and feel safer in it.

By putting forward this argument, I am making a case for the reinforcement of distinctive cultural and spatial identities and for building on differences instead of similarities. This argument is based on Montgomery, Seligman and Wasserfall's concept of learning to live with differences instead of overcoming them: 'Only by learning how to live together differently can we live together at all.'[1] This is a case against the mainstream strategy of the Russian government and other organizations working with migrants – strategies which are predominantly motivated by the idea of integration of migrants and manifested in new laws and policies. In 2010 a special unit was created within the Federal Migration Service to foster the integration of migrants (Dmitriev and Pyaduhov, 2011). In 2012 two important policy documents[2] were introduced by the Russian government which identified the social and cultural adaptation and integration of migrants, and the formation of constructive relationships between migrants and the host community, as their main goals (Mukomel 2013). The Federal Migration Service started working with leaders of migrant diasporas, as well as with religious organizations, such as the Russian Orthodox Church, which is currently very active in offering Russian-language courses for migrants and developing various manuals to teach migrants how to live and behave properly in Russian society.[3]

In the last few years, the idea of the integration of migrants into Russian communities has also received significant attention from local Russian scholars and experts on migration (Ikontcev and Ivahnyuk 2013; Mukomel 2013). The vision of integration varies from scholar to scholar and ranges from recommendations for all migrants to learn how to live the Russian way, to more multicultural perspectives, which leave more room for the migrants' own cultures, languages and traditions. Yet, the general tendency in these reports is to promote the idea of a shared culture, which is expected to unite people of different ethnic groups. In many ways, this idea is reminiscent of the Soviet idea of *druzhba narodov* (Friendship of Peoples), where one supranational identity overarches ethnic differences (Sahadeo 2007). However, as Sahadeo shows, during Soviet times, in spite of people's friendship, Central Asian workers in Moscow and Leningrad were perceived as *chernye* (blacks) and faced discrimination. This is one reason why today as well few authors are optimistic about the potential of such integration. They identify a number of factors that create obstacles on the way to integration, some of which are structural, while others are related to the individual and communal characteristics of the migrant and host communities: strength and encapsulation of diasporic networks; duration of migrants' stay in Russia; language ability and education level of migrants; closed nature of the receiving society; economic difficulties; political instability; migration legislation; changing societal trends, from collectivism to individualism and competition; growing xenophobia and Russian nationalism; etc. The shared pessimism of these authors, a lack of confidence in the success of integration policies, and their very ambitious recommendations, such as to change the 'cultures' of both communities, once again put the whole idea of integration under a big question mark.

In my research I suggest looking at questions of integration and urban segregation from the point of view of an urban planner. I refer to Kevin Lynch and his book *Image of the City* (1960), in which he discusses how a city's image is constructed from various categories of physical elements and strongly argues for the readability of an urban environment as one of its main positive characteristics: the easier we can 'read' urban space and its semantics, the more comfortable we feel in the city. I suggest that we can expand Lynch's conceptualization to include the readability of urban socio-cultural 'text'. Segregation and socio-cultural distinctness of space is not necessarily bad; in some cities it helps us better understand and navigate the contested urban space, thus making everyday urban experience more comfortable. On the contrary, inability to comprehend the urban space and its socio-cultural organization creates cognitive dissonance for the urban dwellers and complicates their relationships with each other. In my study, I compare the readability and legibility of urban space in Kazan with the confusion and ambiguity of urban space in Saint Petersburg. Saint Petersburg is a modern, buzzing metropolis, whereas Kazan is a smaller town. Variations in 'readability' between these cities certainly have something to do with their demographic fabrics, which influence different types of urban experiences. However, I believe that there are other factors at play as well. To understand these, I use a diverse palette of research instruments: observations and mapping; in-depth semi-structured interviews; cognitive mapping; and GIS mapping.

The research team involved in this study walked and biked the streets of the two cities with the purpose of recording on the map all manifestations of Central Asian presence.[4] In Kazan, these were mostly cafes and restaurants with traditional Central Asian cuisine, while in Saint Petersburg there were also many Central Asians working in shops and non–Central Asian cafes and selling fruits.[5] In addition, we made observations on the markets in both cities. Another major block of research involved conducting interviews with both Central Asian traders and long-term urban residents.[6] The interviews were structured around the questions of their daily use and navigation of the city and around their perception of and contact with each other. It so happened that the easiest way to reach the Central Asian migrant community was through the market traders. Therefore, after a few initial attempts to connect to migrants in other professions, we decided to limit our occupational choice to traders. The three main ethnic groups of traders were Kyrgyz, Uzbek and Tajik; in this paper I will refer to all of them as Central Asians. I understand that this is a much-criticized generalization, for example by Abashin (2012). Still, since our main focus is not on ethnicity but on space and on the relationship with the host community, I opted for this larger classification.

Respondents were asked to draw cognitive maps of their respective cities on the basis of their familiarity and everyday experiences. Later, on a printed map, they were asked to indicate places where they live and work and places they frequently visit. While drawing they also elaborated on these daily practices and on the significance and meanings of certain places, and shared stories associated with important locations. The novelty of this research is in the innovative use of GIS software to visualize the cognitive and observational maps. Using GIS capabilities we visualized the answers of our respondents and the physical manifestations of migrant presence. We also visualized places and regions associated with migrants, and places and regions which both communities considered safe or dangerous. These visualizations helped us produce important insights and conclusions about the ways these two communities live and interact in the two cities, which I will discuss in the following sections.

Central Asian traders versus local residents and Kazan versus Saint Petersburg

In this section, I compare the two cities as regards the attitude of local residents and Central Asians towards each other, friendship ties between them, local residents' characterizations of Central Asian migrants and memories of interacting with them, and, finally, accounts of Central Asians' experiences in these cities. One major finding that runs through almost all of the analysis is that the relationship between migrants and locals in Kazan is more positive than it is in Saint Petersburg.

When we compare the attitude of local residents towards Central Asians in the two cities, we can point to some significant differences. We can notice that the majority of locals in Kazan are rather neutral, while in Saint Petersburg attitudes are more diverse: there are twice as many local respondents who perceive migrants negatively, but there are also twice as many who hold a positive attitude (Table 1). Kazan represents a more centrist model, which implies more stability, more tolerance and an unbiased attitude. Saint Petersburg embodies a more polarized attitude, with more opinions at the extreme ends of the spectrum. This means less stability and predictability, and more uncertainty for migrants, who are less sure about what to expect from the locals. In the context of growing xenophobia and nationalism in Russian society, a neutral attitude may indeed seem safer and more preferable for migrants.

Another important factor is friendship between these two communities. As it turns out, more local residents in Kazan (58%) have friends among Central Asians than in Saint

Table 1. Attitude of local residents towards Central Asians in two cities.

	Negative (%)	Neutral (%)	Positive (%)
Kazan	15	80	5
Saint Petersburg	30	60	10

Petersburg (37%). The average number of Central Asian friends per local resident in Kazan is also higher (3.7 versus 1.4). We could observe these kinds of friendship in Kazan's markets. Central Asian traders had many local Russian and Tatar friends, particularly within the trader community. Markets, as spaces of daily interaction of traders of diverse ethnic groups, develop a unique kind of solidarity and sense of belonging. We could observe the intimacy of interaction of market neighbours: traders often joked, teased each other, had lunch together, and looked after each other's merchandise when someone was away. During one of the Federal Migration Service raids, we observed a local Russian trader hiding his Central Asian market neighbour, who had no official registration, behind merchandise inside his own container. Traders in Kazan also shared stories of how they went for picnics together with local friends and invited them for celebrations. Such 'warm relationships' were more difficult to find in Saint Petersburg.

We asked local residents to share accounts of their real-life encounters with migrants or give more extensive comments. In Kazan, half of the accounts were positive and half negative. In Saint Petersburg, two-thirds of the accounts were negative. Saint Petersburg, being the cultural capital of Russia, has a significant layer of *intelligentsia* with progressive outlooks, who not only criticize the xenophobic nationalist discourse and sympathize with migrants, but also volunteer for various kinds of projects helping them with legal assistance or learning Russian. Two programmes implemented in the city are Tolerance-1 and Tolerance-2 (described later), which engage significant numbers of local residents in activities aiming to help migrants integrate. Local organizations like Memorial conduct much advocacy work supporting migrants of different ethnic groups. Yet, Saint Petersburg also has a larger share of local residents from the nationalist camp, many of them representatives of the younger generation (Rozanova 2012).

Finally, to compare the two cities we can look at the experiences of Central Asian migrants. The trend is the same: accounts in Kazan are more positive than in Saint Petersburg. Table 2 shows that while the numbers of negative and neutral accounts are similar, there are twice as many positive stories in Kazan.

Positive stories describe the achievements of migrants and their family members, different kinds of events in their life, the quality of living, etc. One trader boasted of the accomplishments of his son, who became such a successful soccer player in Kazan that he was invited to train for the Barcelona club in Spain. Another trader boasted that he had won four medals in wrestling while living in Kazan. Yet another trader described how his daughters won choreographic competitions and were given tickets to a resort on the Black Sea. Our respondents also shared many stories of economic achievements, such as purchasing apartments and cars. In Kazan particularly, purchasing an apartment was something common for many Central Asian traders. For several of them, Kazan also became a place where they met their future spouses.

There were many stories of positive interaction with locals. One Uzbek boy revealed how he had saved the life of a Russian boy who was almost drowning in a lake. Similarly, a Kyrgyz man described how they were driving to the city centre one day and saw a

Table 2. Experiences of Central Asians in Kazan and Saint Petersburg.

	Negative	Neutral	Positive
Kazan	8	4	39
Saint Petersburg	10	4	17

burning car; they stopped and saved the passengers. One Tajik trader described how he and his friends found a lost child under a bridge and then helped him find his parents. Another Tajik man spent four hours helping a Russian man dig through some trash in order to find a folder of important documents, which he had lost the night before while drinking with his friends. Perhaps less dramatic but just as important are stories that describe how respondents organize celebrations and meals, how they invite their friends from among local residents, and how they participate with them in various holidays organized in the city. Some respondents described how they try to respect people here, for example by offering them their seats on public transport. An Uzbek woman described that she had a very good neighbour across the staircase where she lives, and that they had become like family to each other. In some cases, relations move beyond friendship: one Tajik had fallen in love with a Russian woman and they had been in a relationship for two years. Also there was a Kyrgyz woman who married a local Russian man in Kazan and now has many Russian friends.

Central Asian stories from Saint Petersburg had more emphasis on the quality of living. Saint Petersburg is a very beautiful city, and many Central Asians appreciate the architecture, the urban spaces and the civilized nature of relations between people. Even McDonald's is perceived by some younger respondents as something prestigious: 'With my friends we often go to McDonald's and then walk around with some girls. This is interesting for me. I am planning to live here.' Initiation into this urban environment is sometimes described with a sense of humour: 'When I first stepped on the escalator, I thought this was the metro', said a young Kyrgyz migrant.

At the same time, Central Asian respondents shared negative stories – more so in Saint Petersburg. Such stories included encounters with the police and the local authorities, the experience or perception of racism, and complaints about children forgetting their mother tongue and roots, as well as about boring life. One trader complained that he had had his merchandise stolen in the market, and when he went to the police, the officers did not do anything about it, but instead tried to extort money from him. Several traders mentioned that they always had to be on the lookout for police, and that they hid or fled from the market when the police conducted their raids. There were also many stories of respondents being arrested by the police or by the Federal Migration Service.

Several Central Asians in Saint Petersburg complained about the racist attitude of local residents, about verbal abuse and about the danger of skinheads. One trader said that those skinheads who have already killed someone wear red shoelaces, while those who have not wear white ones. Other migrants complained about their children being discriminated against at school. Perhaps this is one reason why children try to adjust to the local conditions and prefer to affiliate themselves with local Russians rather than with other Central Asians, a process of adaptation that some parents negatively perceive as 'Russification'.

However, the most frequent complaint is about how boring and dull life can be in Russia. For many Central Asian traders, the market is the main place where they spend their day. To earn better, they have to work long hours, and as soon as they finish work, they rush home. Particularly in Saint Petersburg, they try to avoid public spaces, and many have little in the sense of entertainment because they do not have legal status and can be deported if caught by the police. Reeves[7] refers to De Genova's (2002) term 'deportability', which is about not just deportation but the condition of uncertainty that always looms over migrants' heads. She shows how this condition of deportability defines migrants' lives in the city and how very important it is for a migrant to engage in strategies of invisibility, described as *'moskvada korumboybuz'* (we try to be invisible), *'tynch zhashai-byz'* (we live quietly), or *'koidon zhoosh zhurobuz'* (we are quieter than a lamb). This shapes a set of embodied feelings defined by Reeves as 'living from the nerves'. Among our respondents, this condition of deportability also significantly limits their engagement with the city and results in comments such as 'the days are all the same here' and 'there is nothing fun in my life: just work and home'.

The contrast between the two cities does seem a bit grotesque, and of course in Kazan there were also negative stories from both migrants and local residents. However, the cumulative results of our survey presented in this section lead us to conclude that the relationship between long-term residents and Central Asian traders is largely more posi-tive in Kazan than in Saint Petersburg. The big question emerging from such empirical findings is, why is this so? So far, I have provided no explanations. This will be done in the next two sections, where I analyze each city individually and then return to my main argument about urban diversity and readability/ambiguity within the urban socio-cultural environment.

Kazan

Since its establishment in the tenth and eleventh centuries, Kazan has been a place of con-tinuous contestation. From 1552, when the city was completely subjugated by the army of Ivan Groznyi and lost its sovereignty, we can observe a new period in its history – one of coex-istence between its two main ethnic and cultural groups: Russian Christians and Tatar (Bulgar) Muslims. Its early years were a time of repression, when many Muslims were force-fully Christianized, mosques destroyed, and Tatars forced to live outside the city, in an area on the left side of the Kabanka River, which then became known as Tatarskaya Sloboda.[8]

Muslims and Christians were not allowed to live together, and from there on we can observe the formation of a divided city. The traces of this division are still very noticeable today: almost all the churches are on one side of the Kabanka, all the mosques on the other. By the end of eighteenth century, Kazan had expanded its boundaries, and all of its *slobodas*, including two Tatar *slobodas*, became part of the city. Alishev (2005) describes how throughout Kazan's history there was a continuous confrontation between Muslim and Christian city residents, yet the everyday experience of living together over several centuries eventually helped the two communities dissolve barriers and united them in the joint class struggle against feudal and later capitalist exploiters. Kazan also became a place where two cultures, Eastern Islamic and Western Christian, were developing together and contributed to the exchange of ideas and the formation of strong ethnic identities. Perhaps the most prominent manifestation of such development was the for-mation of the Jadidist movement, which combined elements of strong nationalism, a revived Islam and a progressive modernist perspective.

This brief overview of Kazan's history shows how almost a millennium of contestation between Russians and Tatars resulted in the formation of a city divided along ethnic and religious boundaries. Yet at the same time, this was also a millennium of coexistence, which produced to some degree hybrid, but more so distinctive, cultural groups with experiences of how to share this urban space.

The post-Soviet era then brought a revival of religious and ethnic sentiments, which again reinforced these distinctions. That is why today, when Central Asian traders arrive in Kazan, they find environments that are already divided and culturally distinct. According to the census of 2010, Russians make up 48.6% of Kazan's population, Tatars 47.6%. Being Muslims and speaking Turkic languages, the traders share religious and linguistic identities with local Tatars. Upon arrival, most of them settle on the left side of the Kabanka – an area that for five centuries has been primarily associated with Muslims. Thus, they are not perceived as a minority group and have become well embedded in the cultural and spatial structure of the city. They are perceived by local Tatars to some degree as brothers and sisters in Islam, and they are perceived by Russians as members of the Muslim half of the city. This is how they enter into local ethnic and religious dynamics, which seems to play to their advantage.

The spatial organization of contemporary Kazan is strongly connected to its administrative division into seven *rayons* (districts). Respondents in our survey frequently referred to these districts when they talked about the cityscape. These districts also turned out to be important markers of Central Asian migrants' presence in the city, which in the perception of our respondents was associated with two large markets (the Central and the Vietnamese) and various Central Asian cafes and restaurants. Figure 2a shows their location. The largest number of Central Asian cafes (56%) and the largest Central Asian market are in the Vakhitovskii District. The same district has the largest number of Central Asian migrants living there (47% of all surveyed migrants) and is also a region where a majority of migrants (45%) spend their free time (Figure 2b, c).

These maps and statistics show that Central Asian migrants in Kazan are strongly concentrated in one main area in the historical city centre: the western half of Vakhitovskii District. The district is divided into two distinct halves by the Kabanka River. The eastern half is well maintained; it hosts all main administrative buildings, such as the local *kremlin*, and various museums and churches. The western part, the historically Muslim area of the city, where the market is located, is quite run down: buildings are old and in need of renovation, and the roads are in very poor condition. To some degree, the contrast between the two parts of Vakhitovskii District illustrates the policy of the city administration, which for some reason continues the historical tradition of neglecting the Muslim part of the city, as described by Alishev (2005).

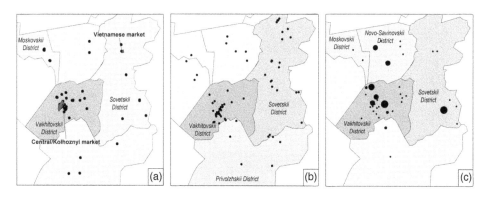

Figure 2. (a) Location of Central Asian cafes and markets. (b) Places of Central Asians' residences. (c) Places where Central Asians spend their free time.

Similarly, the city administration has a negative perception of the Central Market, which it considers a space of vice and informality. Our interviewees from the market mentioned several times the rumours about how the market was going to be wiped out in the preparations for the University Olympic Games. The Central is the largest market in Kazan. It has sections where various food products are sold and sections for other kinds of merchandise – clothes, electronics, kitchenware, etc. The market, with its simple metal and wooden stalls, can be perceived as a very informal place; visually it stands in sharp contrast to the more formal and fancy shopping malls in other areas of Kazan.

The western part of Vakhitovskii *rayon* also has a strong Islamic character. There are many historic mosques and a whole section of streets with shops selling Islamic merchandise. The significant presence of Central Asians only strengthens this Islamic feel. Being in this area, one cannot but notice how different it is from the other half of the city centre: cafes and shops have Islamic names, which often are written in Arabic-style fonts. There are many women wearing long dresses and *hijabs*. On one of our first days of research we had lunch in the Soyombike Cafe on Gabdulla Tukai Street and were very surprised to see it full of young women in Islamic attire. It later turned out that just across the street from this cafe there was a *madrasa* for girls. The language, signs, architecture and dress were all symbols making this space very distinct and readable. Its strong contrast to the western part of Vakhitovskii District also makes this urban territory distinct and legible. The readability and legibility of the urban centre in Kazan thus indicate how physical, cultural and cognitive spaces coincide and reinforce the local urban identity (Figure 3).

The Central and Vietnamese Markets were the main places of employment for our Central Asian respondents. Traders spend significant amount of their time in these bazaars. Accordingly, they try to find places to live not too far away, preferably within walking distance, so that they do not have to use public transport. This is one of the main strategies that helps migrants minimize contact with locals and with the police. Accordingly, markets play a very important role in structuring the migrants' perception of the city. The analysis of cognitive maps of Kazan drawn by such traders on blank sheets of paper and without any specific instructions shows that bazaars are very significant place makers for Central Asians. In some maps, bazaars occupy the central position on the page (Figure 4b); in others they are shown as the main starting/destination points (Figure 4c). In still others they are shown in a very large size, while in some of the maps, there is almost nothing but bazaars (Figure 4a).

Figure 3. Images from the western side of Vakhitovskii *rayon*: a mosque near the market; the Uzbek cafe Uzgen; and an old building illustrating the run-down character of the neighbourhood.

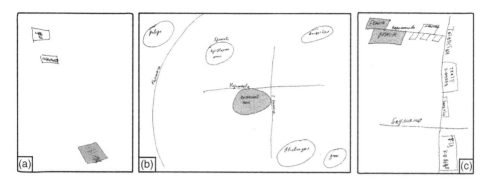

Figure 4. Maps of Kazan drawn by Central Asian traders: (a) nothing but markets on the map; (b) markets occupy the central place on the map; (c) markets are drawn as the main starting or destination points.

Interestingly, this physical presence of Central Asians strongly correlates with the perception of Central Asian presence among the local residents: 61% of local respondents associate migrants with the Vakhitovskii District and the Central Market (Figure 5a). But what is even more interesting, for local residents, the Vakhitovskii *rayon* is also the safest *rayon* in the city (Figure 5b, c). These maps clearly show that local residents do not consider places associated with migrants dangerous. This confirms our findings from the questionnaire survey results: migrants in Kazan are not associated with danger and are not perceived as a threat.

The next map (Figure 6) compares the routes taken from home to work by local residents and by Central Asian traders. The routes do not overlap much, and the majority of traders prefer to live within walking distance from the market. This is also evidenced by the time and mode of their journeys: traders travel to work for only 18 minutes, while locals do so for 38 minutes; 49% of traders walk to work, versus only 9% of locals. In addition, 68% of traders work in the district where they live, as opposed to only 24% of locals. Traders prefer to live near markets and walk to work for the reasons of convenience and safety (to avoid meetings with police).

We can conclude at this point that in Kazan the presence of Central Asians has a very strong spatial manifestation, in real life (as evidenced by the locations of markets and

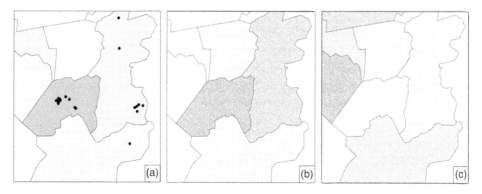

Figure 5. Places and regions (a) associated with migrants among locals; (b) safe for locals; (c) unsafe for locals.

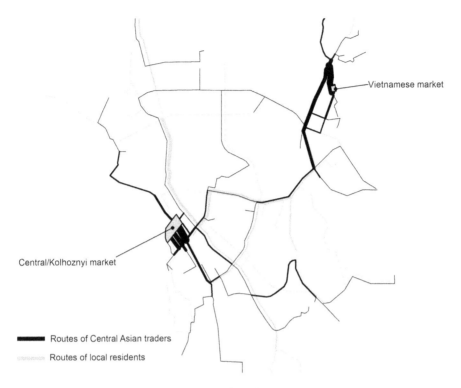

Figure 6. Routes of Central Asian traders and local residents.

Central Asian cafes, traders' residences, their places for spending free time and by their home–work journeys) as well as in the perception of local residents. The main neighbourhood in Kazan associated with Central Asians – the western half of the Vakhitovskii *rayon* – has a run-down appearance and a strong Islamic character, which results in some stigmatization, but not in a negative attitude. This is quite unexpected given all the literature on urban conflict reviewed in the introduction part of this article, and all the fears and warnings of Russian authors about the dangers of ghettoization. To explain this positive outcome, one has to remember that contrary to the many negative case studies of urban segregation, in Kazan there is a thousand-year history of interaction between the two main ethnic and religious communities associated with these places. The two communities 'read' each other very well, and space reinforces that readability, distinction and mutual respect or tolerance. In addition, many local Tatar residents interviewed in our survey still have regard for their historical territory on the left side of the Kabanka River, even if their families long ago moved out. The fact that the spaces and journeys of locals and Central Asians do not overlap much is perhaps another reason why the two communities coexist without significant conflicts.

Saint Petersburg

From its very establishment in the early eighteenth century, Saint Petersburg has been a multilingual and multi-ethnic city, although the vast majority have always been ethnic Russians. Among its main ethnic groups there were Germans, Ukrainians, Finns and Jews. By the time of the revolution in 1905–07 there were about 150 ethno-cultural associations in the city (Rozanova 2012). However, during the repression years of the 1930s, all these organizations were closed down because of the fear of espionage. The siege of Leningrad in 1941–44 reduced the size of the city population to one-sixth of its peak size. In the postwar period, the ethnic composition of the city started to change, with more migrants coming from the Volga region, the Caucasus and Central Asia (Rozanova 2012). The rates of immigration rapidly increased in the post-Soviet period, and today Saint Petersburg is second only to Moscow in the number of migrants. In 2010, the number of migrants in the city reached 1.5 million, out of a total population of 5.1 million. Migrants produced 13% of city revenue (Rozanova 2012). The majority of migrants are from nearby and other regions of Russia, and according to the 2010 census, such traditionally Muslim ethnic groups as Tatars, Uzbeks, Tajiks, Kazakhs, Bashkirs and Turkmens together make up only about 2% of the city.

Unfortunately, Saint Petersburg is also second in the number of hate crimes; 15 people were killed and 39 assaulted in 2008 in Saint Petersburg and the Leningradskaya *oblast* (Rozanova 2012). The westernmost city in Russia, it also has a reputation of being one of the most racist. At the same time, there are many people representing progressive intelligentsia who defend migrants. On a graffiti in Figure 7b the portraits of Hitler and Putin are placed next to each other, perhaps suggesting some similarity between fascism and contemporary Russian migration policies and the sign under it says "Never again". Saint Petersburg has developed and introduced two very ambitious programmes on interethnic tolerance: Tolerance-1 and Tolerance-2. The first, launched in July 2006, aimed to change the public opinion of Saint Petersburg residents about representatives of different ethnic groups. The main idea was to spread the concept of a supra-ethnic identity of *peterburgets* – a resident of Saint Petersburg. The main slogan of this programme was 'Petersburg unites people', and its activities included various kinds of cultural, social and scientific events. While doing our research we came across a graffito with this slogan. Interestingly, next to the main slogan 'Petersburg unites people' someone added the sceptical word *pochti* (almost), which was later painted over (Figure 7a). The programme's outreach was quite significant; its main mistake was that it did not engage the migrant community itself (Rozanova 2012).

The Tolerance-2 programme addressed this failure: its main focus was on the migrants and their children, helping them integrate into city life (Rozanova 2012). During our research we interviewed a local Russian young man who was volunteering for this programme, spending a few hours a week to help the children of migrants learn Russian. The programme, however, remained within the boundary of a joint supra-ethnic identity concept as a solution to the problems of growing racism. As such, it fit well the Federal Migration Service policy of migrant integration.

When we first arrived in Saint Petersburg from Kazan and asked our landlady about the location of Central Asians in the city, we received a puzzling answer: 'What do you mean? They are everywhere!' We thought that maybe she just did not know. However, as we progressed with our fieldwork, we came to understand that she was quite right. In contrast to Kazan, there was not one strong concentration of Central Asians in this city. Rather, these migrants were more or less evenly spread across the whole urban area. Figure 8 shows the location of Central Asian markets, restaurants, food shops and fruit vendors in Saint Petersburg.

Figure 7. Graffiti: (a) 'Petersburg unites people' (with 'almost' added and then painted over); (b) 'Never again'.

Saint Petersburg has three times the area of Kazan, and four times the population. That is why the research team were not able to cover the entire city. We decided to make observations on a diagonal stretch from the south-west to the north-east that cut through the city centre and other main kinds of neighbourhoods. Our analysis does not reveal any large concentrations of Central Asians on the city scale, but it shows small concentrations around metro stations. In contrast to Kazan, administrative districts in Saint Petersburg are not important place markers. People hardly refer to them; instead, when they talk about their use of space, they extensively use the names of metro stations. Interestingly, metro stations have also become the main magnets for Central Asian traders, because the metro is the most popular mode of public transport in the city, and large numbers of potential customers pass through them on a daily basis. The enlarged section of the northern part of the city (Figure 9) illustrates how Central Asians tend to locate near the station or on the streets leading to the stations.

The analysis of Central Asians' places of residence and recreation shows that they are not strongly concentrated either (Figure 10). As in Kazan, traders prefer to live near markets. Their average time to work is 19 minutes, versus 32 minutes for local residents;

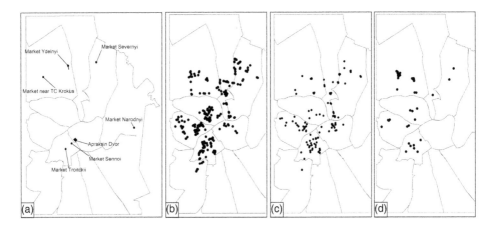

Figure 8. Physical presence of Central Asians in Saint Petersburg: (a) markets; (b) food shops; (c) restaurants; (d) fruit vendors.

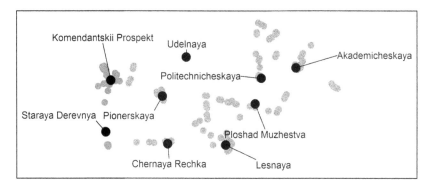

Figure 9. Location of food-shops, cafes and fruit stalls where Central Asians work, in relation to metro stations, in Saint Petersburg.

and 44% of Central Asians walk to work, versus 23% of locals. However, because there are many more markets and they are spread across the city, the map of Central Asians' residence is rather spread out, too. Also, as in Kazan, markets play a very important role in the Central Asian traders' life, which is reflected in how they draw their own maps of the city: in some maps markets occupy almost half a page and have a lot of details, whereas the city is drawn in a very abstract and limited way.

How does the physical presence of Central Asians correlate with the perception of their presence among local residents? In contrast to Kazan, not significantly. In addition, there is little correlation between areas associated with migrants and areas that are perceived as safe or dangerous by locals. Figure 11 shows that some areas associated with migrants are perceived as dangerous, while others are understood to be safe.

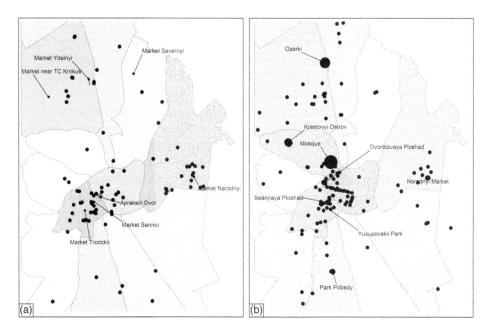

Figure 10. Saint Petersburg: (a) places and regions of Central Asian traders' residence; (b) places and regions where Central Asian traders spend free time.

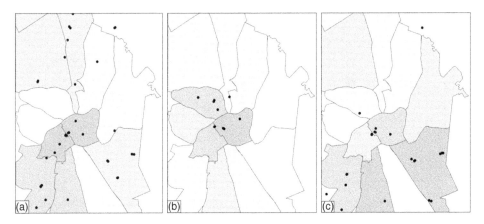

Figure 11. Saint Petersburg: (a) places and areas associated with migrants among local residents; (b) places and areas perceived by local residents as safe; (c) places and areas perceived by local residents as dangerous.

One explanation of this ambiguity again is linked with the metro. The metro, being the main mode of public transport in Saint Petersburg, becomes a place where locals and Central Asians regularly meet. Even though Central Asians prefer to walk to their workplace, some of them (15%) cannot avoid a metro ride. Figure 12 shows that the travel routes of Central Asian migrants and local residents overlap much more significantly than they do in Kazan.

This again shows that the metro creates a parallel urban space – one which is underground and which adds additional layers of complexity to the ways the two communities locate each other in the city. Central Asians referred to travelling in the metro as a dangerous experience, because it is an enclosed space with no options for escape. This is where they are most likely to be stopped by the police or the Federal Migration Service, and sometimes become targets of racist attacks. A clear illustration of this is the case of 'white train' actions, which took place in Moscow in 2013 after the infamous events in Biryulevo, when crowds of Russian young people attacked migrants inside the metro trains.

The visual presence of Central Asians in Saint Petersburg had much more ambiguity than in Kazan. If in Kazan we saw many Central Asian women freely wearing *hijabs*, in Saint Petersburg we saw many Central Asian girls bleaching their hair and fashioning it in such a way that it enclosed their faces on the sides and made them look more like Russians. In contrast to the streets of Kazan – where Central Asian identity was emphasized, particularly in the names and decorations of Central Asian cafes and restaurants – in Saint Petersburg, many Central Asian cafes 'hid' behind more traditional Russian names or different kinds of ethnic food, for example Japanese sushi. According to our observations, every second small shop with daily consumer products had Central Asian traders in it. However, the shops almost never used Central Asian names either.

The analysis of maps in Saint Petersburg presented in this section clearly shows the differences from Kazan. Saint Petersburg, being a larger city with a more complex spatial organization and the metro as its main public transport, does not show a strong spatial concentration of Central Asians. Instead, the spaces of locals and Central Asians significantly overlap, and both communities have many more chances to meet each other on a daily basis. In the case of Saint Petersburg this creates a potential to bring these groups

Routes of Central Asian traders

Routes of local residents

• Metro stations

Figure 12. Routes of Central Asian traders and local residents in Saint Petersburg.

closer, but at the same time it is likely to generate conflicts. This unpredictability and ambiguity of social and spatial organization produces a much more vulnerable urban space, prone to all kinds of unpredictable developments. In addition, Central Asians, being recent arrivals in Saint Petersburg, are clearly a minority group, in relation to their appearance, language, culture and religion. This makes their situation more vulnerable than that of their compatriots in Kazan and forces them to hide their identity. As a result, it makes the urban space even less readable and understandable for both local residents and for migrants and adds to the overall urban confusion. The tolerance programmes introduced since 2006 do not help either of these communities solve these problems, because their main goal is the abstract supra-ethnic identity of *peterburgets*, which complicates matters and – according to local respondents – creates only more confusion.

Conclusion

In this paper I have offered readers an unusual perspective on the relationship between the long-term local residents and more recent arrivals in Russian cities – labour migrants from Central Asia. The methodological uniqueness of this research was based on the rigorous comparison of the two cities, on the use of meso-level research elements, such as urban districts and neighbourhoods, and on the combination of more traditional sociological methods with rarely used instruments from the fields of psychology and urban studies. The main product of data analysis, maps of migrants' presence and their interaction with local communities and urban environment, helped me visualize the image of a 'divided city' and develop a three-step conclusion to this paper, each step building on the previous one.

First, the results of our questionnaire survey reveal that relations between Central Asian migrants and long-term residents in Kazan are much better than they are in Saint Petersburg. Second, the reasons for such differences can be found in the histories of both of these cities and the socio-cultural, economic and political organization of their urban spaces. Kazan, a city with a very long history of struggle and coexistence of Russian Christians and Tatar Muslims, produced very strong ethnic and religious identities that are deeply embedded in the spatial structure of the city. For today's Central Asian migrants and long-term local inhabitants these patterns are well readable and easy to navigate. Saint Petersburg is a city with a more complex and ambiguous spatial matrix. It makes life for both communities less certain, more unpredictable, and also more difficult to comprehend and engage with. This comparison confirms the classic thesis by Kevin Lynch (1960) about the values of urban semantics and their readability and legibility as qualities of the urban environment which make the urban experience more positive and satisfactory. It also confirms more recent critiques of uncertainty and ambiguity (Abashin 2012; Reeves, 2013) as urban conditions, which make the experiences in urban space of migrants very difficult and result in growing xenophobia and racism in the local community. My third conclusion draws on the previous one to suggest that just as clarity and distinctiveness of a spatial identity are necessary for peaceful coexistence of diverse urban communities, a successful policy of migrant integration must not sacrifice their unique cultural and religious identities. Contemporary policies of the Russian government to integrate migrants either by 'Russifying' them or by creating various kinds of supra-ethnic identities so far have failed. I would like to return here to the earlier cited statement by Montgomery, Seligman and Wasserfall: 'Only by learning how to live together differently can we live together at all.'

Notes

1. CEDAR (Communities Engaging with Difference and Religion), http://www.cedarnetwork.org/about-us/mission-vision/, accessed 14 January 2015.
2. 'Koncepciya gosudarstvennoi migratcionnoi politiki Rossiskoi Federatcii na period do 2025g.'; 'Strategiya gosudarstvennoi natcionalnoi politiki Rossiiskoi Federatcii na period do 2025g.' http://kremlin.ru/events/president/news/15635, http://kremlin.ru/acts/bank/36512.
3. 'Russian Orthodox Church Prepared a Textbook for Migrants' (Avesityan 2014).
4. The research team included my fellow researcher Nurzat Sultanalieva and six students of the Anthropology Department at the American University of Central Asia, Kyrgyzstan.
5. Because Kazan is a smaller city, we were able to cover most of its territory. In Saint Petersburg we decided to make observations on a diagonal stretch from south-west to north-east that cut through the city centre and other main kinds of neighbourhoods.
6. All together 300 semi-structured interviews were conducted: 200 with migrants (100 in each city) and 100 with local residents (50 in each city).
7. Madeleine Reeves, 'Living from the Nerves: Deportability, Indeterminacy and the Feel of Law', presentation at Anthropology Club, American University of Central Asia, 18 September 2014.
8. *Sloboda* means a village located just outside of town.

Acknowledgements

I would like to acknowledge the help of my research colleague Nurzat Sultanalieva and the team of students from the Anthropology Department at the American University of Central Asia: Alexei Kosterin, Maria Marchenko, Tynchtyk Bakyt uulu, Aigerim Tabysheva, Rashida Khasanova and Alexei Mun. I would also like to thank Madeleine Reeves and Sergei Abashin for their feedback on my first draft and Philipp Schroder for his continuous encouragement.

Disclosure statement

No potential conflict of interest was reported by the author.

Funding

This work was supported by the Central Asian Studies Institute, American University of Central Asia, under a USAID grant and the Tyan-Shan Policy Center, American University of Central Asia, under a USAID grant.

References

Abashin, S. 2012. "Sredneaziatskaya Migratcia: Praktiki, lokalnye soobshestva, transnationalism [Central Asian Migration: Practices, Local Communities and Transnationalism]." *Etnicheskoe Obozrenie* 4: 3–13.

Alishev, S. 2005. *Vse ob istorii Kazani* [Everything about the History of Kazan]. Kazan: Rannur.

Avesityan, R. 2014, December 11. Izvestia News. http://izvestia.ru/news/580608.

De Genova, Nicholas P. 2002. "Migrant 'Illegality' and Deportability in Everyday Life." *Annual Review of Anthropology* 31: 419–447. doi:10.1146/annurev.anthro.31.040402.085432

Dmitriev, A., and G. Pyaduhov. 2011. "Migranty i sotcium: Integratcionnyi i dizintegratcionnyi potencial praktik vzaimodeistviya [Migration and Society: Potential for Integration and Disintegration in Interactive Practices]." *Sotciologicheskie issledovaniya* 12: 50–59.

Ikontcev, V., and I. Ivahnyuk. 2013. "Modeli integratcii migrantov v sovremennoi Rossii, Karim-Vostok".

Jaffe, R., and E. Durr. 2010. "Introduction: Cultural and Material Forms of Urban Pollution." In *Urban Pollution: Cultural Meanings, Social Practice*, edited by E. Durr and R. Jaffe, 1–29. Oxford and New York: Berghahn Books.

Laruelle, M. 2013. "Introduction." In *Migration and Social Upheaval as the Face of Globalization in Central Asia*, edited by M. Laruelle, 5–22. Leiden: Brill.

Lynch, K. 1960. *The Image of The City*. Cambridge, MA: MIT Press.

Mukomel, V. 2013. *Integratciya migrantov: Rossiiskaya Federatciya* [Integration of Migrants: Russian Federation]. San Domenico di Fiesole: CARIM-East RR, Robert Schuman Centre for Advanced Studies, European University Institute.

Reeves, M. 2013. "Clean Fake: Authenticating Documents and Persons in Migrant Moscow." *American Ethnologist* 40 (3): 508–524. doi:10.1111/amet.12036

Rozanova, M. 2012. "Migration Processes and Challenges in Contemporary Russia: St. Petersburg Case Study." Eurasian Migration Papers, N.6.

Sahadeo. 2007. "Druzhba Narodov or Second-class Citizenship? Soviet Asian Migrants in a Post-colonial world." *Central Asian Survey* 26 (4): 559–579. doi:10.1080/02634930802018463

Vendina, O. 2009. "Kulturnoe raznoobrazie i 'pobochnye' effekty etnokulturnoi politiki v Moskve [Cultural Diversity and 'Side' Effects of Ethno-cultural Policy in Moscow]." In *Immigranty v Moskve*, edited by Zaonchkovskaya, 45–147. Tri Kvadrata.

Assemblages of mobility: the marshrutkas of Central Asia

Wladimir Sgibnev[a] and Andrey Vozyanov[b]

[a]Leibniz Institute for Regional Geography, Germany; [b]Graduate School for East and Southeast European Studies, Regensburg University, Germany

ABSTRACT
This article addresses reconfigurations of urban space in Central Asia through the lens of marshrutka mobility. Marshrutka-based transport is – together with the bazaar trade – a major sector of Central Asian economy. Although precise data are not available, estimates propose that one family in ten gains its income through it. In spite of its economic and social importance, there has barely been any research on marshrutka mobility so far. The marshrutka mobility phenomenon appears at once wide-ranging and elusive. In order to grasp its complexity, we propose a theory framework based on John Law's concept of fluidity and assemblage. Providing empirical insights from Khujand, in northern Tajikistan, the article addresses marshrutka mobility from a local perspective, notably with regard to regulatory processes of marshrutka-based transport. It also covers the trans-local perspective, with particular attention to global flows of ideas, vehicles, and people.

Introduction

Minibuses, locally known as *marshrutka*, are a common sight in urban and rural landscapes of Central Asia; at the same time, marshrutkas are part of a wider trans-local phenomenon. *Dolmuş, matatu,* bush taxi, dollar van, *tro tro, collectivo,* and their cognates serve millions of users daily, primarily but not exclusively in the developing world. In spite of its economic and social importance, the literature on this mobility phenomenon has only recently begun to emerge; and there are barely any English-language overview publications in the field so far.

In spite of the dazzling variety of emic terms for this mobility phenomenon (see also Kumar and Barrett 2008), we suppose that there are also substantial local specifics to be taken into account. For Central Asian marshrutkas this includes a command-planning economy in their background, and a developed Soviet-era infrastructure of electric urban transportation (tramways and trolleybuses) as their transit counterpart. In our eyes, looking at marshrutkas does not only mean looking at a mode of transportation. Instead, we prefer to speak of the *marshrutka mobility phenomenon,* which encompasses vehicles, drivers, passengers and regulators, as well as an entire set of cultural practices connected to marshrutkas.

Marshrutkas are intriguing because they represent a significant deviation from Soviet mechanisms of mobility production. After the breakdown of the Soviet Union in 1991, funding for public transport withered, and the marshrutka emerged, to some extent, as its replacement. Yet the emergence of the marshrutka mobility phenomenon was not the outcome of elaborate policy and top-down action, but rather resulted from the inaction of state actors and the bottom-up initiative of mobility entrepreneurs. At the same time, marshrutka mobility hardly lends itself to a simple definition: we have to deal with a range of characteristics, which vary across the area of marshrutka dissemination. To be considered a marshrutka, the transport system has to possess several of those 'identifiers', yet we can hardly talk about the minimum set, or the primary and secondary among them; the shape of this mobility phenomenon is flexible, but recognizable. Still, together they constitute one highly discernible (both by users and providers) and prominent feature of post-Soviet life.

Marshrutkas mirror and forge particular patterns of social and cultural settings and are thus part and parcel of reconfigurations of urban space in post-Soviet Central Asia. They can be seen as an experimental arena, where a series of post-Soviet societal developments emerged, either before their mass spread or in a particularly salient way. The emergence of marshrutkas necessitated the development of a particular economic framework based on bottom-up regulation of individual economic activity – heralding the entrepreneurial boom of the very early 1990s. The harsh regulation of the marshrutka sector in 2000–2010 (as a trend, albeit with differences in degree from one country to another) is embedded in a general strengthening of authoritarian regimes in the area – and at the same time witnesses their projects of modernization (Figure 1).

With an empirical foundation based on a four-week period of exploratory fieldwork in Khujand, in northern Tajikistan, the article cannot pretend to expand on a wide range of data.[1] Instead, it proposes to present some major conceptual, historical and current socio-

Figure 1. Marshrutka terminus at the 34th *microraion*. Image: W. Sgibnev (2014).

economic cornerstones of the marshrutka mobility phenomenon, and expand on the relevance and the timeliness of research on marshrutka mobility. We will first of all sketch a theory framework, based on John Law's (2002) concept of fluidity, for grasping marshrutka mobility, which appears at once wide-ranging and elusive. The concept of fluidity allows us to present and conceptualize marshrutkas as mobile artefacts of global mobility. We will show how the marshrutka mobility phenomenon is a promising field of study – one which allows insight into the region's socio-economic transformations, on both a local and a trans-local scale. Providing empirical insights from Khujand, we will cover the local perspective, notably with regard to regulatory processes of marshrutka-based transport, before addressing the trans-local perspective, with particular attention to flows of ideas, vehicles and people.

Fluidity and assemblage as frameworks for researching marshrutkas

While research on post-Soviet societies has largely overcome the normative 'transitological' focus of the 1990s (as castigated, *inter alia*, by Pickles 2010, 129–130), research on the emergence of 'new and different orders' (Alexander, Buchli, and Humphrey 2007, 11) is still in its early stages. Overcoming the transitological focus is also at stake when it comes to research on post-Soviet mobility. Institutional change and privatization management was one main focus of research mentioning 'informal transport' solutions (for contributions with a post-Socialist focus, see e.g. Pucher 1995, 1999; Hook 1999; Gwilliam 2000, 2001; Finn 2008; Grdzelishvili and Sathre 2008; Akimov and Banister 2011). Generally speaking, we have to overcome dualistic and hierarchizing frames of reference, which directed the researchers' attention to verticality and decision-guidedness, quantitative growth, long-term planning, and the irreversibility of development processes. The marshrutka mobility phenomenon refutes this paradigm, and thus draws attention to social and cultural aspects of mobility and its role in identity formation and power relations, thanks to the 'mobilities turn' as heralded first of all by Urry (2002, 2004, 2007; for fruitful examples outside the post-Socialist realm see Brownell 1972; Schwantes 1985; Suzuki 1985; Davis 1990; Müller-Schwarze 2009; Edensor 2004; Jensen 2009; Jensen 2011).

The International Association of Public Transport (UITP) classifies marshrutkas as one form of 'informal transport'. In our eyes, this falls short of explaining the breadth and the importance of the phenomenon. Instead, we propose looking at marshrutkas as both 'substance' and carriers of meaning (Cresswell 2006). This is witnessed particularly by the remarkable informal regulation of the sector in the early 1990s; the elaborate interplay between passengers and drivers; and the recently increased attempts at state regulation of this transport sector – not only in the former Soviet Union (Burrell and Horschelmann 2014) but on a global scale. Rather, we should look at the transformation of public transport systems as a part of societal transformation at large, including new forms of state–society relations, new means of livelihood and subsistence, and new networks of trade and migration. The rise of marshrutkas is an essential element of this process.

We understand mobility as a mode of space production. Through mobility, marshrutkas take part in processes of space production in Central Asia and the Caucasus. Marshrutkas are, in this regard, an element helping us understand space – in its physical and social dimensions, and with regard to the forces which produce it. 'Space' has become a prevailing concept for speaking about ordering of social relations and urban life. Bourdieu, de Certeau, Lefebvre, and many others used spatial approaches to analyse the relations between the social and the material, the structure of societies, the organization of the urban everyday. Michel de Certeau's notions of tactics and strategies, in particular, are increasingly employed to overcome the deficiency of bottom-up approaches (see e.g. Thrift 2004; Bissell 2009). The imperfection of this theoretical approach is the risk of redu-cing the users' role to consumerist adaptive patterns opposing a suppressive exercise of power, which poses the threat of semantically producing black-and-white dualities. It also tends to neglect the meaning of unintended actions in system performance (and thus inevitably to view the situation as a conflicting one). The post-Soviet transformations, however, were remarkable for deregulation, the decline of state support, and the emer-gence of unintended outcomes.

Marshrutkas constitute a highly visible phenomenon in vast parts of the post-Soviet space and coevolve with socio-cultural transformations of Central Asian societies. As object and phenomenon, marshrutkas refer to a particular type of vehicle; a particular legal and regulatory environment; a type of organization of the public transit network (including routing, headways, and operation hours); a user–technology interface (a vehicle with particular design and redesign requirements, imposing particular relations and rules on its users); and a pattern of economic relations.

Marshrutkas as an object of research are in many senses elusive – constantly changing as to their vehicles (from private cars via minibuses to privately run full-fledged buses), forms of ownership, modes of state control, tariff structures and rules of behaviour. In spite of local peculiarities in different cities and regions, and the marshrutkas' great adap-tability, we still observe similar patterns of their success and dissemination. Conceiving marshrutkas as a fluid object in a fluid space (Law 2002, 96) allows us to operationalize the space-producing and space-consuming characteristics of mobility, without losing sight of the materiality of marshrutka mobility. Fluid objects have no stable boundaries, changing with the relations in which these objects are involved, but those relations 'need to change bit by bit rather than all at once' (99). At the same time, 'mobile bound-aries are needed for objects to exist in fluid space' (100), otherwise those objects cease to exist. It means that some of its elements are standardized, while some are variable; pre-sently used infrastructure is immanently connected to previous versions (which was noticed already by historians of technology – see Collingridge 1979 and Johnston 1984 on technological progress and decision-making) and to versions that simultaneously exist in other regions[2] – turning here to the notion of assemblage.

In order to describe the social and technological interactions of the marshrutka mobility phenomenon, we turn to the notion of assemblage, which is rooted in Deleuze's and Guat-tari's works (Deleuze and Guattari 1987). Earlier theoretical models approached society as a totality – a system of elements that receive their meanings only in mutual relations within the certain entity. In addition, social theories tend to consider the social world as the reality produced exclusively by human actors. Unlike the (human) elements of totality, 'parts of assemblages may be detached from it and plugged into different assemblage in which its interactions are different' (DeLanda 2006, 10). Then, assemblages are necessarily het-erogeneous multiplicities, including 'networks of its buildings, people, organizational structure and processes, … codes of conducts [sic] and rules, norms, regulations and cul-tural understanding' (Lee 2010). Marshrutka drivers, with their skills and labour force, whole vehicles and spare parts, official ways of regulating the fare, etc., can move from one location (city, region, country) to another and integrate successfully into a new assemblage. The whole assemblage cannot be perceived from any one point inside it: objects are heterogeneous and hard to demarcate; though they tend to stabilize, they are constantly changing. Using Deleuzian (and Latourian) terms, we can speak about a co-production of urban mobility by vehicles, passengers, transport providers, and infrastructure, and to conceive of marshrutka mobility as a broad societal phenomenon in its own right.

Seeing mobility phenomena as assemblages allows grasping their chronological contingency. We thus can convincingly take path dependency and the importance of past decisions, their intentions, and bygone ideas of the future into account (Collingridge 1979; Johnston 1984; Saxenian 1999; Pinch 2001). Indeed, infrastructure has a strong connection to the future – its visions, prognoses, and expectations. Infrastructure may anticipate the development of an area or embody longings for modernity, development, and progress. The notion of assemblage also helps explain why sets composed of seemingly the same elements do not work in similar ways in other regions. Thus, contingency is how a given object is never the same at two subsequent moments, but is also never totally different. Fluidity is what allows an object to be contingent – in other words, to remain itself – or, it is what allows the assemblage to re-assemble without harsh fractures. Being contingent themselves, marshrutkas present changes of variables and constants within the contingency of a city. In other words, marshrutkas reconfigure post-Soviet urban space, changing themselves alongside with it. We would argue that the success of the marshrutka resides in its fluidity – for and within the fluid space of the early 1990s. Recent developments in the marshrutka sector in Central Asia and the Caucasus suggest that the fluidity of this sphere may soon disappear through imposed regulation: authorities are blocking access of marshrutkas to main city streets, imposing free service for low-income categories of the population, and setting requirements for operating hours regardless of actual passenger demand. For this reason, this is the right time to investigate this shift – which is already largely completed in other post-Soviet contexts outside of Central Asia and the Caucasus.

While a broad range of works confirms that the object – be it policies for urban space (McFarlane 2011), health and bioethics (Konrad 2007; Scambler 2012), or discotheques (Jordan 1995) – can be better understood as assemblage, the literature lacks detailed descriptions of this kind. The task is to demonstrate particular examples of assemblages, including their local significance and trans-local connectivity. The nature of investigated objects imposes a qualitative methodology with a variety of sources and techniques, like interviews, surveys, discourse analysis, and 'mobile methods' with an accent on interdisciplinary translation. Summing up, anthropologically grounded research on the (social, everyday) role of infrastructure in post-Soviet transformation deserves more attention. This surely concerns mobility phenomena at large, and public transport networks from marshrutkas to tram and trolleybus systems up to full-scale metro systems; yet also bureaucracies, media and communications, and water and energy provision are concerned.

A local perspective on marshrutka mobility

Looking for the origin of marshrutka mobility in Central Asia, we have to go back to the Soviet era. Thus, marshrutkas are by no means an invention of the burgeoning 1990s.

Marshrutka mobility is inscribed in a long line of Soviet heritage, and its reconfiguration after independence tells us a lot about transformation patterns and processes. As a transport option, marshrutkas appeared in Soviet cities in the 1930s. Regular taxi vehicles were assigned to fixed 'marching routes' – from where they took the name – yet could generally be hailed and stopped at any location *en route*. It was a comfortable, yet quite expensive option on major thoroughfares, or a cheaper alternative to the taxi when heading for 'exceptional' locations, such as train stations, airports, and beaches. Small in size and limited in number, marshrutkas were never thought of as means of mass transportation in Soviet urban planning (Vozyanov 2014a) – even if their importance grew with the construction of the first Soviet-built minibus series, the RAF-10, of Latvian origin.

In the following, we will take a closer look at Khujand – Tajikistan's second-largest city and centre of the Sughd Region, in the Ferghana Valley. Due to a lack of data, it is impossible to say which part of Khujand's modal split is covered by cars, marshrutkas, or buses, and which with other modes such as cars or walking. Still, we can estimate a relative victory of marshrutkas, which are popular even for short distances of one kilometre or less. One additional reason for marshrutka dominance is the division of the city into two parts, with large housing estates on the right bank and the commercial centre and the old town on the left, which generates impressive traffic flows across the Syrdarya bridges. Furthermore, marshrutkas operate on minor streets and even penetrate into the old town, which one respondent attributed to the particular ingenuity and entrepreneurship of the Khujandis (Interview FO).

In Khujand, the first marshrutka route came into being in the early 1980s, running the length of the city's main street, as a supplement to the already overcrowded trolleybus lines on this stretch (Interview TD). Indeed, for the transportation of the bulk of the passenger load, Soviet urban planners mostly relied on electric transportation – that is, trams and trolleybuses. Public transport was utterly important, in terms of both the passenger load and the urban ideology. In Khujand, the trolleybus network began operating in 1970, mirroring the city's main commuter flow: it ran from the *microraions* on the right bank, via the main street, southwards to the silk plant, and was extended over the years.

As in other Soviet republics, the economic decline and political turmoil of the 1990s were mirrored by disinvestment in publicly run transport services. Administrative responsibility was transferred from central ministries to the municipalities, without a corresponding transfer of funding (Gwilliam, Meakin and Kumar 1999, 1). The ageing rolling stock was decaying, and no funding was available for the purchase of new vehicles or the maintenance of overhead lines. Municipalities throughout Central Asia attempted to privatize bus fleets and created legislative frameworks for route tendering in the course of the 1990s (Gwilliam 2003, 8; Akimov and Banister 2011, 9ff.), which eventually proved useful for the regulation of marshrutka-based transport. Marshrutkas, which institutionally reported to taxi companies in Soviet times, were thus able to survive as large-mobility providers, independent of the ailing bus and tram operators.

In the course of the 1990s, trolleybus traffic in Khujand became very irregular. The lack of spare parts and neglect of overhead wiring led to frequent breakdowns. Unstable electricity provision destroyed the image of the trolleybus as a reliable means of transport. For these reasons, the trolleybus network closed 'indefinitely' in 2008 (S ulic Hudžanda isčezli 2008). Surprisingly, it reopened in 2009 (V Sogde posle dolgogo 2009), with two buses running on the north-south line, in an attempt by the city administration to present itself as catering to the population's needs (for a discussion of the unsustainable character of infrastructure investments in Tajikistan, see Sgibnev 2014). In 2010, trolleybuses stopped running once again due to the breakdown of an electric substation. Neither the trolleybus operator nor the city administration contributed funds to repair the substation.[3] The handful of trolleybuses in working condition remained rusting in the garage; the drivers had left for Russia. In early 2014, authorities decided to get rid of the trolleybus system for good. Trolleybuses were sold for scrap, and the overhead wires disappeared from the main street.

New needs and possibilities, a new legal framework, and new struggles for livelihood drastically changed urban transport, as 'new forms of social networking co-evolve with extensive changes to transport and communication systems' (Gillen and Hall 2011, 33). Public transport operators were unable to meet the population's basic mobility needs, and an ever-growing fleet of marshrutkas filled the gap. At the same time, industry plants closed down and released thousands of persons into unemployment. The marshrutka sector was able to absorb a large proportion of the workforce, limited only by the provision of appropriate vehicles. Marshrutka routes therefore opened one by one, sporadically at the very beginning, as soon as vehicles were made available. Yet, as Khujand's buses and trolleybuses were phased out due to tear and wear, the need for marshrutkas grew. In the first half of the 1990s, almost all suitable vehicles in the city ran as marshrutkas. Even the entire fleet of medical emergency vehicles was abandoned and adapted for public transport use (Interview TH).

In the early days, to open a new line, the candidate had only to sketch the route, draft the prospective headways, and get a stamp from the city's transport department. There were, and still are, no obligations with respect to minimum service levels or operating times. Thus, the marshrutka infrastructure was assembled with the help of several other (elder and ailing) types of urban infrastructure, building on gaps in regulation and the decay of some industrial spheres. The emergence of marshrutka-based transport necessitated the development of a particular economic framework based on informal and bottom-up regulation of individual economic activity – heralding the entrepreneurial boom of the early 1990s. The official mechanisms of route licensing and operation, however, have persisted since the Soviet era. *De iure,* each driver has to pick up a route sheet and have it signed by the operator in charge. Moreover, the driver has to pass a daily medical check-up at the operator's office; the same goes for his vehicle. These obligations are generally not fulfilled, and the respective control bodies receive fees merely for retroactively signing the required documents. Drivers usually pay a flat licence fee, and keep the surplus. At the same time, they have to pay out of these funds for maintenance, fuel, insurance, and traffic fines on their own. All together, this is a good business for the operators, who receive guaranteed licence and control payments, yet have no obligations as to the everyday operation of the lines (Figure 2).

In Khujand, Sorbon, the privatized former taxi company, held the status of a monopolist operator until the early 2000s. Due to pressure from credit providers such as the Asian Development Bank and the European Bank for Reconstruction and Development (EBRD) to implement tendering legislation (Interview SB), the transport administration stripped Sorbon of more than half of its lines. Lines were distributed among a handful of smaller operating companies 'in order to help small and medium enterprises' (Interview TH), yet without a tendering process. No new lines have been accepted since 2003, and the

Figure 2. Passengers waiting for a ride in the afternoon rush hour, 19th *microraion*. Image: W. Sgibnev (2014).

transport administration considers the marshrutka market saturated (a performative claim, which can potentially discontinue the fluid character of the phenomenon – unless the new circumstances will channel marshrutka entrepreneurship towards renewed public success). The existing lines are in charge of Khujand's transport administration and provide urban service in Khujand and suburban service to the Ghafurov, Konibodom, and Djabbor Rasulov Districts. In each district and city, local services operate under the responsibility of local transport administrations.[4] In order to deal with lines under the responsibility of several administrations, regular meetings take place, prefiguring some kind of metropolitan governance for the larger Khujand agglomeration.

Apart from drivers joining lines with their own vehicles on a 'route sheet' basis, operators also employ salaried drivers, as well as freelancers with their own or leased minibuses, which makes the marshrutka-based transport system highly flexible and resilient – an element which surely has contributed to its success in the region. In the evenings, profit margins decrease for regular minibus drivers, and unregulated freelancers take over with private cars, plying the most popular routes.

As of late 2014, 92 urban and suburban lines operated in Khujand, deploying at least 1500 minibuses. This adds up to some 400 marshrutkas per hour in each direction on the central stretch of Lenin Street during peak hours (own count). Akimov and Banister (2011, 28) estimate that every sixth vehicle in Tashkent's urban traffic is a marshrutka, and that 1 family in 10 is supported by a member driving a taxi or minibus. The count might be even higher for Khujand, if we consider the number of 1500 vehicles against the urban population of 170,000; that is roughly 1 marshrutka per 100 inhabitants. Furthermore, we have to take into account the service economy, including petrol stations, maintenance, and retail. Marshrutka mobility is therefore a vital pillar of Khujand's economy, and the economy of post-Soviet Central Asia in general. The importance of the phenomenon is such that Wondra (2010, 9) claims that 'without the marshrutka network, many towns would be isolated from governance structures and may cease to function within the greater economy'.

Today, marshrutkas are being widely criticized for being unsafe, uncomfortable, or polluting. Yet they still offer a series of very user-friendly interfaces, for both passengers and drivers, which make them popular for a broad scope of urban dwellers. For passengers, marshrutkas bring about small headways, at least at peak times, and the possibility of getting on and off at will at almost any (convenient) place, as well as connections between almost all important areas, without having to change lines. These benefits are complemented by high speed (surely obtained via fearless and reckless driving). For the driver, the marshrutka implies a direct source of income, flexibility in personal and professional self-organization, and the liberty of taking only paying passengers, thus excluding schoolchildren or the elderly, who enjoy legally imposed fare privileges. These features taken together create a unique style of passengering, characteristic of urban mobility in the last two decades in the former USSR (Figure 3).

Given the role of the marshrutka sector in providing livelihood for thousands of Khujand's citizens, regulation of marshrutka-based transport is a highly sensitive issue (for a comparative post-Soviet perspective, see Vozyanov 2014b). To circumvent regulation, driving without route sheets is becoming more common: in peak hours there are one and a half times as many vehicles on the streets as have been licenced (Interview TH), regulated by informal market access negotiation by marshrutka drivers – reminding one to some extent of organized crime settings, as hinted at by Humphrey (2004) and Mühlfried (2006).

Regulation through licencing and (the threat of) tendering goes hand in hand with strict spatial regulation aimed at providing representative town centres. In Khujand's

Figure 3. Marshrutkas are often blamed for reckless driving. Whose fault was it this time? Image: W. Sgibnev (2014).

city centre, marshrutkas may only use designated stops, and a large marshrutka station has been set up close to the main bazaar. The topography does not allow banning marshrut-kas from the main street altogether, as happened in Dushanbe,[5] since there is no alterna-tive thoroughfare to Lenin Street. Yet there is some official ambition to get marshrutkas off the streets, performing modernity through particular visions of mobility. The EBRD has pledged to provide a credit of USD$ 61.5 million for 600 new buses and trolleybuses. The first hundred Chinese-built buses were due to arrive towards the end of 2011 (Mèr Hudžanda: 100 novyh, 2011), but as of this writing, they have not yet appeared on the streets. One reason for this might lie in the personal involvement of bureaucrats who themselves employ marshrutka drivers and fear losing their income (Interviews NR, LS). Another reason for the delay is a discussion between the EBRD and the city administration on whether to provide the credit in cash or in kind – that is if buses are to be tendered and ordered directly by the EBRD or if the cash flow runs through the city administration accounts (Interview TH).

Focusing on regulatory aspects, we have retraced in this section the spread of marsh-rutka-based transport in Khujand, and have presented its vital importance for the local economy and its role in projects of modernization. In the following section, we will take a closer look at the trans-local ties of the marshrutka mobility phenomenon, notably with regard to flows of ideas, vehicles, and people.

The trans-local perspective

Looking at the trans-local perspective, we now expand on how the marshrutka mobility phenomenon is inscribed in global flows. We will deal here with spreading understandings of modernity referring to car ownership, to global value chains reflected in changing marshrutka vehicles, and to border regimes and (migratory) actor networks, which are co-constitutive of the marshrutka mobility phenomenon.

The spread of marshrutka mobility relates to larger trends typical of the post-Soviet space, such as catch-up motorization. During the Soviet era, private cars were very much sought after and very difficult to obtain, and therefore there were very few on the streets, even more so at the Central Asian periphery. As Fick (Fick 1971, 190) prosaically notes, 'Private cars play a minor role in the urban landscape. Instead, the large number of trucks is noticeable. Bikes are extremely rare.' Indeed, car ownership in the Central Asian republics was distinctly lower than the USSR average, but nevertheless steadily rising.

The spread of marshrutkas is, in this regard, typical for a society on the verge of mass motorization. The rise of marshrutkas notably resulted in a stratification of passengers according to income and status, and consequently according to the choice of a particular mode of transport. Passengers thus preferred marshrutkas to (cheaper and less frequent) municipal buses or trolleybuses. As for Khujand, unstable electricity provision destroyed the image of the trolleybus as a reliable means of transport from the early 1990s. Further-more, the expansion of the line towards the train station in 1999 ironically contributed to further degradation of the image in favour of marshrutkas: the line extension conveniently connected the main bazaars (Atush and Somon) to both the city centre and the railway station. For this reason, sellers and buyers used trolleybuses for cargo transport, since car usage was low and marshrutkas too cramped to carry large bundles or even livestock

(Interview OG), fostering the (urbanites') image of the trolleybus as a means of transport for villagers and all those who could not afford anything better.

Furthermore, marshrutkas represent an alternative branch in the social history of fares. Soviet public transport offered free rides for a few, quantitatively insignificant groups of urban passengers. Later on, legislation throughout the former Soviet Union forced munici-pal and state-owned carriers to provide free transportation services for pensioners, school-children, and some other categories of the local population. This kind of social support (and, simultaneously, social sorting) does not exist on marshrutka routes – a factor which contributed to their 'exclusive' character, to the detriment of trolleybuses (Vozyanov 2014b; Sgibnev 2014). Combined with rivalry on the marshrutka side, this served as a trigger for a new dimension of social stratification in the city according to mode of mobi-lity. Marshrutkas not only offered perceived superiority compared to publicly run transport options, they also bore the promise of accessibility, comfort, and speed – a promise of modernity. Those who in the 1990s could not (yet) afford a car could get a glimpse of it in marshrutka mobility. In this regard, marshrutkas relate to the jitney phenomenon in the United States of the 1910s. The innovation of the assembly line brought hundreds and thousands of Ford vehicles to the streets. Combined with cheap credit, high unem-ployment, absence of regulation, and the desire to take part in automobile-driven moder-nity, jitneys conquered American cities one after another, thus hastening the decline of publicly run transport and heralding the onset of mass motorization (Schwantes 1985). Marshrutkas thus reveal fruitful insight into the emergence of social inequality and irrational sympathy among passengers (Bratanova 2009), and into regimes of justice in contemporary post-Soviet societies (Kuznecov and Šaîtanova 2012).

Car ownership in Khujand relies almost entirely on imported second-hand vehicles. The car trade and transit has evolved into a profitable sector of the economy, with Khujand being the transshipment hub for Tajikistan, southern Kyrgyzstan, and northern Afghanistan. Second-hand vehicles, overwhelmingly from Germany, are sold to Latvia and Lithuania, where Khu-jandi traders routinely buy them.[6] Most vehicles are forwarded by rail. Every day, a freight train arrives in Khujand. On average, it carries 10 autoracks with 10 cars each, meaning that at least 100 cars arrive in Khujand on a daily basis. As for marshrutkas, they are generally for-warded by road. First, they do not easily fit into the autoracks. Second, one marshrutka passage allows transporting four vehicles at once: the minibus itself, one other car as a trailer at the rear, and two automobiles sawn apart and stacked in the interior.[7] The remaining space is generally filled with spare parts, which are particularly difficult to come by in Central Asia. Upon the marshrutka's arrival in Khujand, specialized mechanics fit the interior with pas-senger seats, cut out windows, and install a sliding door, lighting, and loudspeakers.

Marshrutka-based transport lives according to the rhythm of import waves. In the course of the 1990s, the Latvian RAF minibuses were mostly replaced, either by second-hand Western products (domestically refurbished Mercedes-Benz Sprinter and Ford Transit vehicles) or, since the mid-1990s, by Russian Gazel' (GAZ 3221x) minibuses. In the mid-2000s, Chinese eight-seaters manufactured by Hafei were actively imported to Tajikistan and became locally known as Tangem. Since 2010, Tangem cars are banned from Dushanbe and have migrated to the periphery. In the capital they are being replaced by larger Hyundai Starex vans, allegedly in a move by some government-affiliated business circles to boost Hyundai sales and to bring the profitable marshrutka sector under their control (Žiteli Dušanbe krajne nedovol'ny 2010).

It is interesting to note that the composition of the local marshrutka fleet varies widely, in tune with local supply chains and investor interests. We observe the spread of marshrutka vehicles forming concentric circles of modernization: newer vehicles settle in the capitals and regional centres, with older vehicles being squeezed out to the periphery. In this regard, it is still common to see Soviet-built RAF minibuses in service on remote rural routes. This concentric distribution is challenged by recent investments of labour migrant remittances into marshrutka-based transportation. Smaller, less capital-consuming Isuzu/Damas six-seaters have replaced, for instance, the oldest vehicle series in neighbouring Spitamen District.

Turning to remittances, we have to acknowledge the importance of Central Asian labour migration for the marshrutka mobility phenomenon. Migrants constitute the core of marshrutka import networks, and their remittances largely fuel vehicle and license purchases for their (male) family members back home. Furthermore, the transport sector offers exit options for elderly labour migrants who are no longer in condition to do the taxing and exhausting work they used to do (for example on Russian construction sites). Interview partners repeatedly reported that after having paid for their sons' and daughters' weddings, they started to put aside money for vehicle purchases.

Conclusion

The role of the marshrutka mobility phenomenon in the production of post-Soviet urban spaces in and beyond Central Asia tells us about more than just changing patterns of transportation. It is rather a contribution to a larger discussion on post-Soviet transformation in the region – one which questions the still-widespread discourses of decline and deficiency, and focuses on the bottom-up emergence of new orders in the fields of economy, morale, urban development, and migration. The marshrutka mobility phenomenon provides fruitful material for understanding how everyday life is transforming throughout the post-Soviet period.

The Soviet city was conceived with a detailed plan for the future, a long and firm path to follow, secured by a command-planning economy. Transport, along with several other types of infrastructure, responded not only to actual passenger demand but also to state ideology and its politics of the future. After the breakdown of state-provided structures, the need (and the possibility) had come for situative decisions: they considered only short-term perspectives, but have had long-lasting outcomes. If one had said to passengers in 1991, pointing to a marshrutka, 'Look, this is going to be your transport for the coming decades', they would probably have reacted differently from how they did historically. Marshrutkas indeed become (swiftly, yet contingently) something other than they used to be a couple of years earlier. They react much faster to the changing environment than heavy-footed official plans. Marshrutkas, with their parasitizing on infrastructure, their multi-local types of emergence, prefigured and created those developments which over time have come to characterize Central Asian societies. And they continue to do so, through rapid, sometimes retrograde transformations, and incremental, fragmented management. This very fluidity seems to be the foundation of marshrutkas' success. Marshrutkas might have saved post-Soviet passengers from transport collapse at some moment in the 1990s. The ongoing regulation of the sector, however, limits fluidity and therefore puts into question the future existence of marshrutkas as we know them today.

A series of intriguing questions on the marshrutka mobility phenomenon still need to be answered. We surely need more (oral history–based) insights into their massive spread in the early post-Socialist period. Research has barely started on how modes of socializing and gendered mobilities are being performed through mobility.[8] Yet, changes in the perception of urban landscapes induced by the rise of marshrutkas also constitute, in our eyes, a valuable field of study, since they allow insights into how mobility co-produces space. In the same vein, we should take a closer look at how the rise of marshrutkas has changed attitudes towards waiting, and thus brought with it a new culture of time. Disclosing the interrelations between technological development, everyday practices, and urban space will allow us to reflect on the role of mobility in transformation processes – and thus to rebound our research to First World settings. In spite of marshrutkas' being extensively criticized within a 'sustainable mobility' mainstream, they are at the same time applauded by proponents of demand-responsive transportation as 'lessons to be learnt from less developed countries' (Silcock 1981; Enoch 2005, 68). And who knows which of us will be taking a marshrutka to work in some years' time?

Notes

1. Still, it draws from some 20 interviews with marshrutka drivers, owners, experts and passengers, participant observation and archive data collection.
2. Indeed, given the very limited communication options of the early 1990s, it would be extremely interesting to study knowledge transfer mechanisms between pioneers of marshrutka-based transit. Perhaps the picture we would get would be similar to a 'dialect continuum', where the degree of dissimilarity between local versions is proportional to the geographic distance between locations.
3. The necessary investment would have amounted to only two working days with the appropriate equipment (Interview TD). As of 2010, the trolleybus enterprise received only 12,000 somoni (€2000) a year in subsidies from the city administration and was therefore unable to pay for this larger repair out of its own funds.
4. Long-distance marshrutka lines fall under the responsibility of the transport administration of Sughd Region, as do those remaining 'large bus' lines on some routes (to Isfara, Taboshar, and Zafarobod, as of late 2014).
5. A ban on marshrutkas on main streets is in force in many capitals throughout the post-Soviet space: in Tbilisi on Rustaveli Avenue, in Bishkek on Ala-Too Square (in daytime), and in Astana in the entire city. Marshrutkas do not seem 'high-end' enough to appear in representative locations. For a discussion of the representative dimension and the role of public transport in Central Asian nation-building, see also Sgibnev (2014).
6. In August 2014, a much-acclaimed joint investigation by the German newspaper *Süddeutsche Zeitung* and the TV magazine *ARD Panorama* revealed that stolen high-end cars from Germany are shipped to Tajikistan with the tacit approval of local authorities.
7. The halves are welded back together upon arrival in Khujand and brought to the market. Alternatively, they can be cannibalized for spare parts, whichever is more profitable.
8. In this direction, we find an emerging literature in Russian-speaking academia, such as works on oral folklore in a public transport setting, often reflecting upon the conflicting interaction between marshrutka drivers and their passengers (Ivanova 2007; Sanina 2011; Tihomirov 2008).

Acknowledgements

An early draft of the article was presented at the workshop, Tracing Migration and Global Connectedness: Urban Contexts in Central Asia and Beyond, at the Humboldt University in Berlin. We would also like to extend our thanks to Jørgen Burchardt, of the Danish National Museum of Science and Technology, for kindly sharing with us his detailed bibliography on informal systems of public transport around the world.

Disclosure statement

No potential conflict of interest was reported by the authors.

Funding

The article's preliminary empirical findings are based on exploratory fieldwork in Khujand (Tajikistan) in autumn 2014, funded by the Gerda Henkel Foundation's Central Asia programme, to which the authors are greatly indebted.

References

Akimov, A., and D. Banister. 2011. "Urban Public Transport in Post-communist Transition: The Case of TASHKENT, Uzbekistan." *Comparative Economic Studies* 53 (4): 721–755. doi:10.1057/ces.2011.18

Alexander, C., V. Buchli, and C. Humphrey, eds. 2007. *Urban Life in Post-Soviet Asia*. London: Univ. College London Press.

Bissell, D. 2009. "Conceptualising Differently-mobile Passengers: Geographies of Everyday Encumbrance in the Railway Station." *Social & Cultural Geography* 10 (2): 173–195. doi:10.1080/14649360802652137

Bratanova, E. 2009. *Maršrutkite v Sofiâ: b"rzina i risk v gradskaâ sreda* (3-4): 113–138. www.ceeol.com.

Brownell, B. A. 1972. "A Symbol of Modernity: Attitudes Toward the Automobile in Southern Cities in the 1920s." *The Johns Hopkins University PressStable* 24 (1): 20–44. http://www.jstor.org/stable/2711913.

Burrell, K., and K. Horschelmann, eds. 2014. *Mobilities in Socialist and Post-socialist States. Societies on the Move*. London: Palgrave Macmillan.

Collingridge, David. 1979. "The Fallibist Theory of Value and its Applications to Decision Making." PhD Thesis, University of Aston.

Cresswell, T. 2006. *On the Move. Mobility in the Modern Western world*. New York: Routledge.

Davis, D. F. 1990. "The North American Response to the Jitney Bus." *Canadian Review of American Studies*, University of Toronto Press 21 (3): 333–358. doi:10.3138/CRAS-021-03-04

DeLanda, M. (2006) *A New Philosophy of Society: Assemblage Theory and Social Complexity*. London, New York: Continuum.

Deleuze, G., and F. Guattari. 1987. *A Thousand Plateaus: Capitalism and Schizophrenia*. Translated by B. Massumi. London: The Athlone Press.

Edensor, T. 2004. "Automobility and National Identity: Representation, Geography and Driving Practice." *Theory, Culture & Society* 21 (4–5): 101–120. doi:10.1177/0263276404046063

Enoch, Marcus P. 2005. "Demand Responsive Transport: Lessons to be Learnt from Less Developed Countries." *Traffic Engineering and Control* 46 (2): 68–71.

Fick, K. E. 1971. "Die Großstädte in Sowjet-Mittelasien. Entwicklung, Gestalt und Funktion der Siedlungszentren eines kontinentalen Trockenraums." In *Hamburger Geographische Studien* 24 (Festschrift für Albert Kolb), 159–197.

Finn, B. 2008. "Market Role and Regulation of Extensive Urban Minibus Services as Large Bus Service Capacity is Restored – Case Studies from Ghana, Georgia and Kazakhstan." *Research in Transportation Economics* 22 (1): 118–125. doi:10.1016/j.retrec.2008.05.012

Gillen, J., and N. Hall. 2011. "Any Mermaids? Early Postcard Mobilities." In *Mobile Methods*, edited by M. Büscher, J. Urry, and K. Witchger, 20–35. Abingdon, UK: Routledge.

Grdzelishvili, I., and R. Sathre. 2008. "Understanding the Urban Travel Attitudes and Behaviour of Tbilisi Residents." *Transport Policy* 18 (1): 38–45.

Gwilliam, K. M. 2000. *Private Participation in Public Transport in FSU*. Washington DC: The World Bank. http://www.worldbank.org/ … nsport/publicat/twu_40.pdf.

Gwilliam, K. M. 2001. "Competition in Urban Passenger Transport in the Developing World." *Journal of Transport Economics and Policy* 35: 99–118. http://www.jstor.org/stable/20053860.

Gwilliam, K. 2003. "Bus Franchising in Developing Countries: Some Recent World Bank Experience." WB22135. *8th International Conference on Ownership and Regulation of Land Passenger Transport*. Rio de Janeiro, June 2003. http://siteresources.worldbank.org/INTURBANTRANSPORT/Resources/bus_franch_gwilliam.pdf

Gwilliam, K. M., R. T. Meakin, and A. Kumar, eds. 1999. "Designing Competition in Urban Bus Passenger Transport Lessons from Uzbekistan." *6-th International Conference on Competition and Ownership in Land Passenger Transport*. Cape Town, South Africa.

Hook, W. 1999. "The Political Economy of Post-transition Transportation Policy in Hungary." *Transport Policy* 6 (4): 207–224. doi:10.1016/S0967-070X(99)00022-0

Humphrey, C. 2004. "Sovereignty and Ways of Life: The Marshrut System in the City of Ulan-Ude, Russia". Blackwell Publishing Ltd.

Ivanova, T. G. 2007. "Ob''âvleniâ v maršrutnyh taski: Vzglâd folklorista." *Živaâ starina* 4: 35–38.

Jensen, O. 2009. "Flows of Meaning, Cultures of Movements – Urban Mobility as Meaningful Everyday Life Practice." *Mobilities* 4 (1): 139–158. doi:10.1080/17450100802658002

Jensen, A. 2011. "Mobility, Space and Power: On the Multiplicities of Seeing Mobility". *Mobilities* 6 (2): 255–271. doi:10.1080/17450101.2011.552903

Johnston, R. 1984. "Controlling Technology: An Issue for the Social Studies of Science." *Social Studies of Science* 14: 97–113. doi:10.1177/030631284014001008

Jordan, T. (1995). Collective Bodies: Raving and the Politics of Gilles Deleuze and Felix Guattari. *Body & Society* 1 (1): 125–144. doi:10.1177/1357034X95001001008

Konrad, M. (2007). International Biodiplomacy and Global Ethical Forms: Relations of Critique Between Public Anthropology and Science in Society. *Anthropological quarterly* 80 (2): 325–353;.

Kumar, A., and F. Barrett. 2008. "Stuck in Traffic - Urban Transport in Africa." Report. *Africa Infrastructure Country Diagnostic*.

Kuznecov, A. G., and L. A. Šaîtanova. 2012. Maršrutnoe taksi na perekrestke režimov spravedlivosti. *Sociologiâ Vlasti* 2012 (6-7):137–149.

Law, J. 2002. "Objects and Spaces." *Theory, Culture & Society*, 19(5-6): 91–105. doi:10.1177/026327602761899165

McFarlane, C. 2011. "Assemblage and Critical Urbanism." *City* 15 (2): 204–224. doi:10.1080/13604813.2011.568715

"Mèr Xudžanda: 100 novyh avtobusov načnut kursirovat' po gorodu v sentâbre." 2011. *AsiaPlus*, April 15. http://news.tj/ru/news/mer-khudzhanda-100-novykh-avtobusov-nachnut-kursirovat-po-gorodu-v-sentyabre.

Mühlfried, F. 2006. (with Diakonidze A.) "Marshrutki: Public Transportation and the fight against corruption in Georgia." *Caucaz*. http://www.caucaz.com/home_eng/breve_contenu.php?id = 268.

Müller-Schwarze, N. 2009. "Diablos Rojos : Painted Buses and Panamanian Identities." *Visual Anthropology* 22 (5): 435–456. doi:10.1080/08949460701688965

Pickles, J. 2010. "The spirit of Post-socialism: Common Spaces and the Production of Diversity." *European Urban and Regional Studies,* 17 (2), 127–140. doi:10.1177/0969776409356492

Pinch, T. 2001. "Why do You go to a Music Store to Buy a Synthesizer: Path Dependence and the Social Construction of Technology." *Path Dependence and Creation*, edited by R. Garud and P. Karnøe, 381–400. London: Lawrence Earlbaum Associates.

Pucher, J. 1995. "The Road to Ruin?." *Transport Policy* 2 (1): 5–13. doi:10.1016/0967-070X(95)93241-P

Pucher, J. 1999. "The Transformation of Urban Transport in the Czech Republic, 1988–1998." *Transport Policy* 6 (4): 225–236. doi:10.1016/S0967-070X(99)00023-2

Sanina, A. 2011. "The Marshrutka as a Socio-cultural Phenomenon of a Russian Megacity." *City, Culture and Society* 4 (2): 211–218. doi.org/10.1016/j.ccs.2011.12.002

Saxenian, A. 1999. "Comment on Kenney and von Burg, 'technology, Entrepreneurship and Path Dependence: Industrial Clustering in Silicon Valley and Route 128'." *Industrial and Corporate Change* 8 (1): 105–110. doi:10.1093/icc/8.1.105

Scambler, G., ed. 2012. *Contemporary Theorists for Medical Sociology*. Abingdon, UK: Routledge.

Schwantes, C. A. 1985. "The West Adapts the Automobile: Technology, Unemployment, and the Jitney Phenomenon of 1914-1917." *Western Historical Quarterly* 16 (3). http://www.jstor.org/stable/969130. doi:10.2307/969130

Sgibnev, W. 2014. "Urban Public Transport and the State in Post-Soviet Central Asia." In *Mobilities in Socialist and Post-socialist States. Societies on the Move*, edited by Kathy Burrell und Kathrin Horschelmann, 194–216. London: Palgrave Macmillan.

Silcock, D. T. 1981. "Urban Paratransit in the Developing World." *Transport Reviews* 1 (2): 151–168. doi:10.1080/01441648108716456

"S ulic Xudžanda izčezli trollejbusy, soobŝaet ,Narodnaâ gazeta'." 2008. *Asia Plus*, May 15.

Suzuki, P. T. 1985. "Vernacular Cabs: Jitneys and Gypsies in Five Cities." *Transportation Research Part A: General* 19 (4): 337–347. doi:10.1016/0191-2607(85)90069-X

Thrift, N. 2004. "Driving in the City." *Theory, Culture & Society* 21 (4-5): 41–59. doi:10.1177/0263276404046060

Tihomirov, C. A. 2008. "Maršrutnoe taksi kak istočnik fol'klornoj obraznosti." *Fol'klor malyx social'nyx grupp: tradicii i sovremennost'*, 239–251. Moscow: Gosudarstvennyj respublikanskij centr russkogo fol'klora.

Urry, J. 2002. "Mobility and Proximity." *Sociology* 36 (2): 255–274. doi:10.1177/0038038502036002002

Urry, J. 2004. "The 'System' of Automobility." *Theory, Culture & Society* 21 (25): 25–39. doi:10.1177/0263276404046059

Urry, J. 2007. *Mobilities*, Cambridge: Polity Press.

"V Sogde posle dolgogo prostoâ vnov' zapustili trollejbusy." 2009. *AsiaPlus*, August 17. http://www2.asiaplus.tj/news/33/55893.html.

Vozyanov, A. 2014a. "Is Bus Transportation Public Indeed? Marshrutka and Changes of Urban Passengering in Post-Soviet Ukraine" *Paper presented at 12th International Conference on Urban History: Cities in Europe, Cities in the World Lisbon, Portugal 2014, September 3-6.*

Vozyanov, A. 2014b. "L'gotniki v gorode: passažiry staršego vozrasta i ètika mobil'nosti v infrastrukture ukrainskogo obŝestvennogo transporta." *Sociology of Power* 3: 60–80.

Wondra, N. M. 2010. "The Marshrutka—An Overlooked Public Good?" *Russian Analytical Digest* 89: 5–9.

Yu, J. E., and J.-W. Lee. 2010. "Exploring the Management of Social Enterprise from Systemic Perspective: The Application of Deleuze's Theory of Assemblage." *Proceedings of Twenty-eighth International System Dynamics Conference* (Seoul, Korea July 25-29, 2010) http://www.systemdynamics.org/conferences/2010/proceed/papers/P1202.pdf.

"Žiteli Dušanbe krajne nedovol'ny vvedennym zapretom na maršrutki." 2010. *EurasiaNet*, April 24. http://russian.eurasianet.org/node/31089.

Prayer house or cultural centre? Restoring a mosque in post-socialist Armenia

Tsypylma Darieva

Department for Slavic and Caucasus Studies, Friedrich-Schiller-University Jena, Germany

ABSTRACT
Post-socialist urban dynamics in the Caucasus have been characterized by uneven processes of rebuilding and reclaiming of sacred spaces. Exploring re-emerging Shia Muslim lifestyles in post-conflict Armenia around Yerevan's Blue Mosque, I examine how a religious place is perceived and used in everyday life. Built at the end of the eighteenth century in a multi-religious environment, today the Blue Mosque is associated with the political body symbolizing the recent Iranian–Armenian friendship and with Iran's soft-power policy in the Caucasus. The ethnographic research reveals that the mosque complex is not an isolated sacred site emphasizing differences between Iranian migrants and Armenian locals, worshippers, and non-worshippers, but a spatial expression of the coming together of groups from different backgrounds and of the vernacular hybridity that existed in Yerevan in the past. In spite of the invisibility and the silence of the Blue Mosque's past from the point of view of government officials, the physical restoration of the mosque is triggering unembodied memories of people in conscious and unconscious reconstructions of the multi-religious past. The question, is to what extent does the Blue Mosque contribute to a visible rediversification of religious and ethnic life in Armenia?

Introduction

On 1 April 2011, *EurasiaNet*, an electronic newspaper operated by the Open Society Foundation for Central Asia and the Caucasus, reported:

> Over the past two weeks, to celebrate the Persian New Year (Norooz), Yerevan concert halls have offered up an array of banned Iranian music, with performances by Iranian pop singers Andy, Leila, Pouva, Kouros and Sepideh. Restaurants and clubs in Yerevan now offer menus in Farsi, while Iranian and Arab music plays in the background. Such events, though, are not a sudden manifestation of multiculturalism. The large number of Iranian visitors to Yerevan, a city of just under 1.1 million people, nearly requires that local businesses cater to the tourists' tastes.

Iranian middle-class 'pop culture and booze' tourism seems to offer a new form of trans-regional connectedness in the South Caucasus, and yet the presence of Iranians is a not a new phenomenon for Armenia. Until the 1920s, the Iranian-speaking population and

Azeri-speaking local Shia Muslims played a vital role in the history of Yerevan's urban life.[1] By the early nineteenth century, the Muslim community in Yerevan was an important component of the city's multi-religious and multi-lingual population. It was Yerevan which came to embody 'a dusty city of oriental clay houses dominated by Moslem courtyards with gardens', its 'landscape ... defined by the skyline of minarets' (Akopyan 1977, 128). The multi-religious character of urban life in the South Caucasus was the norm, as Ronald Suny (2001, 863) pointed out:

> Baku and Tbilisi [the current capitals, respectively, of Azerbaijan and Georgia] had been models of inter-ethnic cohabitation; Tbilisi at one time had an Armenian majority, and Erivan [Yerevan] was primarily a Muslim town at several points of its long history.

Today, along with a few shisha cafes, Persian restaurants and small sweet shops for Iranian tourists and students, there is one place that is associated with Shia religious practices in contemporary Armenia: the Blue Mosque, on Mashtotz Avenue. Built in 1765, the Blue Mosque was one of Yerevan's eight mosques which, along with seven Armenian and four Russian Orthodox churches, shaped the pre-socialist, multi-religious skyline of this city at the imperial borderland between Russia and Persia. Today, local tourist guidebooks for Yerevan hardly include this site in the cultural repertoire of city tours and urban representations.

In this article, I explore a re-emerging religious place in an Armenian urban landscape characterized by the legacy of socialist atheism and inter-ethnic conflict. Institutionalized Soviet secularism led to the dominant understanding of the socialist city as the equivalent of a transition from rural traditional lifestyles to modern secularity. Consequently, the spectacular decline of public religious life and a high level of socialist urbanization pushed the issues of religious presence in Eurasia's urban spaces to the margins of anthropological interest and have rarely been addressed in the post-socialist urban transformation (Grant 2010; Darieva and Kaschuba 2011). Different actors are involved in uneven processes of restoring and reclaiming sacred sites in post-socialist cities: state authorities, city planners, local oligarchs, official religious institutions, international organizations, migrants, and tourism developers. However, 'practitioners' of the city, such as ordinary worshippers and visitors to religious places, are seldom the focus of these discourses.

Thus, by exploring re-emerging Muslim lifestyles in Yerevan around the Blue Mosque, I examine how a new minority religious place is perceived and used in the everyday life of locals and newcomers. As a public place, the Blue Mosque complex provides a social and metaphorical space for different narratives and debates. It not only provides room for prayer, religious practices, and official politics; it also has a broad symbolic meaning for Yerevan's urban life and reflects the city's uneasy relationship with its heterogeneous past. My approach relies on Doreen Massey's (1995, 188) concept of 'uncertainty of places and their pasts', which suggests that the past and present identities of a place are shaped less by the history of the city or the nation as such than by narratives and legends emerging around the place. Similarly, Michael Herzfeld (1991) observed that contested heritage in a Cretan town creates conflicting perceptions between what he describes as the 'monumental time' appropriated by nationalistic narratives and historical representations used in the present, and the 'social time' of the place as it is lived and experienced by individuals. Following the actor-oriented perspective, I reflect on the

Blue Mosque complex's social life as a 'shared place' and discuss how in the context of Iran's soft-power policy a Shia Islamic place in Yerevan is gaining a multi-vocal character.

Local settings

After the collapse of the Soviet Union, the Islamic Republic of Iran re-emerged as an important regional power (along with Russia and Turkey) in the South Caucasus, and today plays an ever-increasing role in international trade, energy supply, and emerging tourism. In contrast to Azerbaijan and Georgia, relations between the two states, Armenia and Iran, are characterized as 'surprisingly close' (Sharashenidze 2011). During the war between Armenia and Azerbaijan over Nagorny Karabakh (1990–1994) and the resultant period of economic hardship, including an energy crisis, Armenia was unexpectedly offered a strategic partnership by Iran on its southern border. In return, on 13 October 1995, Yerevan authorities transferred the right to use the Blue Mosque complex to Iran's official representatives in Armenia. This transfer released the Armenian state institutions from financial costs for renovation works and provided the Iranian state with a space for promoting Iran's soft-power policy, with a focus on strengthening a new regional interconnectedness between the South Caucasus and Iran.[2] For a long time, the nature of the Iranian–Armenian relationship was stigmatized. In particular during the Soviet period, the image of the southern neighbour became that of 'evil backwardness'. This construction arose from the Soviet ideology of defending the state border between Soviet Armenia and Iran.

In terms of religious and ethnic composition, since the disintegration of the Soviet Union, Armenia has been strongly associated with a mono-ethnic and mono-religious society, combined with an explicit preference for the Armenian Apostolic Church as the national religion.[3] Numerically, ethnic and religious minorities make up less than 2% of the population in Armenia. More precisely, Yezidi, Kurds, Assyrians, and Russian Molokans, the largest non-Armenian ethnic groups, comprise only a few thousand of the approximately three million Armenians. In a historical perspective, by the time of the Russian Revolution in 1917, Yerevan was still a 'patchwork of linguistic and religious groups' with fuzzy boundaries between them. According to the 1897 census, of the 92,323 residents of Erivan Province, 25,218 were Muslim (King 2008, 144).[4] However, after the establishment of ethno-national units in Soviet Transcaucasia in the 1920s, traditions of mixing and religious cohabitation began to disappear, and the notions of ethnic homogeneity within political territories became prevalent after WWII. Similar to what Humphrey and Skvirskaja (2012) outlined in their volume on post-cosmopolitan cities in Eurasia, many elements of the urban 'togetherness' in Yerevan were erased by interethnic hostility and/or indifference in particular by the end of socialism. The Muslim population (Azeri-speakers and Kurds) gradually decreased in the territory of the Armenian Republic and, at the onset of the inter-ethnic conflict over Nagorny Karabakh at the beginning of the 1990s, almost disappeared (the same processes take place for Armenians in Azerbaijan). As a result, dominant conventional assumptions about the existing ethnic homogeneity of Yerevan's population greatly affected the ways minorities and their sacred places were and are interpreted, represented, and treated during and after socialism. Throughout the last century, many non-Armenian sacred places, cemeteries, and residential quarters have been marginalized on the surface of the city, silenced, or completely forgotten. After the geopolitical closure to the world and the era in which religion lost its position as a source of morality and everyday lifestyles, it is not surprising that the 'religious question' has reappeared in the Caucasus in a specific way. In Armenia, it was more often minority religious organizations and alternative religious practices (new Christian sects, neo-paganist movements) which challenged the state and society. The consequences of this dynamic are evident in a strong fragmentation and spatialization of religious minority life in the South Caucasus (Antonyan 2010; Jödicke 2015).

While the notion of intolerance towards new evangelical forms of Christianity in Armenia began in the 1990s, we should not disregard a new trend of the last decade to restore the historical diversity of Armenia's religious landscape. Influenced by global forces and in particular by the process of the incorporation of Armenia into the domain of international policies, Armenian officials and Yerevan's city administration are active in the implementation of the provisions of the UN Declaration of Human Rights, which was adopted by the Armenian government on 1 January 2004. The 'top-down' process aims to reinvent representations of cultural-religious pluralism in Armenia, at least on the level of monuments and the built environment. One of the major domains of this policy in Armenia focuses on the preservation and restoration of non-Armenian historical monuments in the city of Yerevan and other regions of Armenia. As of 30 October 2015, the Ministry of Culture's Agency for the Preservation of Historical and Cultural Monuments presented on its website, in addition to the Armenian Apostolic Church and historical monuments such as a pagan temple and Chalcedonian churches, the official list of monuments under protection, which includes three Russian Orthodox churches (in Yerevan, Gyumri, and Vanadzor), a Catholic church in Gyumri, the Blue Mosque (Goekcami) in Yerevan, the Abbas Mirza Mosque in Yerevan, two Assyrian churches, two Greek churches in the Lori region, one Jewish cemetery in the Vayatz Dzor region, one Kurdish cemetery in Aragatz, and around 50 Azerbaijani monuments within the territory of the Republic of Armenia, mainly in cemeteries (http://www.gov.am/en/religion, accessed 30 October 2015). These objects are registered and claimed by the Armenian government as 'preserved' or 'to be preserved' in Armenia.

Placing Goekcami in Yerevan: one place, many histories

> From Surb Zoravor one may readily regain the Tiflis road and pass in a southerly direction along the central park. Thence it is no great distance to the principal mosque of the city, Gök-Jami or mosque of heaven. This edifice is situated in the western half of Erivan, and surrounded by dwellings of Tatars in considerable number, overlapping into the Armenian quarters. It is approached from the narrow streets of a bazaar consisting of booths, and is entered by a handsome doorway at the side of an imposing minaret, of which the surface is diversified by designs in polychrome tiles. You pass through a vaulted passage in to the great court. It is a vast place, shady and serene. Lofty elms of great age shadow the basin of overflowing water which bubbles in the center of the paved spaces. (Lynch [1910] 1965, 297)

Built in 1765 by Hussein Ali Khan, the local mayor at the time, the Blue Mosque, also known as Goekmeschit, Goekcami (in Turkish), Голубаямечеть in Russian, and Masjid-I Juma'a or Jami-iShahr in Persian, is a clear-cut brick architectural complex with an internal courtyard equipped with a water-filled pool and an elegant rose garden. The Muslim complex is one of the oldest buildings in central Yerevan and consists of three prayer halls with a large blue dome in the middle, a 24-metre-high minaret, and 24 arcade cells looking onto the pool. It is located on the main street (formerly Lenin Street), opposite the Covered Market (built in 1952), and its brick buildings contrast with the surrounding modern Armenian stone architecture. The congregational mosque, with three *mihrabs* (sacred *kiblah* niches, showing the orientation to Mecca), is one of the largest and most unique mosque edifices in Transcaucasia, and was described by Markus Ritter (2009, 252) as 'the main model for the early Qajar mosque architecture of the Iranian period'. Akopyan (1977, 132) emphasized the meaning of the religious complex for the history of Yerevan's material culture, noting, 'Especially the long minaret was very beautiful and it was the highest point in old Yerevan.' Nowadays the 24-metre-high brick minaret, with its staggered tiled patterns, can be seen only from the internal court or from the windows of the neighbouring high-rise residences. The quarter is one of the busiest parts of central Yerevan and is surrounded by galleries for contemporary art, travel agencies, snack bars, bank offices, and grocery and clothing shops. However, in spite of its central location, the Blue Mosque is hardly visible from the street; incorporated into a streetscape of socialist housing blocks, it is hidden behind these high-rise residential buildings.

Placing the Blue Mosque in the multi-layered history of the city of Yerevan between different political regimes, one can identify continuity in its form and architecture, and a striking discontinuity in its content and functions. Four different trajectories can be distinguished on the basis of the functions and of the names used for the mosque complex over the last two centuries. Although all of these trajectories are linked with a specific way of conceptualizing this site, the processes of interacting with the 'Other', and mixing boundaries, seem to be common for this 'transitional zone'.

Originally, the Blue Mosque functioned as a Friday mosque for Yerevan's Muslim (mostly Azeri-speaking) population, until the middle of the 1920s, when it was closed under pressure from the anti-religion campaign. The intensive process of physical concealment, symbolic marginalizing, unmaking, and desacralization of the pre-Soviet multi-religious past in Yerevan was legitimized by the rhetoric of the struggle against 'feudalistic backwardness' and the opium of the people. In particular, Islam and the Russian Orthodox Church were stigmatized as 'backward' and as the most conservative institutions shaping the everyday life of ordinary people. The first key step towards physical desacralization occurred in the 1920s, marking the start of the anti-religion campaign in Yerevan and investing the Blue Mosque with secular functions. The sacred system of entrances into and exits from the mosque complex was radically changed. The southern main gate, located to the right of the minaret and close to the main prayer hall, was blocked and has never since been used as the main entrance. Depicted in a painting by the Armenian artist Gurjan in 1930, the southern gate appears to be a wide arched entrance with columns protected by a roofed construction. The western gate was incorporated into a residence complex and became hardly recognizable as an entrance. Only the northern entrance remained accessible and visible from the outside (Figures 1–3).

Despite the physical modifications to the building, the act of turning the Blue Mosque into a secular space did not marginalize it. On the contrary, it provided the mosque complex with a new social meaning and cultural status. In the middle of the 1920s, the courtyard was turned into a creative space for Armenian artists, writers, poets, and intelligentsia, facilitating the production of a new cultural and aesthetic order for socialist Armenia. The courtyard was protected by large elm and plane trees, and in this way provided the hot and dusty city with a shaded refuge. Because of the lack of urban parks,

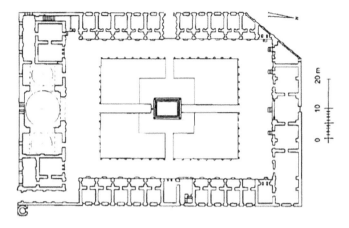

Figure 1. Sketch of the layout of the Blue Mosque, by Anahit Meliksetyan (December 2010).

modern exhibition halls, and houses of culture at that time, the courtyard and a large *chai-hane* (teahouse) inside the complex offered a unique urban space for public gatherings. Regular visitors included Yeghishe Charents, Martiros Saryan, Gabriel Gyurdjan, Aksel Bakunts, and international guests like William Saroyan, Osip Mandelshtam, Andrei Belyi, and Boris Kuzin.[5] Inspired by Socialist Realism and united by the Tovarishestvo Rabotnikov Iskusstva (1923–1930),[6] Armenian artists and intellectuals used the courtyard for exhibitions and as a laboratory for new socialist spirituality. By depicting the life of ordinary urbanites and peasants between markets, mosques, churches, and caravan-sarays, the Blue Mosque served as a background for the creation of a lyrical 'Oriental' landscape of

Figure 2. 'The Old Yerevan', by Gabriel Gyurjan (1930), Repository of the Yerevan History Museum.

Figure 3. The Blue Mosque (southern entrance and the minaret) in March 2011.
Source: Photograph by the author.

vanishing old Yerevan. This image of the vanishing old city stood in contrast both to the Russian European imperial architecture style and to the modernist built environment of socialist Armenia (Ter-Minassian 2007; Episkopyan 2011).

The next step in the physical desacralization of the Blue Mosque occurred during the 1930s and 1940s as part of the implementation of the socialist master plan developed by Alexander Tamanyan in 1924. Tamanyan's master plan for the city included the construction of wide, paved avenues, the removal of small streets, and the elevation of the ground level of Yerevan's streets by more than two metres. The strategy of promoting a new modernist plan for the socialist city centre was reached through 'downplaying' the area of the mosque and by situating it in a hollow. This act led to the visible separation of the religious space from the urban fabric. Even today, entering the mosque complex requires descending a flight of steps. During the next period, between 1935 and 1991, the former place for Islamic prayer was utilized further as a secular educational site. In the 1930s the mosque was turned into the Anti-Religious Museum, and later into the Museum for Antifascism; and in 1950 the complex was divided into two institutions: the Museum of Natural Sciences, mainly promoting the ideology of Darwinism, with a planetarium inside the main prayer hall; and the Museum for Yerevan's History. The attitude of Yerevan's population towards the mosque building during the late Soviet era was indifferent. As the relationship between Armenians and Azerbaijanis worsened throughout the 1980s, the Blue Mosque was not damaged during the inter-ethnic conflict, because it was positively associated with being 'Persian', not Azerbaijani, and it was known as the museum of the city's history.[7]

As a religious place the Blue Mosque complex (Goekcami) reappeared on the city map in 1996 after reconstruction work had been completed. The significant restoration works were funded and carried out by Iranian companies, in cooperation with local architects.

The Iranian Cultural Centre was opened in the Blue Mosque as one of the public relations institutions of the Iranian Embassy in Armenia. Since that time, in local media and in official discourses, the Blue Mosque has been strongly associated with the new expatriate political body symbolizing the recent Armenian–Iranian friendship. This dominant reading of the place defines the Blue Mosque exclusively as the 'Persian Mosque', and only a few local experts remember the original name of the mosque, Goekcami.

However, the dominant 'exclusionist strategy' to represent the mosque as an expatriate Persian subject may be read differently by individuals. Having disappeared from daily life, the multi-religious past still resonates in contemporary interpretations. We cannot state that the Blue Mosque is a monolithic space with clearly defined religious boundaries. On the contrary, I argue that remnants of vernacular hybridity can still be traced in urban myths, imaginaries, and local narratives. By providing some examples below, I want to draw attention to how the phenomenon of 'shared sacred space' implicitly finds its expression in urban narratives and activities around the mosque. Glenn Bowman (2012) pointed out the notion of 'shared sacra' in different societies when differ- ent religious groups, whose beliefs are factually opposed and whose conceptions and practices would seem incommensurate, gather reverentially around the same site. Prac- tices and concepts of the usage around the Blue Mosque may be viewed through this lens. This approach helps highlight the local imaginaries of intercommunal interaction between Moslems and Christians as much as between the secular and religious realms (Bowman 2012). The assemblage of different groupings is not identical with practices of 'nostalgia' for the cultural mixing identified in the Mediterranean societies such as Turkey, Greece and in the Balkans (Bowman 2012; Couroucli 2012), yet to some extent it is comparable with the situation around the Blue Mosque in Armenia. The assemblage of different metaphors, materialities, and interactions does not seem to be the result of the top-down tolerance policy.

One important component of the narratives around the 'shared' place is focused on materiality and physical structure as evidence of a local symbiosis. Those who were involved in the restoration of the mosque associated the mosque building not only with the recent Armenian–Iranian friendship but more with the long history of Iranian– Armenian cultural interconnectedness, which binds Christianity and Islam and elements of them through the idea of sharing a space. In spite of the mosque's fixed interior design, equipped with traditional Shia Islam attributes such a minaret, mihrabs, holy inscriptions, a shoe shelf at the entrances of prayer halls, and boxes containing small sand stones (called *muehir* in Persian[8]) for Shia Islam worshippers, this study has revealed a shift in reading the meaning of the place that modifies the authoritative discourses.

According to these narratives, some Christian architectural canons were incorporated in the process of (re)constructing the Blue Mosque. For example, the 12 windows cut into the dome's drum are associated with the 12 Christian apostles. Another link to imagining the religious hybridity is manifested in the interior architectural design. During my fieldwork in Yerevan, Anahit Meliksetyan, a local field assistant and architecture student, told me that the existence of three mihrabs inside the mosque halls is related to the symbol of the Christian Trinity. Moreover, over the central mihrab, the sacred site inside mosques facing towards Mecca, one can see three windows with beautiful stained glass. The fact that the middle window is larger than the two others and that there are three windows in all led local experts to see the windows as a linkage to one of the postulates of the

Christian Trinity: God the Father, God the Son, and God the Holy Spirit (Muradyan and Saakyan 2008, 5).

Another interesting interpretation is related to the 'trinity' of mihrabs inside one single mosque complex. According to an explanation put forward by local architects as to why one mosque needs three different mihrabs in three halls, they represent three different religious communities that once shaped Yerevan: Shia Muslims, Sunni Muslims, and Armenian Christians. The size and design of the niches do not differ, and all three are decorated with Arabic and Persian scripts from the Koran. However, the central main mihrab bears an inscription of the name of the *sardar*[9] Husseyn Ali, who was governor of Erivan during the period when the mosque was constructed (1762–1783). The northern mihrab, opposite the entrance to the prayer hall, has lost its sacred meaning. During my fieldwork in 2011–2012, the space remained unused in terms of religious activities; instead, the niche was pragmatically used as a profane space to store vacuum cleaners and other technical equipment. The hall with its large dome (planetarium) is the embodiment of the central prayer hall for male visitors, public community gatherings, and religious celebrations. The third, smaller hall offers space for female worshippers and is separated from the larger male halls by a curtain. As indicated by the librarian of the mosque, this niche was associated with the Sunni tradition.

In a way, one could say that these interpretations of the sacred material composition in the context of multi-religious connectedness make the mosque complex unique and exotic at the same time. Though it can hardly be proved by historical documents, we should look at this phenomenon from a different angle. As was mentioned in the introduction, the past and present identities of a place are shaped less by the 'monumental time' and the conventional history of the nation-state as such than by narratives and legends emerging around the place.

The three marble niches in the Blue Mosque point to the sacred orientation of this Islamic religious place, yet the building also contains narratives of 'sharing', syncretism, and local hybridity. This particular way of constructing a unique syncretism is in line with that defined by the anthropologists Simon Coleman and Peter Collins (1996), who suggested that ethnographic examination of culture as actually lived in everyday existence can show how ideal aesthetic and moral principles embodied in architecture are constantly subject to multiple appropriations, interpretations, and transformations.

Cultural centre

In this section I look at the mosque as a socially constructed religious and cultural place frequented by different social groups, including Iranian migrants and the local Armenian population. During my fieldwork, together with Satenik Mkrtchyan (National Academy of Sciences / Ivane Javakhishvili State University in Tbilisi) and Anahit Meliksetyan (Yerevan State University / Bauhaus Universität), who assisted me in the period between November 2010 and February 2011, we used a situational approach by combining passive but regular observations during weekdays, and focused participant observations at larger events and religious rituals – such as 19 October, the Birthday of Imam Reza; 17 November, the Qurban holiday of sacrifice; 16 December, Ashura of Imam Hussein; 25 December, birthday of Jesus (Christmas), which is a celebration integrated into the final session of the Persian-language courses; 25 January, the 40th Day of Imam Hussein's Martyrdom Anniversary; and 21 March, Novruz celebration.

Like any mosque, the Blue Mosque offers a place for worship and socializing for community members. However, it explicitly combines two main functions. It is a religious place for 'insiders' (Iranian migrants in Yerevan), and it is a secular Cultural Centre for local 'outsiders' (Yerevan city urbanites), offering space for cultural events, education, and exchange. Muslim holiday ceremonies are organized mostly for Iranian students and business people and their families living in Yerevan.[10] Outside of the seasonal influx of Iranian pop-culture-and-booze tourists during the Novruz holiday in the spring, there are about 2000 Iranian students and migrants who make up an invisible minority in Yerevan. The number of Iranian expatriates, students, and trade migrants fluctuates, but Iranians comprise a new important part of the city's international make-up and play an increasing role in the development of local entrepreneurship and transnational trade networks. I use the term 'newcomers' for those Iranians in Armenia who have recently arrived in Yerevan to study or for business purposes. The 'booze-tourists' usually do not frequent the Yerevan mosque during their holidays in Armenia.

In general, three groups can be distinguished on the basis of the type of migration. The first group of Iranians came as bazaar merchants and small or middle-sized entrepreneurs during the economic crisis of the 1990s. In addition to the impact of the post-Soviet breakdown, Armenia suffered from the effects of both the 1988 earthquake and the armed conflict with neighbouring Azerbaijan, which led to the country's isolation, economic blockades, and a serious energy crisis. At this point, the early Iranian–Armenian trade networks in food and everyday goods supply stemmed mostly from northern Iran, and many of these traders and entrepreneurs were coincidently ethnic Azeri from Iran.

The second group of Iranians in Yerevan arrived in the late 1990s and 2000s as students, with the intention of staying in Armenia only temporarily. Due to the high costs of education in Iran and the geographical proximity to Armenia, some young Iranians in small cities choose to move to Yerevan to study medicine, architecture, engineering, and the humanities. Some of them come to Armenia already holding a master's degree and go on to do a PhD at Yerevan State University, and they bring their families along. Numerically, they form the largest group of Iranians in Yerevan, and are mobile, young, and mostly male.[11] Though only a minority of Iranian students visit the Blue Mosque on a regular basis, they are still linked to Iran's official representation in Yerevan through the Islamic Students' Association.

The third group can be characterized as expatriates and highly skilled professionals who socialize around the Cultural Centre at the Blue Mosque. Together with their families, they constitute the core group of worshippers. Some of these families are involved in certain larger international businesses in Armenia, such as energy supply and transportation. On Thursday evenings and on special holy days one can see five to seven cars with so-called 'red numbers', the diplomatic car registration plates, stopping in front of the mosque on Mashtotz Street.

Integrated into the mosque complex is a large library for Persian literature, containing more than 8000 items. The opening ceremony for the new Centre for Persian Literature, named after Hafiz (1325–1389), one of the most celebrated Persian lyric poets, took place in the Blue Mosque in October 2014. The mosque library and tourist guides are managed by an Iranian-Armenian lady in her sixties who was born and brought up in

Iran but studied in Armenia and Russia. She emphasized that in the 1960s, it was socialist ideals that attracted a group of young male and female Iranians to go to Moscow and Yerevan to study. At the library entrance, there is a desk for regular announcements in Persian regarding religious festivals, days of mourning, and restaurants for 'insiders', who are mostly Iranian students and diplomats and their families. Besides the library and prayer halls, inside the mosque one can find a large kitchen, a bathroom for ritual purification, a room for the local police, an exhibition room with Iranian crafts, and a computer room for Iranian students who do not have Internet access. Between the room for the Persian-language classes and the police room, there is a dentistry office, run by Doctor Lutfi. He is also known as the informal 'director' of the mosque complex, whom policemen call each time they have visitors or tourists in the evenings. During the daytime, visitors consult with the librarian, who takes over the responsibility of conducting tours through the mosque complex. The area of the mosque complex is secured by Armenian policemen, who receive state wages and are additionally paid by the mosque administration.

During the daytime, inside the mosque complex, the Iranian Cultural Centre offers free Persian-language courses on a regular basis, which are popular among young Armenians, in particular female visitors. Along with other secular cultural activities, the free access to lessons seems to be the major attraction for the local population. Three groups, each of about 20 students of different ages, meet once or twice a week. It is young female students who form the majority in the groups, and they express different motivations for taking part in the language courses. A group of students explained that their interest was due to the growing popularity of learning an 'oriental language', the Persian culture, and in particular classical Persian poetry, in Armenia. Some class members are local academics doing Iranian studies, and they attend the classes 'to refresh their level of knowledge'. A young participant gave a pragmatic reason for learning the Persian language: 'to communicate with Iranian tourists, those who want to rent an apartment or a house in Yerevan'. At the same time, the free courses provide an opportunity to meet Iranians. As one of the teachers mentioned, the main intention of some young female students is not to study but to find an Iranian husband.

The popularity of free Persian-language courses among Armenians inside Yerevan's mosque complex demonstrates the attractiveness of Persian aesthetic values in Armenia. In this specific case, it is an expression of the symbolic power of culture that leads to better acceptance and greater prestige of the Iranian community in Armenia. Iranian officials pursue the strategy of inclusiveness and sharing that can be traced in activities around the Cultural Centre. The Persian-language teacher and students emphasized that the room in which discussions regarding the culture and history of Iranian society take place is called the Saint Mariam room. The room, of medium size and decorated with an image of the Virgin Mary mixed with Iranian folk elements and numerous educational materials, is intended as a place for 'serious communication' between local students, teachers, and Iranians. Occasional devotion to Saint Mary by Muslims is not unique to Yerevan. Mary (Mariam in Arabic) has been and still is venerated by Muslims in the Middle East and the Mediterranean (Albera 2012).

I heard another example of the Blue Mosque's inclusive strategy towards the local population in Yerevan when the Persian-language teacher and Satenik were talking to each other. In December 2011 the head of the Cultural Centre entered the classroom and expressed his surprise as to why they still did not have a decorated Christmas tree in the room. This example describes a situational form of local 'cohabitation' contributing to the promotion of Iran's soft power in Armenia; nevertheless it can be extended to the moments when overlapping interests give rise to shared practices.

Religious practices

The mosque is accessible to all visitors and tourists during the daytime. However, Thursday evening after sunset is the time when the mosque is turned into a place for discrete Shia religious practices. However, in the Blue Mosque there is no strong attachment to the religious behavioural norms or dress codes known in contemporary Iranian society. Locals and newcomers seem to be drawn to the mosque as a liberal place for social and cultural gatherings. One of the regular visitors to the mosque, a male Iranian who also serves as a cook during Muslim holidays, identified the centrality of the social meaning of the mosque in the following manner:

> In Iran we have a special dress code which is very strict, and here everything is free: Girls do not follow the rules, they do not wear headscarves, and every Armenian can enter the mosque. It is a cultural place, and not only for praying, many Iranians gather here just to see each other.

There is no regular imam in the mosque; for major religious holidays imams are invited from Iran. Migrants who are registered at the Iranian Embassy and the Cultural Centre regularly receive information about prayer times via mobile phone, a centralized 'SMS-*azan*'. This practice reminds the recipient of the official call to prayer in Iran, which is transmitted by a centralized radio broadcast – unlike the *azan* in Sunni Muslim societies, where every mosque performs its own *azan* publicly. However, the striking point of the SMS-*azan* is its discreet modus. In his interview with me on the significance of this and the lack of 'voiced' *azan*s in Yerevan, the leader of the Cultural Centre at the time, Mr Shakiba, stressed the modern aspect of this call to prayer:

> The function of the minaret belongs to the past; it just signifies that this building is a mosque. Instead of the minaret, we use computers and mobile phones and send our members the azan call by email and SMS.

To some extent, this statement may correspond to historical records on the Muslim communities in the Caucasus, in particular in Georgia and Armenia. Asatryan and Margaryan (2004, 44) noted in their study of the development of Muslim communities in Tiflis:

> The religious life of the Muslims was focused in two mosques located inside the fortress: the third one had by that time been abandoned. Yet the limitations noted by J. Chardin remained in force: 'the muezzins would have never dared here to announce the hours of prayer from the high minarets on the fortress mosques: the people would have stoned them'.

However, the story of the silent *azan* in contemporary Yerevan goes back to an official agreement between the Islamic Republic of Iran and the Republic of Armenia.

The Blue Mosque seems to be far more than the central source for a feeling of belonging to the urban space for Iranian tourists and students. One of the Iranian students expressed her indifferent attitude to religious life inside the mosque, instead emphasizing its secular and pragmatic value. She came to the mosque not for prayer, but for dentistry. On another occasion, she came to give her cat to the mosque before going to Iran.

At the same time, she admired the 'positive energy' of the mosque courtyard and the sacred building, comparing it to other spiritual places such as a church or a synagogue.

As mentioned above, this 'cultural place' is regularly transformed into a distinct space for prayer during major religious holidays, which are accompanied by different preparations and practices. On Thursdays, one can come to the mosque to buy *halal* mutton, properly slaughtered according to religious prescriptions and Islamic dietary laws. A distinctive preparation for a feast is expressed not through additional religious decorations, public performances or specific spiritual metaphors, but rather through a material agent of transformation: cooking communal food inside the mosque. There is a large kitchen inside the mosque connected to a water system and gas supply. Refrigerators, several large rice cookers and saucepans, and a number of teapots are used for food-sharing practices during major Shia Islamic holidays: Qurban, Ashura, and Shia martyrdom mourning prayer ceremonies. This food-sharing practice is evident during the Qurban holiday: it is celebrated by preparing *gheimeh*, which is not a distinctly sacred food. However, it acquires a specific communal dimension during this holiday, as it is usually served for 600–700 visitors simultaneously.

According to the cook, Rahman, a large amount of ingredients (60–70 kg Persian rice, 40 kg lamb or beef meat, 15 kg red lentils, 50 kg potatoes, and 7 kg onions) is delivered to the mosque, provided by community members who either sacrifice an animal (usually a lamb) a day before or donate money to this event. Rahman compared the practice of donating meat or money for religious events at the mosque to the Armenian *matagh* tradition of sacrificing an animal for individual and family purposes.[12] Similarly, Muslim community members donate food for the success of their business or for the recovery of their son or one of their family members. Another important donor of the food shared in the feast is the Embassy of the Iranian Republic. Satenik Mkrtchian, the Armenian co-investigator, perceived the act of sharing food inside a public sacred place as unusual for Armenian practices. In response to her question as to why Iranian migrants prepare and share meals inside the mosque, Rahman, the cook, explained this practice by referring to both secular purposes and religious aspirations:

> For example, you [Armenians] have Independence Day and celebrate it; we have Revolution Day which we celebrate, and that is a merry day, a good day. But now we have a sad occasion, a sad holiday (the 40th day of Imam Hussein's death). We have a joint feast just to get together, celebrate or mourn, remember the day, also to get to know one other. ... Another reason is because everyone is equal that day, as if we want to symbolize that everyone is equally appreciated by God, and there are no social and other hierarchies.

The cooking team included three male volunteers, who were engaged in preparing food for two days. When asked why only men are involved in the cooking process, Rahman explained that the mosque kitchen work would be too exhausting for women, as large amounts of food must be served in big vessels, while women usually cook at home on a much smaller scale in the private sphere.

Food ingredients were supplied from the local market. However, Rahman emphasized the sacred dimension of the meat used in preparing *gheimeh* and *adas polo*. He explained the difference between the Armenian way of slaughtering and the *halal* way (actually, according to both traditions, the blood must be drained from the veins) in the following manner:

First of all, the one who kills the animal should be Muslim. Second, we make the animals drink water and eat salt before killing them, only in cases of *matagh* you give them salt. While cutting the head of the animal, we keep the animal's face turned towards Mecca, and we cut in a way that the animal does not choke and all the blood from its body bursts out. That's why our halal meat has no scum on its surface while cooking and has a lighter colour.

A young male student expressed the value of consuming halal food in a rational manner:

I am not religious, but you know, I am used not to eating pork, because it is not healthy. The Islamic religion emerged in Saudi Arabia, where the climate is very hot – also people used to drink a lot there, that is why this taboo was invented. And also the way the Muslims kill animals for meat is very healthy, it does not leave blood in the meat. So I like the concepts, but now, when Islam is mixed with politics, I do not like it. I know someone who of course goes to mosque, before that he changes his clothes, but afterwards does other things. I do not like when freedom and wisdom are suppressed. That is why I do not go to the mosque; I prefer to go out in nature.

The dish was served after the worshippers had performed a collective prayer on the carpet, which was covered by a plastic tablecloth. The prayer was conducted in two separate halls, one for male and one for female guests. Each individual then received a disposable plastic plate, napkins, and cutlery. Visitors shared sweets and biscuits. On the occasion of Ashura and other mourning festivities, female worshippers bring *halva* (sweets) as a special symbol of solidarity with the mourning event and distribute it among the visitors.

The process of simultaneous usage of the same site as cultural centre and religious place offers a dynamic stage for binding worlds between the sacred and the secular. From this perspective, the practices are embedded in a specific local context, which is shaped by the positive image of migration, post-socialist uncertainty, and the geopolitical constellation of regional powers. Religious forms of expression can be constructed as desirable for the purposes of secular governmentality (Asad 2003; Burchard and Becci 2013). In the Iranian context, mosques offer public spaces for communication of political messages and cultural symbols. In Yerevan's Blue Mosque, by combining religious practices for Iranians and cultural activities for local Christian visitors in a single edifice, the official Iran is engaged in the promotion of Iran's soft-power policy on the international stage (Hiva and Babak 2012). In this context, the inclusive strategy of Iran's Cultural Centre in Yerevan aims to create a cultural sense of regional reconnectedness, based on the idea of shared cultural and aesthetic values, which is also apparent in the public celebration of the Norooz holiday and other pre-Islamic festivals in Yerevan. Marking the beginning of spring, Nooruz (New Day) is rooted in the rituals of the Zoroastrian tradition, which was widespread in ancient Iran and the Caucasus. This strategy seems to play an important part in the formation of Iran's new positive image in Armenia.

Conclusion

The purpose of the Blue Mosque in Yerevan has changed radically several times: from religious gathering place, to ideologically driven secular museum, and back to a prayer house. However, the multiple decontextualization of the mosque within the city's history has not marginalized the site within the urban fabric. The prayer house may be both sacred and non-sacred in different respects and circumstances and has created its own social life.

In this particular case there is a dynamic space of multifunctionality between sacred and secular that may be a specific characteristic of the urban context defined in its general sense by heterogeneity, temporality, and modernity (Simmel 1950; Desplat and Schultz 2010).

The analysis has also revealed that the Blue Mosque cannot be seen as a monolithic 'expatriate' in the city, a closed place of a religious minority; it is rather a site of interactions and interplay between locals and newcomers, Muslims and non-Muslims – a 'sharing' place shaped by Yerevan's multi-religious past. The Shia Muslim religious lifestyle in Yerevan is not only about emphasizing differences between Iranians and Armenians. Rather, the Blue Mosque enables the coming together of different groups, Muslim Iranians and Christian Armenians, and the interactions taking place in its courtyard can be understood as a spatial expression of vernacular hybridity imagined by both local people and newcomers. In spite of the invisibility and silence of the Blue Mosque's past from the point of view of officials, the physical restoration of the mosque triggers unembodied memories of people in conscious and unconscious reconstructions of the shared multi-religious past. The extent to which the Blue Mosque contributes to a visible rediversification of religious life in the region, and its eventual impact on local identities and relations, remain to be seen.

Notes

1. Until the Russian–Persian war, 1826–1828, the territory of modern Armenia was under the control of the Persian Empire.
2. The concept of soft power is based on attracting others and co-opting, people rather than coercing them, by emphasizing cultural values and cultural diplomacy as means to reach that outcome (Nye 2005).
3. According to the Armenian constitution the centrality of the Armenian Apostolic Church is protected by Armenian Law. One can say that over the twentieth century the institution of the Armenian Church has been transformed into a kind of 'cultural Christianity', which emphasises the link between the ethnic group and its religion. In the Armenian experience, the mainstream religion was actually present and visible in different spheres of social and cultural life during the socialist period.
4. The rapid rise of the Armenian population in the city was due to forced migration from the territory of the Ottoman Empire at the end of the nineteenth century (Bournoutian 1982, 61–77).
5. Yeghishe Charents (1897–1937) was an Armenian writer and public activist, a member of the Bolshevik party, who was persecuted and killed during Stalin's Big Purge; Axel Bakunts (1899–1937), a writer of short stories and a member of the Armenian Association of Proletarian Writers, was also killed in the purge; Gabriel Gyurjan (1892–1987) was an Armenian painter, professor at Yerevan's Institute of Fine Arts, and leader of the Armenian Union of Artists; Martiros Saryan (1880–1972), a Soviet Armenian painter famous for his impressionist pictures of Armenian and Middle East landscapes, designed the coat of arms for the Armenian SSR.
6. Community of Art Workers (1924–1930) – played an important role for Armenian painters, artists, poets, and writers.
7. In 1990, the small Shia mosque on Vardanats Street was bulldozed by young Armenian nationalists. According to the British journalist Thomas de Waal (2003, 79), 'The Armenians didn't harm the Blue Mosque, because it was known as a museum of history of Yerevan, as the Armenian Cultural Centre, and moreover, it became known as a "Persian mosque".'
8. *Muehir* is the Persian word for 'sign' or 'stamp', analogue to *turbah*, a term for the Shia sand stone used to pray on. It is considered that the sand stone (clay or mud) symbolizes the earth from sacred Kerbela, the pilgrimage site for Shia Muslims.

9. *Sardar* is the Persian equivalent for 'governor' or 'ruler' of a settlement.
10. Though the Blue Mosque operates as a mosque and functions as a public place for prayer, there is no officially registered Muslim religious minority in Armenia.
11. This type of migrant is not new for Armenian–Iranian relationships as this migration goes back to the Soviet period. A group of leftist Armenians from Iran received special permission to enter Soviet Armenia to study.
12. *Matagh*, the Armenian tradition of giving alms to the poor and asking for health or prosperity, includes the ritual of offering a slaughtered rooster or lamb to God in front of the church. It is considered a ritual that involves a local synthesis of pagan and Christian beliefs. See for example Abrahamian (2006), Manning and Meneley (2008), and Tuite (2011).

Acknowledgement

The research for this article was based on ethnographic fieldwork I conducted in Armenia (November 2010–April 2011), supported by a grant from the Japan Society for the Promotion of Science and assisted by Satenik Mkrtchyan, at that time a doctoral student at the National Academy of Sciences and Ivane Javakhishvili State University in Tbilisi, and by Anahit Meliksetian, a student at Yerevan State University. Part of this research was discussed in a previous publication (T. Darieva, 2012, 'Placing a Mosque in Yerevan: Invisible Place, Multiple Names', in *Die postsowjetische Stadt: Urbane Aushandlungsprozesse im Südkaukasus*, special issue of *Berliner Blätter: Ethnographische und ethnologische Beiträge* 59: 54–73). I was able to go deeper into this topic within the ongoing research project, Transformation of Sacred Spaces in the post-Soviet Caucasus (2013–2016), funded by the Volkswagen Foundation, at the Friedrich-Schiller-University of Jena. I am grateful to my field assistants, in particular to Satenik Mkrtchyan, to the editor of this special issue, and to anonymous reviewers for their valuable comments.

Disclosure statement

No potential conflict of interest was reported by the author.

References

Abrahamian, L. 2006. *The Armenian Identity in a Changing World*. Costa Mesa: Mazda Publishers.
Akopyan, T. 1977. *Ocherki istorii Yerevana*. Yerevan: Izdatelstvo Erevanskogo universitita.
Albera, D. 2012. "Combining Practices and Belief: Muslim Pilgrims at Marian Shrines." In *Sharing the Sacra. The Politics and Pragmatics of Intercommunal Relations around Holy Places*, edited by G. Bowman, 10–24. London: Berghahn.
Antonyan, Y. 2010. "Reconstituting' Religion: Neo-Paganism in Armenia." *Laboratorium. Russian Review of Social Research* 1: 103–128.
Asad, T. 2003. *Formations of the Secular: Christianity, Islam, Modernity*. Stanford: Stanford University Press.
Asatrian, G., and H. Margarian. 2004. "The Muslim Community of Tiflis (8th-19th Centuries)." *Iran and the Caucasus* 8 (1): 29–52. doi:10.1163/1573384042002966.
Bournoutian, G. 1982. *Eastern Anatolia in the Last Decades of Persian Rule. 1807–1828: A Political and Socioeconomic Study of the Khanate of Erevan on the Eve of the Russian Conquest*. Malibu: Undena Publications.
Bowman, G. 2012. *Sharing the Sacra. The Politics and Pragmatics of Intercommunal Relations around Holy Places*. London: Berghahn.
Burchard, M., and I. Becci. 2013. "Introduction: Religion Takes Place: Producing Urban Locality." In *Topographies of Faith. Religion in Urban Spaces*, edited by I. Becci et al., 1–21. Leiden: Brill.
Coleman, S., and P. Collins. 1996. "Constructing the Sacred: The Anthropology of Architecture in the World Religions." *Architectural Design Profile* 124: 14–18.

Couroucli, M. 2012. "Saint George the Anatolian: master of frontiers." In *Sharing Sacred Spaces in the Mediterranean. Christians, Muslims and Jews at Shrines and Sanctuaries*, edited by D. Albera and M. Coucoucli, 118–140. Bloomington: Indiana University Press.

Darieva, T. 2012. "Placing a mosque in Yerevan: Invisible place, multiple Names." *Die postsowjetische Stadt. Urbane Aushandlungsprozesse im Südkaukasus*. Berliner Blätter. Ethnographische und ethnologische Beiträge special issue 59: 54–73.

Darieva, T., and W. Kaschuba. 2011. "Sights and Signs of Post-socialist Urbanism. An Introduction." In *Urban Spaces after Socialism. Ethnographies of Public Places in Eurasian Cities*, edited by T. Darieva, W. Kaschuba, and M. Krebs, 3–21. Frankfurt: Campus Verlag.

De Waal, T. 2003. *Black Garden. Armenia and Azerbaijan through Peace and War*. New York: NY University Press.

Desplat, P., and D. Schulz. 2010. *Prayer in the City: The Making of Muslim Sacred Places and Urban Life*. Bielefeld: Transcript. 9–35.

Episkopyan, S. 2011. "Semiotic Organization and Transformation of the Urban Space in Central Yerevan." In *City, Migration, and Market. New Views on Socio-cultural Issues in the South Caucasus*, in Russian, edited by N. Lejava, 13–46. Tbilisi: Heinrich Boell Foundation.

Grant, B. 2010. "Cosmopolitan Baku." *Ethnos* 75 (2): 123–147. doi:10.1080/00141841003753222.

Herzfeld, M. 1991. *A Place in History. Social and Monumental Time in a Cretan Town*. Princeton: Princeton University Press.

Hiva, F., and T. Babak. 2012. "Iran's Soft Power Borne of Necessity and Complexity of Its Multi-dimensional Audience." *Exchange: The Journal of Public Diplomacy* 3 (1): 48–52.

Humphrey, C., and V. Skvirskaja. 2012. *Post-cosmopolitan Cities: Explorations of Urban Existence*. Oxford: Berghahn Books.

Jödicke, A. 2015. "Religion and Politics in the South Caucasus." *Caucasus Analytical Digest* 72: 2–3.

King, C. 2008. *The Ghost of Freedom: A History of the Caucasus*. Oxford: Oxford University Press.

Lynch, H. [1910] 1965. *Armenia: Travels and Studies. Volume 1. The Russian Provinces*. Beirut: Khayats.

Manning, P., and A. Meneley. 2008. "Material Objects in Cosmological Worlds. An Introduction." *The Ethnos* 73 (2): 1–18.

Massey, D. 1995. "Places and Their Pasts." *History Workshop Journal* 39: 182–192. doi:10.1093/hwj/39.1.182.

Muradyan, A., and V. Saakyan. 2008. "Pervaya Gazeta." *Caucasus Media Institute* 6: 5.

Nye, J. 2005. *Soft Power: The Means to Success in World Politics*. New York: Public Affairs.

Ritter, M. 2009. "The Lost mosque(s) in the citadel of Qajar Yerevan: Architecture and Identity, Iranian and Local Tradition in the Early 19th Century." *Iran and the Caucasus* 13 (2): 239–279. doi:10.1163/157338410X12625876281109.

Sharashenidze, T. 2011. "The Role of Iran in the South Caucasus." *Caucasus Analytical Digest* 30: 2–5.

Simmel, G. 1950. "The Metropolis and Mental Life." In *The Sociology of Georg Simmel*, edited by K. Wolff, 409–424. New York: Free Press.

Suny, R. 2001. "Constructing Primordialism: Old Histories for New Nations." *The Journal of Modern History* 73 (4): 862–896. doi:10.1086/340148.

Ter-Minassian, T. 2007. *Erevan: la construction d'une capitale à l'époque soviétique*. Rennes: Presses Universitaires de Rennes.

Tuite, K. 2011. "Believer-nonbeliever Shrines in Highland Central Caucasia." Paper presented at the symposium Sacred Spaces and the emergence of the Caucasus at 109th Congress, American Anthropological Association Montréal, November 16.

Index

Page numbers in bold denote tables. Page numbers in italics denote figures. Page numbers with "n" refer to notes.

For Product Safety Concerns and Information please contact our EU
representative GPSR@taylorandfrancis.com
Taylor & Francis Verlag GmbH, Kaufingerstraße 24, 80331 München, Germany

www.ingramcontent.com/pod-product-compliance
Ingram Content Group UK Ltd.
Pitfield, Milton Keynes, MK11 3LW, UK
UKHW031043080625
459435UK00013B/548